The ULTIMATE Book of DINOSAURS

This is a Parragon Publishing Book
This edition published in 2002

Parragon Publishing
Queen Street House
4 Queen Street
Bath BA1 1HE, UK

Copyright © Parragon 2000

Produced by
Monkey Puzzle Media Ltd

ISBN 0-75254-813-1

Printed in the EU

AUTHORS
Paul Dowswell, John Malam, Paul Mason, Steve Parker

ILLUSTRATORS
John Butler, Chris Christoforou, John Egan, Roger Goode,
Philip Hood (Wildlife Art), Mark Iley (Wildlife Art), David McAllister,
Martin McKenna (Sarah Brown Agency), Michael Posen,
Steve D White and Brian Williamson, Tim White

DESIGNERS
Tessa Barwick, Sarah Crouch, Tim Mayer, Victoria Webb

EDITOR
Katie Orchard

ARTWORK COMMISSIONING
Roger Goddard-Coote

PROJECT MANAGER
Alex Edmonds

ADDITIONAL EDITORIAL ASSISTANCE FROM
Michael Flaherty, Caroline Hamilton, Lynda Lines
and Connor Sweeney.

Contents

OTHER CREATURES OF THE DINOSAUR AGE 177

DEATH OF THE DINOSAURS 201

HUNTING FOR DINOSAURS 213

DINOSAUR DATA 235

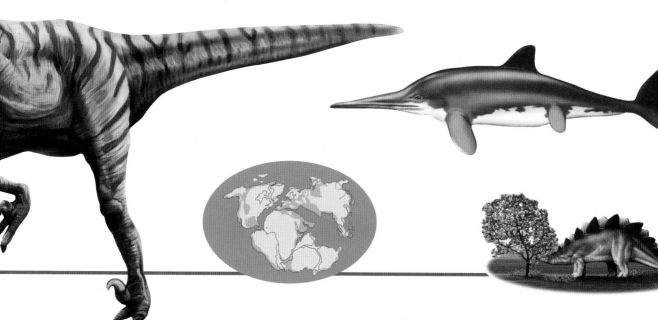

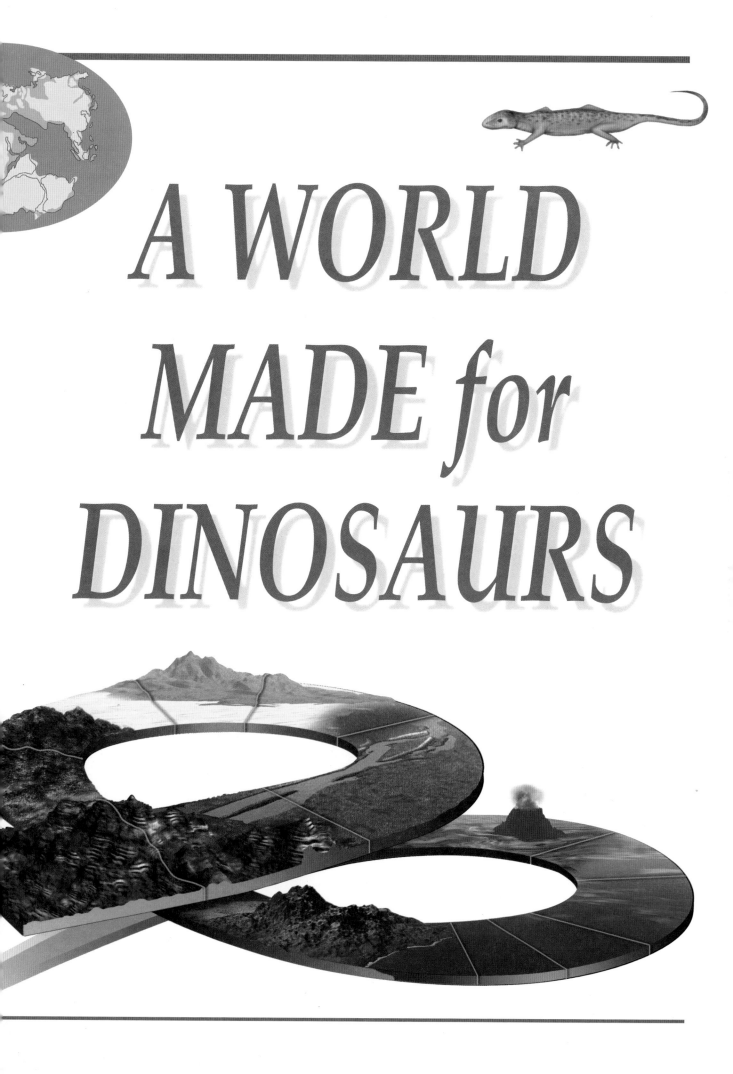

A WORLD
MADE *for*
DINOSAURS

What is a Dinosaur?

THE YEAR OF THE DINOSAUR

Every story has a beginning, and for the magnificent creatures we call dinosaurs their story begins in 1841. In that year, the British Association for the Advancement of Science held its annual meeting at Plymouth, a town on the south coast of England. One of the speakers was Professor Richard Owen, a scientist and animal expert, who was also a friend of Queen Victoria.

For several years Owen had been studying animal fossils, particularly the huge bones of ancient reptiles. Most scientists believed these bones were the remains of prehistoric crocodiles and gigantic lizards, but Owen thought that this was wrong. The more he looked at the old bones, the more certain he was that they came from a new group of animals—a group that was completely unknown to science.

At the meeting in Plymouth, Owen spoke for more than two hours to the leading scientists of his day. What astonished them was the fact that

CHINESE DRAGONS

The Chinese were the first people to write about dinosaurs, although they didn't know it at the time. About 1,700 years ago, Chang Qu, a Chinese writer, described how "dragon bones" had been found in Wucheng, a region in the middle of the country. Today's scientists think that they were dinosaur bones, and the area that they came from is one of the best places in China to search for their ancient remains.

Owen wasn't talking about the discovery of just one new animal. Instead, he was talking about a completely new group that might contain tens, hundreds, or even thousands of different animals. It was one of the greatest discoveries of the 1800s, and it changed the way that people thought about life on Earth.

Tyrannosaurus rex **was probably one of the most fearsome of the "terrible lizards" and the best-known of the dinosaurs.**

Richard Owen

In 1854, Richard Owen helped to open a dinosaur park in Crystal Palace, London, England. The park contained life-sized models of dinosaurs.

DINOSAUR CHARACTERISTICS

Today's scientists use the following basic rules to decide whether the ancient creatures they are looking at are dinosaurs:

- dinosaurs lived between 250—65 million years ago;
- they lived on land;
- they could not fly;
- they had straight legs tucked underneath their bodies;
- they were reptiles.

FINDING A NAME

Owen's group of animals needed a name. At his talk in 1841, Owen had not used a name, but when he wrote about his ideas in 1842 he used the name "Dinosauria." He made the name from two Greek words: *deinos*, meaning "terrible" and *sauros*, meaning "lizard." From then on there was a new word in the English language—dinosaur.

WERE ALL PREHISTORIC CREATURES DINOSAURS?

Although many other animals lived at the same time as the dinosaurs, they belonged to different groups. Some could fly, and some lived in the seas and oceans, so these prehistoric creatures were not dinosaurs. However, their story is just as interesting and important as that of the dinosaurs, since they, too, have played their part in the development of life on Earth.

When Did Dinosaurs Live?

WHEN EARTH BELONGED TO THE DINOSAURS
The animal kingdom is a huge collection of species—one estimate suggests there are as many as 10—15 million different kinds of creatures alive on the Earth today. Animals come in all shapes and sizes, and live in all environments, and it was just like this when dinosaurs lived on Earth, too.

A popular name for the time when dinosaurs lived is the "Age of Dinosaurs." This was a long time that lasted for about 185 million years. Humans, on the other hand, have lived on Earth for only about 2 million years. It is very difficult to imagine such great spans of time, since we are more used to thinking about time in terms of days, months, and years. A simple explanation is that planet Earth belonged to the dinosaurs for about ninety times longer than it has belonged to humans.

THE AGE OF DINOSAURS
Earth is an old planet. Scientists think that it formed about 4,500 million years ago. They divide the whole of Earth's long existence into intervals of time, each of which represents a chapter in the story of the planet.

About 600 million years ago, a new chapter began. Scientists call this the Phanerozoic Eon. It is divided into three smaller parts called eras. The oldest part is the Paleozoic Era, which was followed by the Mesozoic Era, which in turn was followed by the Cenozoic Era.

The Mesozoic Era is the scientific name for the Age of Dinosaurs. It was during the Mesozoic that dinosaurs appeared, and then died out. Humans appeared during the Cenozoic Era, an interval of time that continues right up to the present day. The following table shows how the three eras fit together.

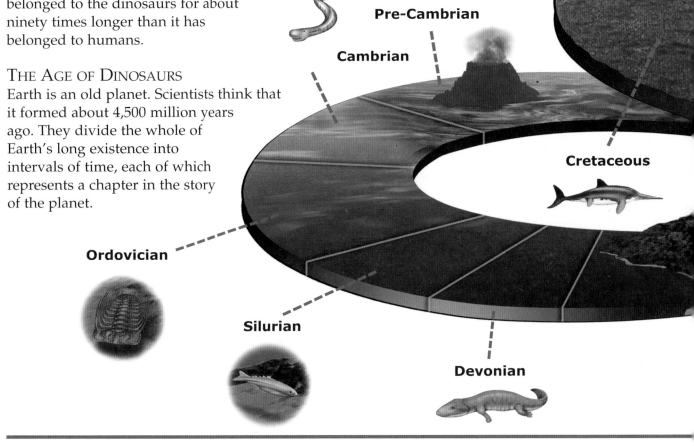

Pre-Cambrian

Cambrian

Cretaceous

Ordovician

Silurian

Devonian

Era	Meaning	Millions of years ago	Which animals appeared?
Cenozoic	"recent life"	65 to the present day	mammals, including humans
Mesozoic	"middle life"	250—65	dinosaurs
Palaeozoic	"ancient life"	600—250	fishes, amphibians, reptiles

THE MESOZOIC ERA

The Mesozoic Era is divided into three periods—the Triassic, Jurassic, and Cretaceous. You can see how these periods fit together in the following table:

Period	Millions of years ago	What happened to dinosaurs?
Cretaceous	144—65	the last dinosaurs
Jurassic	206—144	the greatest time for dinosaurs
Triassic	250—206	the first dinosaurs

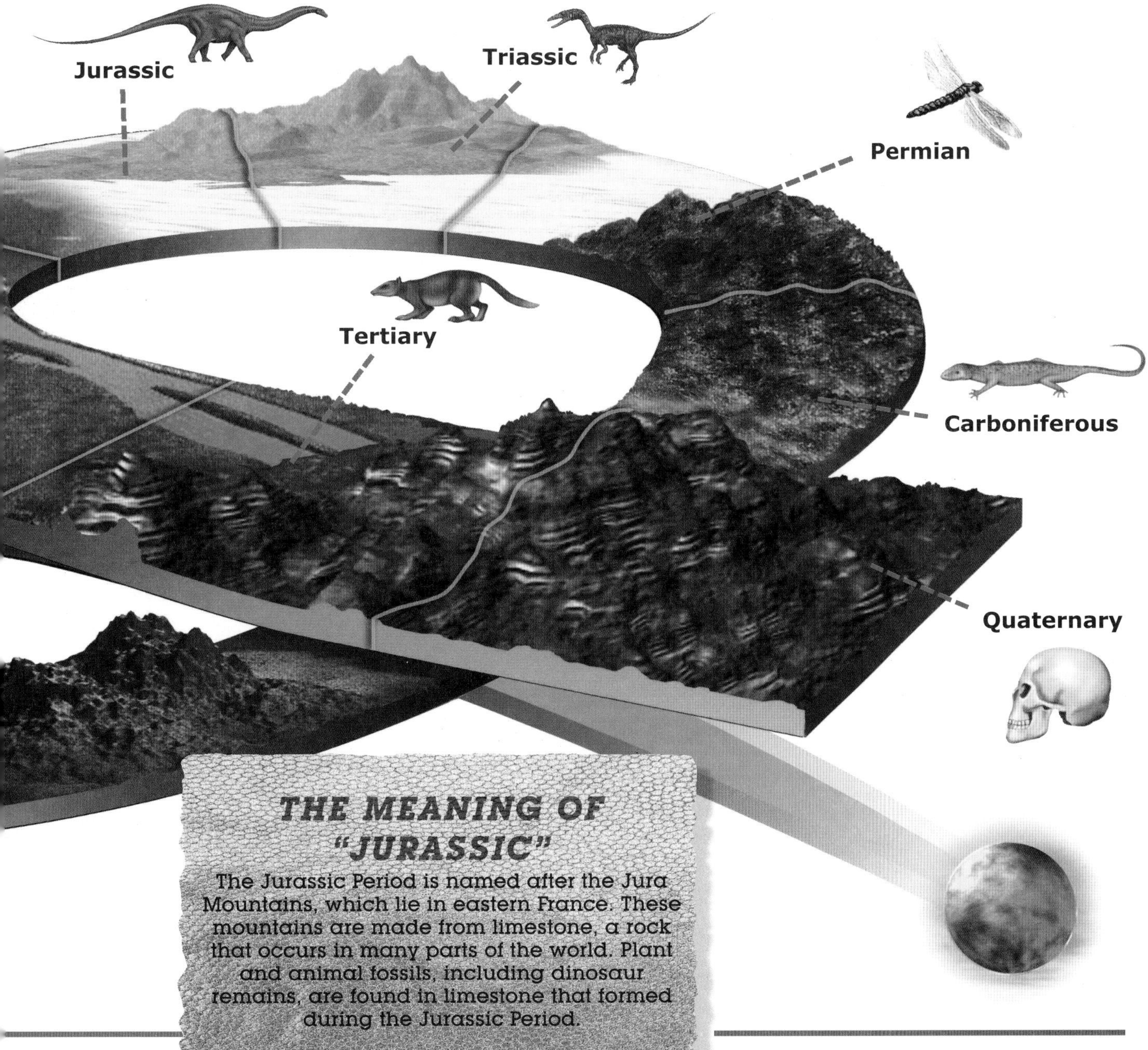

Jurassic

Triassic

Permian

Tertiary

Carboniferous

Quaternary

THE MEANING OF "JURASSIC"

The Jurassic Period is named after the Jura Mountains, which lie in eastern France. These mountains are made from limestone, a rock that occurs in many parts of the world. Plant and animal fossils, including dinosaur remains, are found in limestone that formed during the Jurassic Period.

The Earth's Changing Shape

The world in the Triassic Period
250—206 million years ago

In the Triassic, Earth's land was joined together in one huge supercontinent known as Pangaea. The animals that lived on Pangaea, including the first dinosaurs, were free to wander in all directions since there were no oceans to stop them from crossing the continent.

The world in the Jurassic Period
206—144 million years ago

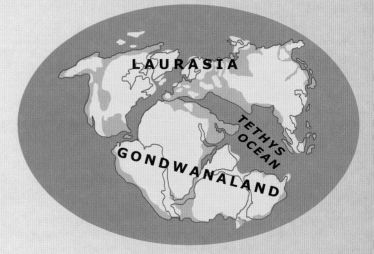

During the Jurassic, Pangaea was split apart by huge cracks that opened up in the Earth's crust. The process of continental drift had begun, pulling North America, Europe, and Asia away from South America, Africa, and Australia. Oceans flooded the gaps between the continents, creating watery barriers that land animals— including dinosaurs—could no longer cross.

A RESTLESS PLANET

Throughout its long history Earth has been shaped by the forces of nature. It is these powerful forces that gave the land and oceans their shape, and which continue to change the planet even today. The action of some forces, such as volcanoes and glaciers, is easy to see. But the action of other forces is far less obvious.

THE GIANT JIGSAW PUZZLE

When we look at a map of the world, it is as if we are looking at the pieces of a giant jigsaw puzzle. It seems that if we could move the continents around some of them would fit together. For example, the bulge of South America seems to fit into the hollow of Africa— the only problem is that they are separated by the Atlantic Ocean.

For hundreds of years, scholars had been puzzled by the shape of the continents. As early as 1596, Abraham Ortelius suggested that America had been torn away from Europe and Africa by earthquakes and floods—but his ideas were not taken seriously. It wasn't until 1915 that a German scientist, Alfred Wegener, came up with a solution to the mystery.

SLOWLY BUT SURELY

Continents move incredibly slowly, at a rate of as little as ⅜–1½ inches (1-4 centimeters) a year. Over the course of millions of years, these tiny measurements add up to account for the drift of the continents across the Earth.

These maps show how the shapes of the Earth's land masses have changed during the last 250 million years. The land is colored yellow, and the oceans blue. The areas that make up today's continents are shown outlined in dark blue.

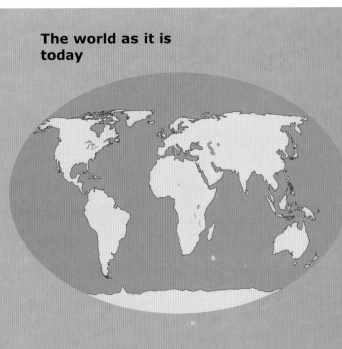

The world in the Cretaceous Period 144—65 million years ago

LAURASIA

TETHYS OCEAN

GONDWANALAND

The world as it is today

By the time of the Cretaceous the continents had more or less reached their present-day positions. Each continent was stocked with its own variety of unique animals.

The world today is divided into seven continents —but as the process of continental drift is never-ending, these land masses continue to move little by little each year. In the future, the map of the world will look different again.

Wegener said that the Earth's continents had started off as one huge mass of land—a supercontinent that he called Pangaea, meaning "All Earth." He said that during the Mesozoic Era, forces from deep inside the Earth began to crack Pangaea into smaller pieces. Then, over millions of years, the pieces drifted across the face of the Earth until they reached the stage they are at today.

A POWERFUL FORCE
For many years no one knew what force was strong enough to move continents. The answer was found in the early 1960s when scientists discovered that the Earth's top layer, or crust, was cracked into giant pieces of land, which they called plates. On top of these plates were the continents.

Under the oceans, magma, which is molten rock from deep inside the planet, is constantly forced up to the surface. The magma makes new crust, and pushes outward the older crust already formed. It is this force coming from within the Earth itself that moves the plates, which carry the continents with them. This process is called continental drift.

The World of the Dinosaurs

TRIASSIC PERIOD (250—206 MILLION YEARS AGO)

LAND All land was joined together in the supercontinent named Pangaea.

CLIMATE The temperature on land was constantly dry and warm.

PLANTS Trees such, as conifers and ginkgoes, flourished, as did tree ferns, horse-tails, and cycads. There were no flowering plants.

DINOSAURS The first dinosaurs appeared, small two-legged meat eaters and larger plant eaters that walked on two or four legs.

OTHER ANIMALS Insects, crocodiles, small mammals, frogs, turtles, fish, gliding lizards, and flying pterosaurs.

Triassic landscape

JURASSIC PERIOD (206—144 MILLION YEARS AGO)

LAND Pangaea began to crack apart, forming smaller land masses separated by sea.

CLIMATE The temperature became cooler and rainfall increased.

PLANTS Conifer forests covered vast areas of land, and ginkgoes, palms, tree ferns, and horse-tails flourished in the moist climate. There were still no flowering plants.

DINOSAURS Giant-sized plant-eating dinosaurs appeared, which fed on the lush vegetation. Large meat eaters lived at this time, too.

OTHER ANIMALS The first birds appeared, but pterosaurs ruled the skies. The ancestors of present-day bees and flies buzzed through the air, while icthyosaurs, plesiosaurs, fish, and mollusks lived in the sea.

Jurassic landscape

KEEP OFF THE FERNS!
Grass did not exist during the Age of Dinosaurs. To dinosaurs, the equivalent of grass was ferns.

CRETACEOUS PERIOD (144—65 MILLION YEARS AGO)

LAND The continents reached their present-day positions, and mountain ranges were formed where plates pushed into each other.

CLIMATE The temperature continued to cool down. There were wet and dry seasons, which gradually changed into summer and winter seasons.

PLANTS The first flowering plants appeared. They spread quickly and became the main type of ground-covering plants. Oak, maple, walnut, and beech trees grew alongside the still abundant conifers, cycads, and ferns.

DINOSAURS Herds of small plant-eating dinosaurs roamed across open country, preyed upon by meat-eating predators. Some dinosaurs developed body armor to protect themselves from attack.

Cretaceous landscape

OTHER ANIMALS Snakes and small mammals appeared on the land, crocodiles lived in freshwater pools, and huge reptiles flew through the skies, as did many kinds of birds and the first moths. Giant turtles and lizardlike animals swam in the seas, feeding on the plentiful supplies of fish and mollusks.

IN the
BEGINNING

Life Begins

THE FIRST SIGNS OF LIFE

Scientists believe that the Earth was formed 4,500 million years ago and that for the first 1,000 million years of its existence there was no life here. It was a lifeless planet, just like thousands of others in the universe. But then, about 3,500 million years ago, the first signs of life appeared.

LIFE WITHOUT OXYGEN

The air that we breathe today contains oxygen, a gas which living things need in order to stay alive. But the farther back you look in time, the less oxygen there was in the atmosphere. In the beginning there was no oxygen at all.

When Earth was a young planet, its atmosphere was made from a mixture of gasses, such as carbon dioxide, methane, and hydrogen sulfide—the gas that makes rotten eggs smell so bad. These gasses colored the sky pink, not blue. To oxygen-breathing dinosaurs—and to humans, too—this is a recipe for death, not life. But it was in these hostile conditions that life on Earth began.

Many scientists believe that life on Earth first began in conditions like these, about 3,500 million years ago.

THE "SPARK" OF LIFE

The question "How did life begin?" is one of the biggest questions of all, and it is one that has no easy answer. A simple explanation is that life began as the result of a chemical reaction. It began in Earth's oceans, where energy from lightning, the Sun, or even from meteorites that came crashing down provided the all-important "spark." As the energy was released it set off a chain reaction among chemicals in the oceans. As the chemicals reacted with each other, structures called organic molecules were made. Among the new molecules were amino acids—the building blocks of life, from which all living things stem. The story of life on Earth had begun.

ALGAE, THE OXYGEN MAKERS

The first living things on Earth were simple, tiny organisms named bacteria. They lived in the oceans, which were not blue as they are today, but rusty red. There were algae too, organisms that lived in shallow water and that spread out across the ocean floor in vast colonies, like huge, sticky blankets. These microscopic specks of algae changed the Earth's atmosphere. In their daily lives they made a waste product that they pumped into the oceans. The waste product was oxygen gas.

At first, the oxygen was dissolved into the oceans. Oxygen changed the water's color from red to blue. Then, after the oceans were filled with oxygen, the time had come for the atmosphere to change, too. Oxygen bubbled up from the algae in the oceans and escaped into the sky. As oxygen filled the atmosphere it took over from carbon dioxide, methane, and hydrogen sulfide. With an atmosphere containing oxygen, the sky's color changed from pink to blue. This oxygen-rich air could be breathed in—it was time for new forms of life to appear.

LIFE IN A TEST TUBE

In 1953, the scientist Stanley Miller carried out an experiment in a laboratory at the University of Chicago, Illinois. He created an atmosphere similar to the one that existed on Earth 3,000 million years ago. It was a mixture of the gasses methane, hydrogen, and ammonia, to which he added water. Into this "chemical soup" he passed electrical charges, which released energy. After a few days Miller found that amino acids had formed—he had the ingredients for life.

Before the Dinosaurs

TIMELINE OF EARLY LIFE ON EARTH
There was life on Earth for about 3,250 million years before the first dinosaurs appeared. The story of early life can be broken down into stages, each one marking a crucial step along the path toward the emergence of the first dinosaurs, some 250 million years ago. This chapter traces the evolution of early life, to the point at which dinosaurs came onto the scene.

PRE-CAMBRIAN PERIOD
3,500—570 MILLION YEARS AGO
For the first 3,000 million years of life on Earth, all life was microscopic—it would have been too small to see with the naked eye. Today, you can only see the remains of these tiny ancient creatures, preserved as microfossils, with the help of a microscope. All life was in the oceans—there was no life on land.

CAMBRIAN PERIOD
570—510 MILLION YEARS AGO
The first creatures big enough to be seen with the naked eye appeared. These were creatures without backbones, the invertebrates, such as mollusks, sponges, worms, jellyfish, and starfish. All life was in the oceans.

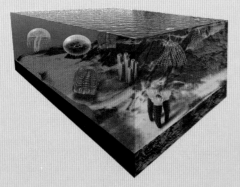

ORDOVICIAN PERIOD
510—440 MILLION YEARS AGO
Creatures with backbones, the vertebrates, appeared. The oceans were home to corals, trilobites, sponges, jellyfish, and graptolites, which lived in colonies and floated through the water. All life was in the oceans.

SILURIAN PERIOD
440—410 MILLION YEARS AGO
The first fish with jaws evolved. Coral reefs flourished in the oceans. The first plants grew on land. Scorpions and millipedes came out of the water and adapted to living on land.

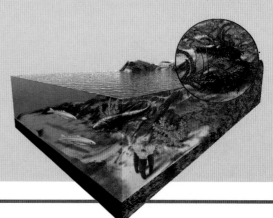

THE FIRST MASS EXTINCTION

The first great mass extinction of animals happened at the end of the Permian Period, 250 million years ago, when about three-quarters of all amphibian and reptile species died out on land and half of all species in the oceans. This event is the most catastrophic loss of life ever known on Earth —greater even than the extinction of the dinosaurs. The reasons why so many animal species disappeared at this time are unclear, although most scientists think that it was because of massive changes that happened on a global scale, such as alterations in the climate and the drying up of the oceans.

DEVONIAN PERIOD
410—360 MILLION YEARS AGO

This was the "Age of Fish." Fish dominated life in the oceans. The first insects appeared. The first amphibians evolved—creatures that can live in water and on land. Primitive plants formed the first forest on land. Horse-tails and club mosses appeared.

CARBONIFEROUS PERIOD
360—290 MILLION YEARS AGO

Snails, centipedes, millipedes, cockroaches, and giant dragonflies thrived in the warm, damp climate. The first small insect-eating reptiles, which evolved from amphibians, appeared. Giant tree ferns, horse-tails, and conifers formed forests.

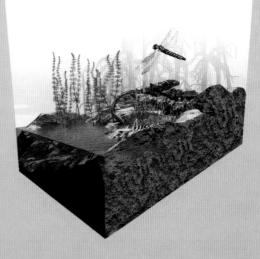

PERMIAN PERIOD
290—250 MILLION YEARS AGO

New species of larger reptiles evolved and took over from amphibians. Ferns, horse-tails, and conifers were widespread on the land.

The First Reptiles

The 3-foot- (1-meter-) long amphibian *Gerrothorax* led a double life, able to crawl on land and swim under water, using its webbed feet.

WHAT IS A REPTILE?

A reptile is an animal that has all of the following characteristics:

• It must have a backbone;
• It must be cold-blooded;
• It must lay eggs;
• It must have scaly skin.

Turtles, crocodiles, lizards, and snakes are examples of living reptiles, but there are many examples of reptiles, such as the dinosaurs, that have died out.

Hylonomus

Hylonomus was an anapsid reptile. It lived 310 million years ago and was one of the first reptiles. Only about 8 inches (20 centimeters) long, its remains have been discovered in Canada, inside the stumps of hollow trees where it may have crawled in search of insects to eat.

FROM AMPHIBIANS TO REPTILES

Toward the end of the Carboniferous Period, about 290 million years ago, the very first reptiles appeared. They evolved from amphibians, which were animals that could live in both water and on land. The very name—amphibian—means "double life." Amphibians were the first animals with backbones to develop legs with feet instead of fins. Having feet meant that amphibians were able to move on the ground. Although amphibians were able to survive on land, they still needed to spend some of their time in water. Unlike amphibians, reptiles lived entirely on dry land. This important difference meant that reptiles did not have to live close to water. Instead, they could wander wherever they liked on land.

Hyperodapedon

Hyperodapedon was a diapsid reptile from 250 million years ago. About 4 feet (1.3 meters) long, it lived on a diet of vegetation that it tore up with its powerful beak. Its remains have been found in Scotland.

Kannameyeria was a synapsid reptile that lived 250 million years ago. It was about 10 feet (3 meters) long and fed on plants that it bit through with its beak and two large doglike teeth. Its remains have been found in South Africa.

Kannameyeria

Reptiles before the dinosaurs

Toward the end of the Triassic Period, about 230 million years ago, several major groups, or families, of reptiles had evolved. Scientists sort these families into groups based on the appearance of their skulls. Some animals had holes in their skulls that allowed their jaw muscles to contract, or tighten, while others had skulls without holes. There are three main groups of early reptiles, based on the number of openings in their skulls:

• Anapsids—reptiles of the "no-hole" group had skulls with no muscle holes in them;

• Synapsids—reptiles of the "one-hole" group had skulls with one muscle hole on either side;

• Diapsids—reptiles of the "two-hole" group had skulls with two muscle holes on either side.

Dinosaurs and other prehistoric creatures, such as pterosaurs in the sky and ichthyosaurs and plesiosaurs in the oceans, evolved from this group of reptiles. Present-day diapsids include crocodiles, lizards, snakes, and birds.

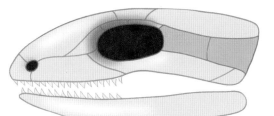

Anapsid skull

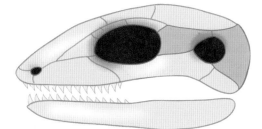

Synapsid skull

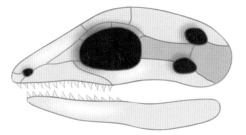

Diapsid skull

IS LIZZIE THE FIRST REPTILE?

Scientists are not certain which animal counts as the world's first reptile. In 1988, a creature was found in Scotland in rocks that are 350 million years old. Some scientists believe it is the first reptile, but others think it is an amphibian. They have named it *Westlothiana lizziae* after the region of Scotland where it was found. Its nickname is Lizzie.

The First Dinosaurs

The Age of Dinosaurs Begins

The first dinosaurs appeared about 228 million years ago. Their ancestors were reptiles that belonged to the diapsid group of animals. For 185 million years dinosaurs were the dominant, or ruling, animals on Earth. But it is important to remember that in all this time dinosaurs were not alone on the planet, since there were many other animals with backbones that lived alongside them. Some of these other prehistoric creatures lived on land too, but others were able to fly and swim. The whole incredible range of these ancient animals formed a worldwide ecosystem in which every creature had its place and in which dinosaurs were the leading animals on land.

***Erythrosuchus* was an archosaur, an ancestor of the dinosaurs. This meat eater measured up to 16 feet (5 meters) long.**

Erythrosuchus

How Dinosaurs Evolved

In order to know where dinosaurs came from we have to look closely at their diapsid ancestors. Among the diapsids were a number of animals that scientists have called archosaurs, which means "ruling reptiles." These animals were beginning to dominate life on the land. The dinosaur family tree begins with the earliest of the archosaurs—a group of large crocodilelike animals with sprawling legs. Known as thecodonts, which means "socket toothed," they were big, heavy reptiles that crawled on all four legs. Thecodonts were meat-eating animals with long jaws and long tails.

Not all reptiles changed from the sprawling gait to the semi-erect and erect gaits. Some, like the crocodiles, are still "sprawlers" today.

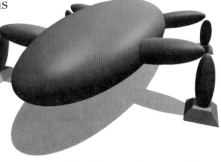

1. Sprawling gait

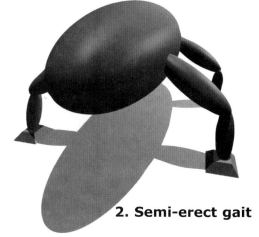

2. Semi-erect gait

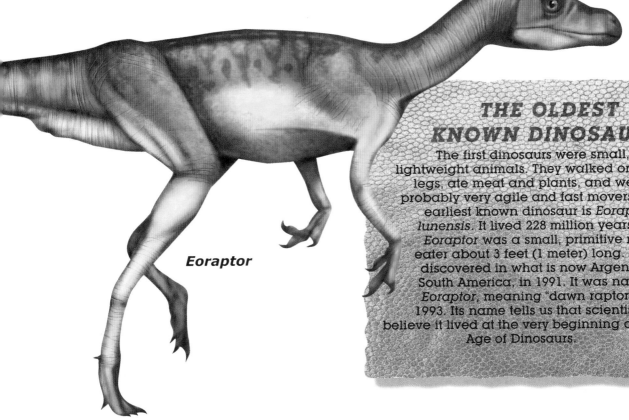

Eoraptor

THE OLDEST KNOWN DINOSAUR

The first dinosaurs were small, lightweight animals. They walked on two legs, ate meat and plants, and were probably very agile and fast movers. The earliest known dinosaur is *Eoraptor lunensis*. It lived 228 million years ago. *Eoraptor* was a small, primitive meat eater about 3 feet (1 meter) long. It was discovered in what is now Argentina, South America, in 1991. It was named *Eoraptor*, meaning "dawn raptor," in 1993. Its name tells us that scientists believe it lived at the very beginning of the Age of Dinosaurs.

Eoraptor walked on two legs and may have been a fast runner. It had light, hollow bones, a long head with many small, sharp teeth and five fingers on its hands.

FROM CRAWLING TO WALKING

With the emergence of thecodonts, a major stage in the evolution of dinosaurs was complete. But there was still a long way to go before the first true dinosaurs appeared. Early thecodonts walked like modern crocodiles do, with their knees and elbows at right angles to their bodies. They held their bodies close to the ground. Over millions of years, thecodonts evolved and the positions of their limbs changed. Later thecodonts walked in a more upright position and they were able to run, but they still moved on all fours. Smaller, lightly-built thecodonts were the first animals to run for short distances on their back legs. For some animals walking on two legs became the normal means of movement. True dinosaurs came from these creatures.

3. Pillar-erect gait

4. "Typical" erect gait

How Dinosaurs are Classified

THE TWO DINOSAUR ORDERS
In 1887, British geologist Harry Seeley came up with a way of dividing dinosaurs into two basic groups, or orders. Over many years he had made a careful study of dinosaur skeletons in museum collections, noting their similarities and differences. He noticed that dinosaur hip bones were either shaped like those of lizards or birds. This important observation led him to propose a new idea —that dinosaurs should be divided into the order *Saurischia* ("lizard-hipped" dinosaurs) and the order *Ornithischia* ("bird-hipped" dinosaurs).

SAURISCHIA— THE "LIZARD- HIPPED" DINOSAURS

Dinosaurs whose hip bones were shaped like those of lizards fall into two types: the agile, meat-eating theropods and the slower-moving, plant-eating sauropods.

THEROPODS

Name means "Beast foot"
Description Dinosaurs that walked on three-toed, birdlike feet with sharp claws. They had powerful legs, small arms, a short compact chest, a long muscular tail, a curved and flexible neck, large eyes, and long jaws with daggerlike teeth.
Examples *Allosaurus, Baryonyx, Deinonychus, Oviraptor,* and *Tyrannosaurus.*
Diet They were carnivores—meat-eating dinosaurs.

SAUROPODS

Name means "Lizard foot"
Description Large-to massive-sized dinosaurs, that walked on all four feet. They had small heads, long necks, bulky bodies, and long tails.
Examples *Apatosaurus, Brachiosaurus, Diplodocus,* and *Seismosaurus.*
Diet They were herbivores—plant-eating dinosaurs.

Ilium

Pubis

Ischium

In the skeletons of saurischians the pubis bone of the hip points downward and to the front.

DINOSAURS

All dinosaurs were descended from reptiles called thecodonts, which first appeared on Earth during the Triassic period.

ORNITHISCHIA —THE "BIRD-HIPPED" DINOSAURS

Dinosaurs whose hip bones were shaped like those of living birds were far more varied than the "lizard-hipped" dinosaurs. These dinosaurs are divided into five types: ankylosaurs, ceratopsians, ornithopods, pachycephalosaurs and stegosaurs.

Ilium

Ischium

Pubis

In ornithischians the pubis bone points downward and toward the tail. The pelvis is wider than that of saurischians. This may have made ornithischians more stable while moving.

ANKYLOSAURS
Name means "Fused-together reptiles"
Description Small to medium-sized dinosaurs. They had low, squat bodies with massive limbs. Their bodies were covered in flexible, bony armor of slabs, plates, and spikes, and they had small teeth and weak jaws.
Examples *Ankylosaurus* and *Euoplocephalus*.
Diet They were herbivores—plant eaters.

CERATOPSIANS
Name means "Horned faces"
Description Small to large dinosaurs that moved about on two or four legs. Some had horned and frilled heads and some had narrow parrotlike beaks. They probably lived in large herds.
Examples *Psittacosaurus* and *Triceratops*.
Diet They were herbivores—plant eaters.

ORNITHOPODS
Name means "Bird feet"
Description Small to very large dinosaurs that walked and ran on their two back feet. Some lived in large herds. Some had crests on their heads.
Examples *Lesothosaurus*, *Iguanodon*, and *Parasaurolophus*.
Diet They were herbivores—plant eaters.

PACHYCEPHALOSAURS
Name means "Bone heads"
Description Small- to medium-sized dinosaurs. They were slow-moving, had thick skulls and moved about on two back legs. They lived in herds.
Examples *Pachycephalosaurus* and *Stegoceras*.
Diet They were herbivores—plant eaters.

STEGOSAURS
Name means "Roofed reptiles"
Description Medium-sized dinosaurs. They moved about on all fours and were slow-moving. Their skins were covered in bony plates or spikes, and they had short, weak teeth.
Examples *Kentrosaurus* and *Stegosaurus*.
Diet They were herbivores—plant eaters.

DINOSAUR
LIFE STYLES

Meat-eating Dinosaurs

SNAPPERS AND CHOMPERS

Most animals today are meat or plant eaters. Just as lions and leopards hunt grazing wildebeest and gazelle, dinosaurs such as *Tyrannosaurus* and *Allosaurus* hunted *Triceratops* or *Iguanodon*.

Hunters need special skills and features to survive—after all, if they do not catch their food, they do not eat. Meat eaters today usually have big teeth, savage claws, sharp eyes, and fast legs. Most meat-eating dinosaurs had all these features and more. But not all of them were big-jawed monsters on the lookout for an equally vast walking supper. Some were tiny, vicious pack hunters, barely bigger than a chicken, and some just ate insects, lizards, and eggs.

A herd of *Coelophysis* chasing prey. Living in a group gave the smallish dinosaurs some protection from larger predators.

AN EARLY MEAT EATER

Speed was important to many meat-eating dinosaurs. *Coelophysis*, one of the earliest dinosaurs, is a good example of this. It stalked the dry desertlike lands of what is now New Mexico during the Late Triassic Period. Its upright posture, hollow bones, light build, and powerful legs made it a very fast runner.

Although *Coelophysis* was not a large dinosaur, its long neck gave it a good view of approaching prey and predators. It hunted small reptiles and even ate other young *Coelophysis* when there was no other food around.

Like many meat eaters, *Coelophysis* hunted in packs. This allowed it to kill prey far bigger than itself.

Tyrannosaurus rex

WATCH YOUR STEP!

Tyrannosaurus rex was so heavy and tall, it would probably have smashed its skull if it tripped over while chasing prey. Its tiny arms were too small to protect it from a fall.

SHARP TEETH AND TALONS

Many dinosaurs relied on special features, such as teeth or claws. *Compsognathus* may have been the smallest meat-eating dinosaur. It roamed the sprawling forests of Germany and France, during the Late Jurassic Period. Including its tail, it was about 2 feet (0.7 meters) long and weighed little more than a chicken. But, despite its size, *Compsognathus* was a deadly predator. It hunted other small animals, such as lizards and insects, which it caught with its small, sharp teeth and grasping talons. With its light build and long legs it shared many of the same features as the earlier dinosaur, *Coelophysis*.

A POWERFUL GIANT

Tyrannosaurus rex was one of the largest meat eaters that ever lived. It lurked in the forests of North America and Asia, waiting to ambush the hefty plant eaters that shared its habitat. At 7 tons (7 tonnes), it weighed more than an African elephant. Its size made it safe from any other dinosaur on the planet, although *Tyrannosaurus* did occasionally fight each other. But its size and build made it a lumbering, clumsy beast. It would certainly have been a lot less agile than other meat eaters. However, *Tyrannosaurus* had a secret weapon—what it lacked in speed, it more than made up for with its powerful jaw. Its mouth was packed with 60 serrated-edge teeth, which could snap off 500 pounds (230 kilograms) of meat in one bite. Its sight and sense of smell were especially good, too. Because it was not a fast runner, it probably lay in wait for its prey, darting out of the forest to kill unsuspecting plant eaters with a single, massive bite.

When *Tyrannosaurus* bit into flesh, it probably pulled back each side of its jaw, in turn, to slice through the meat with its sharp teeth.

Like *Tyrannosaurus*, *Carcharodontosaurus* was a fierce meat eater with massive jaws and very sharp teeth.

Carcharodontosaurus

DEADLY WEAPONS

The *Velociraptor* was one of the most fearsome predators of the Cretaceous Period. Able to run at 40 mph (60 kph), in short bursts, it terrified slow-moving plant eaters on the baking plains of what is now Mongolia and China. Armed with slashing talons on all four limbs, and around 30 very sharp, curved teeth, *Velociraptor* also had a single, retractable, long claw on the middle toe of each foot. It used the claw like a dagger to stab its prey. Although it was relatively small, it hunted in a pack, so it could attack animals much bigger than itself.

One extraordinary fossil find, unearthed in Mongolia in 1971, gives us a clue to the last violent moments of a *Velociraptor's* life. It shows the predator in a duel to the death with a lumbering *Protoceratops*. The *Velociraptor* is grasping the *Protoceratops'* head shield, while slashing at its belly. The *Protoceratops* has pierced the chest of the *Velociraptor* with its horny, beaklike mouth. Both animals died in the battle and crashed to the ground, to be preserved forever in their final deaththroes.

THE DINOSAUR WITH A SAIL ON ITS BACK

Some dinosaurs, such as the *Spinosaurus*, had very unusual features. *Spinosaurus* hunted other dinosaurs around Northern Africa, during the Late Jurassic Period. Almost as big as *Tyrannosaurus rex*, it measured 39 feet (12 meters) from nose to tail. Its most impressive feature is the big sail on its back. This may have helped the *Spinosaurus* to control its body temperature. It may also have been used to attract female dinosaurs, or frighten male rivals away. Whatever its use, it seems an awkward attachment for a hunter—making it clumsy and vulnerable to attack.

Spinosaurus was different from most meat eaters in other ways, too. Its teeth were straight, rather than curved and serrated. It also had unusually long arms, so it may have occasionally walked on all fours.

As well as hunting for food, *Spinosaurus*, like many other large meat eaters, was probably a scavenger. It was fierce enough to frighten off all but the largest predators from their own kills.

Spinosaurus probably used its claws and crocodilelike jaws to snap up fishes from lakes and rivers.

Spinosaurus

Ornithomimus

Ornithomimus looked very much like an ostrich. It lived on fruit, small insects and animals, and possibly eggs.

A DINOSAUR WITH A BEAK
Some dinosaurs, such as *Ornithomimus*, were omnivores—they ate plant food as well as meat. *Ornithomimus* was about the same size as an ostrich. It lived during the Late Cretaceous Period, in North America and Asia. *Ornithomimus* had a horny beak rather than teeth. It used its clawed fingers to grasp and kill smaller animals, such as lizards and mammals. *Ornithomimus* may have been an egg-eating nest-raider, too. If it was disturbed by an angry parent, it could sprint away at 30 mph (50 kph). Fossil remains show that the *Ornithomimus* had a large brain. It is thought by dinosaur experts to be one of the most intelligent dinosaurs.

The skull of the meat eater Allosaurus

BIG BRAINS
Meat eaters had bigger brains than plant eaters. Finding, chasing, and catching prey required considerably more thought than wandering around in a herd, eating plants.

Plant-eating Dinosaurs

Plant-eating Dinosaurs

Plateosaurus

Plateosaurus rears up to reach leaves in the trees. It may have used its arms to pull down branches too.

GRAZERS AND GRINDERS

Probably two-thirds of all dinosaurs were plant eaters. During the Mesozoic Era—the time dinosaurs walked the Earth—the type of plants available to eat changed a lot. Dinosaur dynasties rose and fell according to the plants they ate.

As one type of plant became rare, so the dinosaurs that ate it starved. As another plant took hold and spread across the land, so the dinosaurs that ate that became more numerous.

At the beginning of the Mesozoic Era the most common plants were conifers, such as redwoods and pines, and horse-tails and cycads. Their leaves and seeds were low in calories and difficult to digest. But by the Cretaceous Period, flowering plants, such as sycamores, magnolias, and laurels had appeared and thrived. These were much more nutritious, and grew in much greater numbers. The availability of such a rich supply of food meant that in the Cretaceous Period there were more dinosaurs than ever before.

Each type of plant-eating dinosaur had its own way of feeding and dealing with the meat eaters that preyed upon it. The biggest dinosaurs ever were plant eaters. Unlike most meat eaters, many plant eaters walked on all fours. Their teeth were usually flat, to strip and chew the plants they ate.

DINOSAUR FOOD CHAIN

Without plants there would have been no plant-eating dinosaurs. Without them, the meat eaters would have had nothing to eat, either. This process is called a food chain, and the panel below shows an example of one:

Meat eaters (Secondary Consumers) *Spinosaurus*

Plant eaters (Primary Consumers) *Iguanodon*

Plants (Producer) Fern

EARLY HERDS

Plateosaurus was one of the earliest known plant-eating dinosaurs. It traveled in large herds, searching for conifers and ferns in Europe during the Late Triassic Period. Its long neck helped it to reach the leaves that smaller plant eaters left behind. It could probably rear up on its back legs to nibble even higher. It had sharp teeth to break up the tough leaves it ate and probably swallowed stones to help it grind up the food in its stomach. *Plateosaurus* had small claws on its limbs, but its main defense against predators was probably its huge size—it grew to around 23 feet (7 meters).

REACH FOR THE SKY

The tallest dinosaur found so far was *Brachiosaurus*. Towering at about 40 feet (12.5 meters) above the ground, *Brachiosaurus* ate from the tops of tall trees, pulling off leaves with its 52 chisel-shaped teeth. It swallowed its food without chewing, leaving the entire process of digestion to its massive gut. It belonged to an order of dinosaurs called sauropods—the largest land animals to have ever lived. Its fossil remains, dating from the Late Jurassic Period, have been found in North America and Africa. Unlike most plant eaters, whose lives were constantly threatened by meat-eating predators, the *Brachiosaurus* could probably graze in peace, as it was well over twice the size of the largest predators around.

Brachiosaurus

As well as eating vegetation high above the ground, *Brachiosaurus* may have swung its head from side to side, cutting off ground-level plants like a lawn mower.

Even the sharp horns of *Triceratops* would not have saved it from the massive jaws and razor-sharp teeth of *Tyrannosaurus*.

BEAK-FACE

Triceratops was a type of dinosaur called a ceratopsian, meaning "one with a horn." Such dinosaurs existed toward the end of the Cretaceous Period. They lived in much of North America and central Asia. Ceratopsians owed their success to the way they ate. With a sharp, parrot-shaped bill of a mouth, chopping teeth and powerful jaws, they could eat even the toughest plants. They chewed their food, too, making it easier to digest. Like many plant eaters, *Triceratops* was probably a herd animal. It may have traveled large distances in search of food.

Triceratops had a huge skull, with three horns and a bony neck plate. These were its greatest defense against meat eaters. But even its size could not frighten off its chief enemy, *Tyrannosaurus rex*.

Triceratops

Tyrannosaurus rex

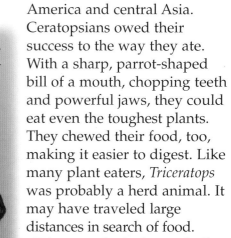

SUIT OF ARMOR

Some plant eaters were heavily armored. *Saichana* was built like a tank. It was a type of plant eater named an anklyosaur. This one lived around Mongolia during the Late Cretaceous Period.

Saichana's low-stooping posture suggests it was a grazer, and it probably nibbled at grasses and bushes with its bill-like mouth. It had a bony plate inside its mouth that allowed it to chew up even the toughest plants.

As well as their fearsome set of body armor, anklyosaurs also had a lethal bony club on the end of their tail to protect them from attackers. The armor must have worked, as anklyosaurs were numerous around North America and East Asia.

Saichana's name means "beautiful lizard." It was called this because of its ornate body armor.

Saichana

Triceratops' skull made up about one-third of its entire length. Experts think that it may have used its long horns to bend down branches to bring them within reach of its mouth.

SPIKES AND PLATES

Other plant eaters had different forms of defense. *Stegosaurus* had its own built-in protection. Its bony back plates were probably too fragile to act effectively as armor, but the spikes on its tail could have been very useful against any attacker.

Stegosaurus lived in North America in the Late Jurassic Period. They weighed 2 tons (2 tonnes), and were at least 20 feet (6 meters) long. Unusually, their back legs were twice as long as their front legs, so their heads sloped forward toward the ground. The hind legs were probably strong enough to allow *Stegosaurus* to rear up to feed on tree branches.

Stegosaurus had a toothless bill at the front of its jaw, with small chewing teeth at the back, to help it mash up the tough ferns, mosses, and conifers it ate.

NEW TEETH FOR OLD
One group of dinosaurs, called hadrosaurs, had no teeth at the front of their mouth, but had rows of cheek teeth in their upper and lower jaws. Old teeth, worn out by endlessly chewing a tough plant diet, were continually replaced by new ones. No other type of dinosaur had this natural advantage, and it helped the hadrosaurs become some of the most

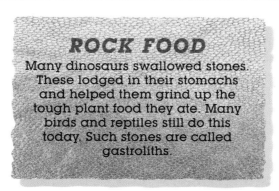

ROCK FOOD
Many dinosaurs swallowed stones. These lodged in their stomachs and helped them grind up the tough plant food they ate. Many birds and reptiles still do this today. Such stones are called gastroliths.

common, successful dinosaurs of their time.

Hypacrosaurus was a 30 foot (9 meter) long hadrosaur, and it grazed in herds in the forests of North America, during the Late Cretaceous Period. It probably moved on all fours as it searched for pine needles, fruit, and magnolia leaves. But unlike most other plant eaters, if threatened it could run away at some speed on its powerful hind legs. *Hypacrosaurus* ate all kinds of plants, as the period it lived in saw a huge spread in plant life across the globe. Their success as a species may well have led to the extinction of other plant eaters, such as *Iguanodon*, and giant sauropods, such as *Brachiosaurus*, which were too slow to compete with them.

In the Cretaceous Period, the first trees and flowering plants appeared. Ferns, conifers, and gingkoes were still plentiful.

Built for Fighting

Any animal that eats meat has a natural advantage over a plant eater. Meat is the most nutritious food of all and it is easy to digest. A large meal can keep a carnivore going for days before it needs to eat again.

But meat eaters use up a lot of energy to catch a meal. They have to track down their food, then they have to fight it. Their prey may escape, or they themselves may be fatally wounded during the struggle to kill it. While they eat, they may be chased off by larger carnivores, eager for an easy meal. Even worse, unless they are the largest carnivores of all, they may even be hunted and eaten by other predators.

With all these problems, surprise attack and fearsome weaponry were essential for carnivores to survive. Meat-eating dinosaurs had the sharpest brains, the keenest senses, (fossil records show carnivores had noticeably larger areas of their brains controlling sight and smell), and most of all, they had the sharpest teeth and claws.

SHARK-TOOTH KILLER

Tyrannosaurus rex may have ruled the Cretaceous landscape of North America and Asia, but *Carcharodontosaurus* (its name means "Shark-tooth lizard") was the top predator in Africa at that time.

The massive head and jaws of *Tarbosaurus*, a Late Cretaceous predator.

Along with other gigantic theropods, such as *Allosaurus*, *Carcharodontosaurus* was blessed with the most ferocious weapon of all—a skull about 6 feet (2 meters) long, with a massive mouth stuffed to bursting with narrow, curved, serrated-edged teeth. Such teeth made perfect tools for both killing and feeding. Once contact had been made, powerful jaw muscles clamped the teeth tight around the target, and the *Carcharodontosaurus*'s thick neck would jerk backward and forward, wrenching huge chunks of flesh away from its victim. As if this wasn't enough, such giant killers had ferocious claws on their hind legs, which could cause lethal wounds to any plant eater. The small front limbs had claws, too.

Although it could run fast on its powerful hind legs, the size of *Carcharodontosaurus* and its cousins probably meant a long chase was out of the question. They probably lay in wait for their prey, then dashed out to ambush it. Rushing forward with open mouth, at a speed of about 20 mph (30 kph), they would have aimed at their victim's weakest spot—probably the back of the neck.

GANG WARFARE

Smaller meat eaters could hunt lizards and small mammals alone, but together they could bring down a dinosaur over ten times their own weight. Their hunting techniques may have been similar to those of today's lions and jackals, which create diversions and ambushes to bring down their prey. Then again, perhaps

Deinonychus just attacked together, hoping to bring down plant-eating prey by sheer ferocity and weight of numbers. Like *Carcharodontosaurus*, *Deinonychus* had a large head filled with sharp teeth. It also had three spindly claws on each hand, and a ferocious 5-inch- (13-centimeter-) long dagger among the claws on its feet.

This illustration is based on an actual fossil find in Montana. The fossil remains show a *Tenontosaurus* alongside several *Deinonychus*—brought down as they tried to overcome the massive plant eater.

Deinonychus

Tenontosaurus

Built for Defense

The big plant eaters had two major problems. The first was finding enough to eat. Plant food is low in nutrition, and a plant-eating animal as big as a dinosaur probably spent almost every waking hour trying to eat enough vegetation to keep it alive. The second problem was being eaten by the most ferocious, terrifying creatures that ever walked the Earth. To cope with this, many plant eaters were well protected, with horns, claws, spikes, and armor. Others grew to extreme sizes—becoming the biggest land animals to ever exist. Others, still, were fast enough to run away from trouble. Plant eaters, such as the hadrosaurs and ceratopsians were herd animals, like wildebeest and antelope are today. The herd would have offered safety in numbers, and also allowed most to feed while a few kept an eye out for predators.

ARMOR PLATES

Euoplocephalus was a short and stocky type of dinosaur named an ankylosaur. Covered with heavy bands of armor plates and spikes, it was almost completely protected from above. Thick spines protected the side of its face, and even its eyelids were armored. But underneath, its softer underbelly was much more vulnerable. To turn it over, a predator had to brave a deadly weapon. Like all ankylosaurs, it had a solid ball of bone at the tip of its tail. Swung around forcefully, it could crush the legs or ribs of an attacker, leaving them with massive internal injuries or broken limbs.

Such powerful defenses, together with an ability to eat most kinds of plants, meant that ankylosaurs, such as *Euoplocephalus,* were able to thrive in great numbers.

Euoplocephalus

Despite its heavy armor, *Euoplocephalus* was able to move fairly quickly when being chased.

Tuojiangosaurus

Yangchuanosaurus

The four tail spikes were *Tuojiangosaurus*'s only defense against attacking predators.

VICIOUS TAIL

Threatened by a ravenous meat eater such as *Yangchuanosaurus*, a *Tuojiangosaurus* could defend itself with its four-pronged tail. These bony spikes were well over 2 feet (0.7 meters) long, and could easily inflict a fatal injury if they pierced a predator's innards.

Attack was the *Tuojiangosaurus*'s main means of defense. It was too heavy and lumbering to escape by running away. Its small brain and low intelligence, and the fact that it spent most of its waking life with its head down, grazing the grass, meant that it must have been particularly easy to stalk.

Its 15 pairs of bony back plates might have offered some protection, too. But dinosaur experts are not sure about the use of the spikes and plates found on the backs of stegosaurs like *Tuojiangosaurus*. They certainly look sharp and dangerous enough to put off an attacker, but may have been quite fragile. If this is the case, they would have been used mainly to threaten rival males and impress females.

HORNS AND PLATES

The *Styracosaurus* was a ceratopsian—one of the most successful types of plant eaters of the Cretaceous Period. Like the ankylosaurs, their abundance was based on a winning combination of efficient eating habits and ferocious defenses. *Styracosaurus* was not as well armored as the ankylosaurs, but perhaps this made it faster. However, its neck, often one of the most vulnerable spots in any plant eater, was extremely well defended. It had a heavy armor plate, topped with a collar of vicious spikes. The great nose horn would have been very effective, too. Being the wrong end of a charging 5 ton (5 tonne) *Styracosaurus* would be a disastrous experience for even the largest carnivore.

The Way they Walked

Dinosaurs walked in one of two ways. Some walked on their hind legs. These are known as bipeds. Some walked on all four limbs. These are known as quadrupeds. Some two-legged dinosaurs spent time grazing on all fours, but ran on their hind legs.

Dinosaurs developed a way of walking that was far superior to the way their reptilian relatives walk now. Look at any lizard or crocodile, and you can see that their limbs are attached to the sides of their bodies. Some can move incredibly fast, but their muscles have to work extra hard to do this.

Dinosaurs, on the other hand, had their legs directly under their bodies, like birds and mammals do today. This gave them two distinct advantages. The two-legged ones could run faster, and the four-legged ones could carry their weight more easily.

Struthiomimus

A SURVIVOR

Alamosaurus was one of the last of the massive sauropods. It still roamed the Earth at the time of the great dinosaur extinction at the end of the Cretaceous Period. It was named after an American fort defended to the last man against the Mexican army in 1836.

Struthiomimus had to be quick and agile to catch the small, fast-moving prey on which it fed.

Alamosaurus

The large sauropod dinosaurs, such as *Alamosaurus*, *Apatosaurus* and *Diplodocus*, were not designed to move quickly.

SPEED KILLS

Almost every meat-eating dinosaur walked on its hind legs. From the huge *Tyrannosaurus*, right down to the chickenlike *Compsognathus*, carnivores had to chase—and that meant outrunning their prey.

The ostrichlike *Struthiomimus* darted around the riverbanks of Late Cretaceous North America, snapping up small animals and insects. Its long, light legs, driven by powerful thigh and hip muscles, could run at over 30 mph (50 kph).

Struthiomimus's foot, like the feet of all meat-eating dinosaurs, was held so that it was always balanced on its toes. This increased the length of its legs, giving it a longer stride.

HEAVYWEIGHT CHAMPIONS

Anything that weighs over 30 tons (30 tonnes), and is nearly 70 feet (21 meters) long needs a lot of support. Plant eaters, such as *Alamosaurus,* had no option but to walk on four legs, and they were superbly designed to do so.

Most plant eaters needed very big stomachs, to digest the enormous amount of food they ate. This is one reason why *Alamosaurus* grew so big. Its body was held on four stout elephantlike legs, which were designed to carry its weight rather than allow it to move quickly. Each leg ended in a set of stubby toes, supported by a thick heel pad.

Not all plant eaters walked on four legs, but almost all the four-legged dinosaurs were plant eaters. *Alamosaurus* could probably rear up on its hind legs to reach the very tops of trees. It would have used its long tail as a "fifth leg" to steady its balance.

DINOSAURS
in
DETAIL

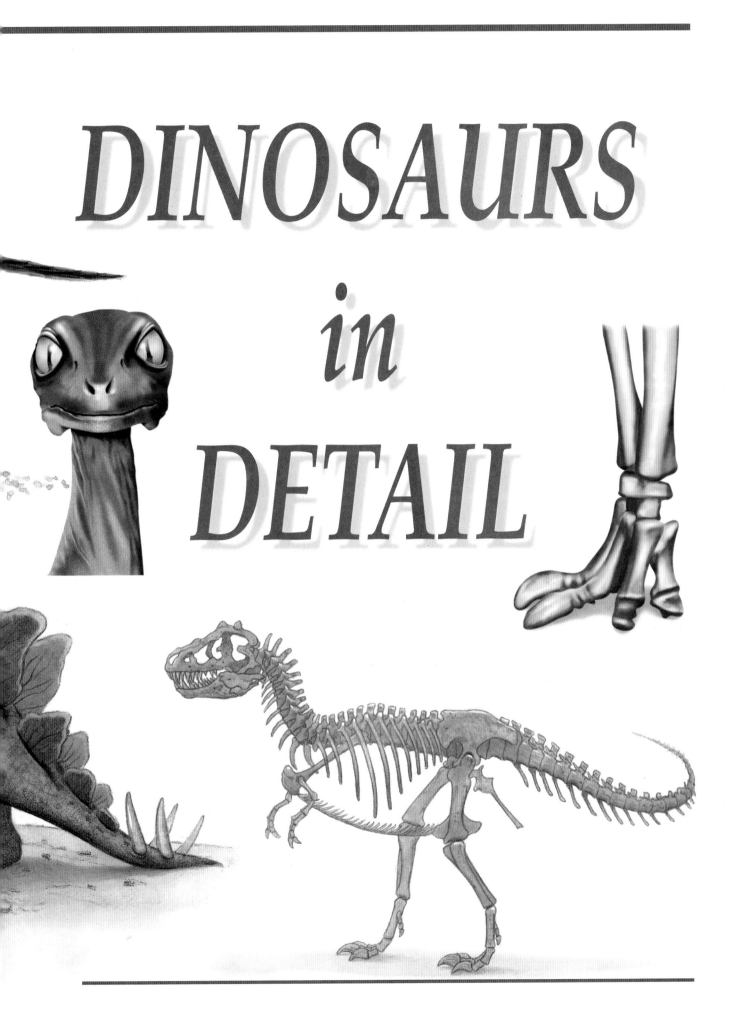

Brains and Intelligence

If anyone knows one fact about dinosaur intelligence, it is usually "they had brains the size of a walnut." Some of them did, but that did not stop them from being extremely successful animals and thriving on the Earth for millions of years. While it is true that dinosaurs were not the most intelligent of animals, they had the brains they needed to survive.

Much of what we do know about dinosaur brains is based very much on guesswork. Brain and nerve tissue decay very quickly after death, and ideas about dinosaurs' intelligence are based on the size of brain cases and nerve channels in fossilized skulls and backbones. Even this kind of research has only been carried out in around 5 percent of all known dinosaur types.

Tröodon's large eyes and brain were the secret of its success as a hunter, enabling it to catch small scuttling mammal and lizard prey that would have eluded less intelligent dinosaurs with poorer sight.

On average, dinosaur intelligence can probably be compared with that of bony fish, amphibians, such as frogs, and reptiles, such as crocodiles. What we do know is that the meat eaters had bigger brains than the plant eaters. The more an animal had to do, the more brain power it needed to do it. There is also some evidence, based on what we know about how the brain works, that meat eaters had a more highly developed sense of vision, and plant eaters had a more highly developed sense of smell.

BUSY BRAIN

Tröodon is considered to be the most intelligent of all dinosaurs. Scientists have worked this out by comparing its brain size to the rest of its body. It was probably smarter than an average emu, and at least as clever as a possum. Its way of life required a lot of brain power. Large grasping hands, with slim fingers would have allowed it to be able to grasp and pull. It was very fast on its feet and could probably move with great agility. Studies of the brain case suggest that it had a good sense of balance. It also had very large eyes for a dinosaur, and may even have been a night hunter.

Kentrosaurus

Heavily armored and with little more to concentrate on than munching leaves, *Kentrosaurus* had no need of a large brain.

Tröodon

NOT VERY SMART

Scientists work out dinosaur intelligence by comparing the size of a dinosaur's brain with the size of its body. This is called the "Encephalization Quotient" (EQ). They match the dinosaur EQ with the EQ of living animals such as fish, crocodiles, and small mammals and assume their intelligence to be similar.

NUT-SIZED BRAIN

Kentrosaurus belongs to the stegosaur family. Its tiny head really did contain a brain the size of a walnut, but this was enough to control its bulky body. Its protective armor plates and spikes meant that it did not need to think quickly when facing an attacker.

Sight and Sound

Little is known about how dinosaurs saw their world and what kind of noises they made. We can make some guesses about their eyesight based on fossil remains of optic nerve channels and brains cases, and on what we know about animals today. Most hunters have sharp color vision, and it is likely that the meat-eating dinosaurs had this, too. Many plant eaters today have poor vision and some only see in black and white. Perhaps many plant-eating dinosaurs were like this as well.

There is even less evidence available relating to the sounds that dinosaurs made. But from howling to attract a mate or calling to warn others of danger, to bellowing in fear or snarling in anger, sound is an essential part of the animal world. No doubt dinosaurs made these noises, too.

Tröodon's eyes were large and forward-facing.

STEREOSCOPIC SIGHT

The position of the eye sockets in an animal's skull gives it various advantages and disadvantages. If the eyes are placed squarely on the side of the head, then it is likely that an animal has a good all-around view of its surroundings. It can watch pretty much everything around it without even having to move its head. If the eyes are placed more to the front of the head, so that their field of vision overlaps, this all-around view is lost. But it is replaced by something much more useful—stereoscopic sight. Fossil skull remains show us that tyrannosaurs, such as the *Alioramus*, had this stereoscopic vision. This gives an animal the ability to judge depth—vital for a hunter who needs to time a surprise ambush to the split second, or judge a leap on to the back of a ceratopsian precisely, to avoid its lethal horns.

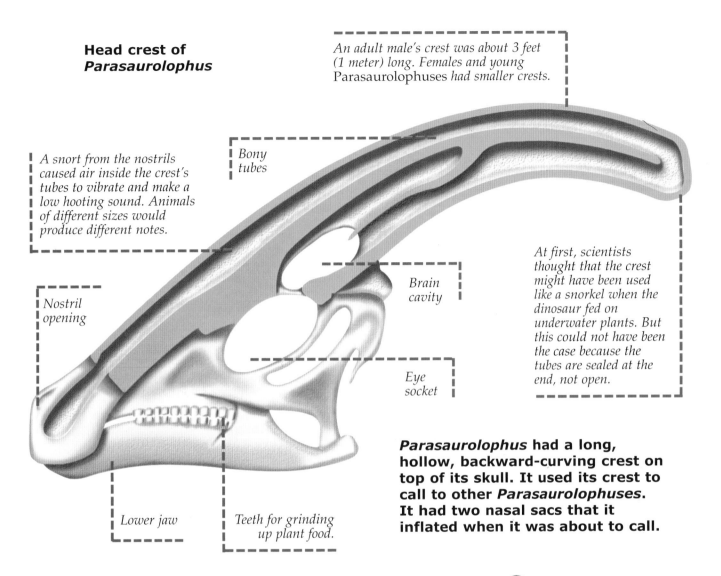

Head crest of *Parasaurolophus*

An adult male's crest was about 3 feet (1 meter) long. Females and young Parasaurolophuses had smaller crests.

Bony tubes

A snort from the nostrils caused air inside the crest's tubes to vibrate and make a low hooting sound. Animals of different sizes would produce different notes.

Brain cavity

Nostril opening

At first, scientists thought that the crest might have been used like a snorkel when the dinosaur fed on underwater plants. But this could not have been the case because the tubes are sealed at the end, not open.

Eye socket

Lower jaw

Teeth for grinding up plant food.

***Parasaurolophus* had a long, hollow, backward-curving crest on top of its skull. It used its crest to call to other *Parasaurolophuses*. It had two nasal sacs that it inflated when it was about to call.**

MUSICAL CRESTS

Some of the plant-eating hadrosaurs had curious crests and crescents on their heads. Many theories have been put forward regarding their use, from breathing apparatus to mating displays. The most likely one is that they generated sound. Inside the crest of the *Parasaurolophus*, were a series of passages. Recent research with a reconstructed crest has shown that this would have made a great, deep, reverberating note. Such a noise would have traveled long distances over the forests of Late Cretaceous North America, where *Parasaurolophus* made its home. Perhaps *Parasaurolophus* made such noises to make contact with others of its kind. (Whales are able to communicate over vast distances today, using similar low-frequency sounds.) Deep notes are also ideal as a warning, as it is difficult to identify where they came from. This would be essential for any plant eater not wanting to draw attention to itself from a predator on the prowl.

ABLE TO SEE IN THE DARK

During the Mesozoic Era dinosaurs lived in the Antarctic region of the Earth. Although it was warmer than it is today, there were still long periods of continuous darkness during the winter. Fossil evidence shows that animals such as *Leaellynasaurus* who lived there had especially well-developed eyes to help them see during these dark days.

Color

Nobody knows what color dinosaurs were. Their bones may remain with us as fossils. The texture of their skin may imprint itself in mud that turns to rock. Even their footprints have left their mark in the Earth. But color is something that has not survived the 70 million-year gap between extinction and today.

When the Victorians first became aware of dinosaurs, in mid-nineteenth-century Britain, they thought that the gigantic creatures they found would have been a dull green, brown, or gray. These were the colors of the largest animals, such as elephants, or reptiles, such as crocodiles or monitor lizards, which their dinosaur finds slightly resembled.

Today, we are not so sure. Much of what we imagine dinosaurs looked like is based on what we know about animals now. Animals survive and thrive because they have specific features, or adaptations, that give them some natural advantage in the world they inhabit. Some,

including dinosaur descendants, such as birds, snakes, and lizards, use colors as camouflage, warning signals, and to communicate with each other. The colors in this book are based on successful color adaptations seen in animals today.

CAMOUFLAGE

Prosaurolophus grazed and foraged for pine needles, magnolia leaves, seeds, and fruits in the Cretaceous forests of North America. Its likely coloring may have reflected the dark, shaded world of the forest floor. Browny and dark- and light-green patches would help it blend among the tree trunks, leaves, and shafts of sunlight.

It is thought that many hadrosaurs like *Prosaurolophus* had this kind of coloration. And it was not only plant eaters that had such markings. The stalking carnivores had just as much need to hide themselves from their prey, and many were probably colored in this way, too.

A *Stegosaurus* flushes its back plates bright pink to scare off a threatening *Allosaurus*.

DON'T MAKE ME ANGRY!

Imagine this scene: An *Allosaurus* approaches a *Stegosaurus*, and they circle each other, ready for a fight to the death. As they roar and snarl, the *Stegosaurus* flushes its diamond-shaped back plates bright pink, sending an alarm signal to its enemy.

Many animals today use a similar tactic—named a "threat display"—to avoid a real fight. The idea is to show your opponent that you are extremely angry and prepared to do battle. When it was courting female *Stegosauruses*, a male probably also flushed its plates at rival males, to warn them off.

This is still just a theory. Research has suggested that the plates on *Stegosaurus's* back were too fragile to be much use as armor.

With its coloring helping it to blend in with its forest surroundings, *Prosaurolophus* could forage safely, hidden from predators.

They were also rich in blood vessels, which could have made the plates flush pink. Like many predators today, *Allosaurus* probably had sharp color vision. Instinct or experience would have warned it that a *Stegosaurus* with bright pink spines was likely to put up a fight.

TOO BIG TO BOTHER

The biggest dinosaurs were probably dull browns, greens, or grays, as the Victorians thought. Once an animal reaches a certain size, camouflage becomes useless. It is too big to hide, and it is also unlikely to be attacked for the same reason.

Eggs and Nests

Eggs had lumpy surfaces to stop them bunching together in the nest.

Some dinosaur babies were able to look after themselves immediately after birth—others were not.

Eggs were often arranged in groups in the nest.

This illustration is based directly on that most rare of dinosaur finds—an actual egg with an embyro inside it.

Egg shells had tiny pores to allow the babies to breathe.

A few dinosaurs gave birth to live young, but most dinosaurs laid eggs. The eggs and nests that have been found have much to tell us about how dinosaurs lived. Like most reptiles today, dinosaurs had many young, but did not usually look after them. Only a few seem to have nurtured their babies once they had hatched.

There have been no egg finds for whole dinosaur families, such as the stegosaurs and ankylosaurs. But what we do know is very revealing. Communal egg sites tell us that the dinosaurs who made them were sociable. Massive nesting sites tell us that, like birds, some dinosaurs returned to the same spot year after year to lay their eggs.

Some nests were carefully constructed. They had leaf linings, or earth rims. The eggs inside were often laid and arranged with care. But other eggs were laid as the dinosaur walked along, absent-mindedly depositing her offspring in the tracks behind her. (Chameleons still do this today.)

BABY FACE
Fossil evidence reveals that in one dinosaur family, the hadrosaurs, the young looked noticeably different from the adults. They had all the classic, cute baby features of big eyes, round heads and shortened snouts, that scientists think trigger nurturing instincts in animal parents.

INSIDE THE EGG

Curled up snugly, an *Orodromeus* baby grows inside its egg. Eggs were often one of as many as 19, laid in a carefully arranged spiral, by a small, two-legged plant eater. Typical vertebrate eggs had a hard shell that let gases in and out. This would enable the growing dinosaur inside to take in oxygen. When the baby was ready to hatch, it was also ready for the outside world. *Orodromeus* hatchlings entered the world fully able to look after themselves. Their parents may have guarded the unhatched eggs, but would not have looked after the babies.

We know this because nest finds show eggs that have opened but remained untrampled. This shows that the baby left the nest immediately. Whether it discovered its new world in the relative safety of a small clutch of other baby *Orodromeus*, or struck out alone, we do not know.

HELLO, MOM!

A female *Leaellynasaura* stoops over her hungry hatchlings. As they chirp for food, she spits out a nourishing paste of half-digested plant food. The nests were hollowed in the ground and lined with insulating leaves. They generated warmth as they decayed, and kept the eggs at a temperature necessary for the life within them to flourish.

The babies would have been about 1 foot (30 centimeters) when they hatched, and were totally dependent on their parents. Their bones were too weak to allow much movement, so they would have had to be fed in their nest.

We know that some dinosaur babies were like this because nest finds have shown egg shells trampled into small pieces. One find showed a nest full of babies. The instinct to stay must have been very strong because they all died there. Perhaps a parent was killed while foraging for food to bring back for them, and the abandoned chicks starved to death.

Unusually for dinosaurs, *Leaellynasauras* invested a lot of care and attention on both their nests and hatchlings.

Feet and Footprints

During their life on Earth dinosaurs evolved extremely effective ways of getting about. From the speedy two-legged meat eaters to the huge four-legged plant eaters, all of them walked on their toes. This did not necessarily make them as graceful, but it did mean that they could move their bodies with minimum effort and maximum efficiency.

These feet also left the only evidence, aside from eggs and teeth marks, of what dinosaurs actually did during their lifetimes. Dinosaur tracks were first found in 1836, but it took a while for science to realize the importance of this discovery. It is difficult to believe that something as fleeting as a footprint could survive for the 65 million years or more since the dinosaurs became extinct. But survive they did, and dinosaur footprints have much to tell us about their owners.

Ankle joint

Leg bones could be as thick as tree trunks.

The foot bones were locked together to make a long extension to the leg and give a longer stride.

The toes were probably covered by round, horny pads.

Toes were broad and splayed to spread the weight over a wide area.

Birdlike toes

Sharp claws

The feet of two-legged theropod carnivores (left) were built for speed and balance, while those of four-legged sauropod herbivores (above) were designed to support the dinosaur's great body weight.

TWO TYPES OF FEET

There are two different types of dinosaur feet (shown left). The bone structure of these two types gives a lot of information about how dinosaurs moved around. The first foot belongs to a two-legged, or bipedal, theropod predator. The long, slender, birdlike toes gave a solid grip on the ground and kept the animal as well balanced as possible—all vital skills in the acrobatic twists and turns of a chase. Walking on toes also increased the length of the leg, so this dinosaur would have had a longer stride. This meant that it could walk or run faster.

The second foot belongs to a four-legged, or quadrupedal, sauropod plant eater. It had to hold and transport a huge amount of weight, and is remarkably similar to the foot of a modern-day elephant. The toes were shorter and broader than in the theropod foot. Although the dinosaur walked on its toes, the hind foot was supported by a thick, fibrous wedge, which acted like the heel of a shoe. Like elephants do today, sauropods probably walked with their legs held stiffly. This wedge would have saved them the effort of having to lift the entire foot off the ground whenever they took a step.

DINOSAUR FARMERS
Because of their enormous weight, dinosaur footprints did much to churn up the soil and vegetation where they walked. Such disruption to the local environment would have created ideal conditions for the new flowering plants of the Cretaceous Period to take root and flourish.

Apatosaurus footprints left in riverbank mud

OUT FOR A STROLL

A group of *Apatosauruses* trek across the soft mud of a riverbank, one misty Late Jurassic morning. Although they are difficult to read very accurately, the tracks dinosaurs left behind give us some clues about their appearance and habits. For example, the deep indentations left by these *Apatosauruses* give a strong impression of great weight. The sets of tracks are side by side, suggesting they were sociable, herd animals. Tracks left in mud flats, sand dunes, and swamps have now been found all over the world. Far more meat eater tracks have been discovered than plant eater tracks. This is almost certainly because meat eaters were much more active than plant eaters, and probably spent much of their lives patrolling their territory searching for prey.

Teeth

The teeth increased in size from the back of the jaw to the front.

Tyrannosaurus's sawlike, backward-curving teeth sliced through flesh and tough dinosaur skin with ease.

Some of the teeth grew up to 7 in (18 cm) long.

Dinosaur teeth tell a fascinating story. They come in all shapes and sizes and show what a dinosaur ate and how it ate it. Killing teeth, tearing teeth, plucking teeth, grinding teeth—all worked to suit the diet and life style of the dinosaur they belonged to.

Dinosaurs were constantly replacing teeth throughout their lives. This is something reptiles and some other animals still do today. The plant eaters ground down their teeth with their endless chewing, and the meat eaters left teeth in the corpses of their victims.

Some dinosaurs, such as the ornithomimids did not even have teeth. They had a sharp, bill-like mouth that was well-adapted to their omnivorous (plant- and meat-eating) diet. Other dinosaurs, such as the plant-eating hadrosaurs, had over a thousand teeth packed into their jaws.

With its fearsome array of sharp teeth and powerful jaw muscles, *Tyrannosaurus* held its prey in a vicelike grip. Then it simply twisted its head to rip off a chunk of meat.

OUCH!

As you might expect, the carnivore *Tyrannosaurus rex* had a skull full of ferocious bone-crunching and flesh-tearing teeth. Other top predators in the dinosaur world had teeth with many similar features. The sharp, cone-shaped spikes were ideally suited to the task of killing and eating the hadrosaurs and ceratopsians that they hunted. Designed to aid the *Tyrannosaurus* in a quick kill, the curved teeth would sink farther into struggling prey, making escape or fighting back even more unlikely.

The teeth were attached to a heavily built jaw that was over 4 feet (1.2 meters) long. The jaw was even hinged at the top of the skull to allow the snout to tilt up and down. This would absorb the shock of the first killing bite, and allow the *Tyrannosaurus* some flexibility while feeding. The jaw had some give at the sides, too, and could bulge out, to accommodate a particularly large mouthful of meat.

Tyrannosaurus shared many features of its teeth with another terrifying predator—today's shark. Not only were the teeth replaceable, but they were also serrated, like a kitchen carving knife. This was particularly useful when it came to tearing off enormous chunks of meat.

SLICE UP

Ceratopsians such as *Triceratops* probably benefited from the most efficient plant-eating apparatus. Well-muscled jaws like these could cope with a wide variety of plant food, from the toughest cones and branches, to the more succulent and easily-digested flowering plants. There was certainly plenty of choice in the *Triceratops's* habitat—the upland forests of North America.

The sharp, horny bill was used to snip up tough leaves, stems, and branches.

The teeth were self-sharpening

FULL STOMACH

Not all plant eaters relied on their teeth to eat. Some, such as the enormous sauropods, just used their teeth to strip leaves from trees, and did not chew their food before they swallowed. They relied entirely on their enormous stomachs to break up their food.

Triceratops's bill got worn down by tough plants, but it continued to grow during the dinosaur's life.

The front part of the jaw, a parrotlike bill, was designed for cutting. Behind the bill were hundreds of sharp, interlocking teeth, which moved up and down like guillotine blades, slicing up vegetation as the *Triceratops* chewed. Its large, muscular tongue would push its food between its cheeks and teeth before swallowing and further digestion in the stomach.

Skin

We can take a good guess at what kind of shape dinosaurs were from the bones they left behind. Put together, like an enormous jigsaw puzzle, the bones also tell us how big they were. But what did they look like on the outside? Although we can only guess at their color, we do have a little more idea about what their skin was like. Over the years, some remarkable fossils have come to light that have preserved the texture of dinosaur skin. They show quite clearly that dinosaurs had a scaly reptilian surface, much like the hide of a crocodile today.

But a few skin imprints on mud that has turned to stone can never tell the whole story—especially in a class of animals as wide-ranging as the dinosaurs. Because they are so delicate, fossil skin impressions are very difficult to find and preserve. We also have no idea at what stage of an animal's decay the impression was made. An imprint could be anything —from a dinosaur that died and was preserved almost immediately—to one that was shriveled and dried up like an Egyptian mummy. As might be expected, the skin that has been found shows many variations. Some skins have horny spines and bumps among the scales. Others have a warty texture. These extra patterns would have helped to toughen a dinosaur's outer layer.

Cetiosaurus's **thick skin would not have protected it from predators such as** *Stegosaurus*.

Chasmosaurus's **thick, scaly skin covered the openings between the bones of the horn frill.**

Scales produced a tough skin.

Tubercle gives extra protection to the animal's body.

Tail had tubercles for extra protection from enemies.

Cetiosaurus *was as big as six elephants.*

Hexagonal scales

Dinosaur skin resembles that of modern crocodiles.

HEXAGONAL SCALES

Dinosaur skin was first discovered in the 1800s, and the first sample to come to light was sauropod skin, like that of the *Cetiosaurus* pictured here. It took several years for scientists to realize that it belonged to a dinosaur, rather than a giant crocodile, which was what they first thought. When they were first pieced together in museum models, and as illustrations in books and magazines, people thought that the huge sauropods would have smooth, scaleless skin, like that of other large animals today, such as whales and elephants. But the reptilian, hexagonal scales on the skin clearly showed that this was not the case. More recent fossil finds suggest that some sauropods may also have had spines along the skin of their backs, like the fringes on iguanas.

LUMPS AND BUMPS

Fossil skin samples of a ceratopsian called *Chasmosaurus* show that, not only does it have scales, but it also has bumps placed among them. These bumps, known as tubercles, would add an additional protective covering to the hide, and may have been more numerous around vulnerable areas of a dinosaur's body, such as the neck, thigh, and tail. The scales on ceratopsian skin samples have been found to be much larger than scales on iguanodonts, for example. The larger scales would have made the hide thicker and given the dinosaur more protection from the claws and teeth of predators.

KEEP YOUR COOL
Some scientists think that the extra lumps and bumps on dinosaur skin were to give them a greater overall surface area. Because there was more of the body to lose heat from, this would have helped them to stay cooler when it was hot.

Feathers

Fossils of Sinornithosaurus millenii seem to show that some dinosaurs had feathers, probably for insulation.

During the mid-1800s, scientists realized that birds and reptiles shared some characteristics. Ever since then, people have wondered whether these two types of animal also had common ancestors in the dinosaurs. The discovery of *Archaeopteryx* in 1861 added fuel to this debate. *Archaeopteryx* is considered to be the first bird, but its skeleton is strikingly similar to the theropod dinosaur *Compsognathus*.

In the mid-1990s other extraordinary fossil finds, unearthed in China, set dinosaur experts reeling. One dinosaur, named *Sinosauropteryx prima*, was a tiny theropod, about 3 feet (1 meter) long, dating from about 135 million years ago. Like *Archaeopteryx,* this dinosaur was also similar in many ways to *Compsognathus*. But what made it so unusual was the fact that its body was covered in tiny 1-inch- (3-centimeter) long feathers. The structure of the feathers made them unsuitable for flying, so they probably acted as insulation. This discovery was important evidence for the argument that birds were descended from small dinosaurs that had evolved feathers. Such fossil-finds are making us re-think our ideas about what dinosaurs looked like, particularly the meat-eating theropods.

Long dinosaurlike tail

Sinornithosaurus millenii had strong back legs because it could not fly.

Winglike upper arms

Sinornithosaurus millenii

NEXT STOP, BIRDS?

Protarchaeopteryx, which dates from the same period as *Sinosauropteryx prima*, is thought to be another ancestor of *Archaeopteryx*. It had a birdlike appearance. Although it could not fly, its bones were hollow, and it had sprouted feathers instead of scales. Most of its body was covered in short, downy feathers, but it had longer feathers on its front limbs and tail. Like other early, birdlike dinosaurs, the feathers were intended to keep it warm. This also suggests that this dinosaur was warm-blooded, like its bird descendants. Two other recent finds, named *Sinornithosaurus millenii* (see left), and *Archaeoraptor liaoningensis*, also resemble a curious halfway stage between dinosaurs and birds. Fossil remains show clear evidence of feathers, and they both have winglike upper limbs, and lightweight hollow bones. But they also have long dinosaur tails, and could almost certainly not fly.

It was many millions of years before the feathers that had originally evolved to keep their owners warm were used for gliding, and eventually, powered flight. But it is feathers, more than any other physical characteristic, that make birds the greatest flyers in the animal world.

Tyrannosaurus's whole body may have been covered in feathers.

Short arms were typical of Tyrannosaurus rex.

Feathers are thought to have been more "shaggy" than birds' feathers.

Tyrannosaurus rex baby

It is possible that a newly hatched baby *Tyrannosaurus* had a fluffy down covering, which it would gradually shed as it grew bigger.

FLUFFY T-REX!

The tough-guy image of the *Tyrannosaurus rex* has taken a serious bashing. Fossil-finds suggest that tyrannosaur hatchlings may have been covered in downy feathers, much like those of baby birds. Many of *Tyrannosaurus's* relatives had feathers, so it may have had them, too. If the adult did have feathers though, they would have been used to attract the attention of a mate, rather than to keep warm. Large animals, such as the *Tyrannosaurus*, had little need for the extra insulation that feathers would bring, especially in the warm, humid environment in which they lived. But baby animals lose heat from their bodies much more quickly, and need to be kept warm.

Dinosaur Blood

All animals are either warm- or cold-blooded. Cold-blooded animals, such as reptiles, have bodies that are as warm or cold as their surroundings. Warm and cold weather affects them more than warm-blooded animals. If they are too cold they become slow. If they are too hot, they dry up and die.

Warm-blooded animals, such as birds and mammals, burn up food to make their own heat in their bodies. They have to stay the same temperature, no matter what their environment is like.

Dromiceiomimus

Dromiceiomimus is one of the dinosaurs that has been used by scientists to prove that dinosaurs were warm-blooded.

Komodo dragon

There are advantages and disadvantages to both systems. For example, warm-blooded animals tend to be more active, but have to eat all the time to keep their bodies going. Cold-blooded animals can make a meal last for weeks. There has been a great deal of discussion about whether dinosaurs were warm-blooded or cold-blooded. No one knows for sure. Dinosaurs themselves could be so completely different—compare a huge four-legged plant eater, such as *Diplodocus*, with a tiny meat eater, such as *Compsognathus*—that it is entirely possible that some were warm-blooded and some were cold-blooded.

WARM-BLOODED THEORY

This *Dromiceiomimus* stalks the forests of Alberta, Canada, its keen eyes straining in the dark, looking for any unwary lizard or scurrying mammal foolish enough to think that night-time was a safe time to venture out. Night hunters, such as *Dromiceiomimus,* provide one of the arguments for dinosaurs being warm-blooded. The lower temperatures at night would make it much more difficult for a cold-blooded animal to move with any speed and agility.

It is the dinosaurs' fleet-footedness, more than anything else, that makes many people believe that they were warm-blooded. Supporters of this theory also point out that dinosaur hearts were similar in structure to other warm-blooded animals, such as mammals. Finally, they say that birds, who are direct descendants from dinosaurs, are warm-blooded, too.

COLD-BLOODED THEORY

When dinosaur remains were first discovered in the nineteenth century, their similarity to cold-blooded reptiles made people think that they must be cold-blooded, too. When it was discovered that dinosaurs evolved from animals who were unquestionably cold-blooded, this argument held even more weight.

Other supporters on the cold-blooded side, point to the *Stegosaurus* and its massive back plates. Cold-blooded animals need to bask in the morning sun before they are warm enough to move around. It has been suggested that these plates were built-in temperature control devices. Turned flat to the sun, they would absorb heat rapidly, letting the *Stegosaurus* quickly reach the correct temperature. When the *Stegosaurus* was too hot, the plates could be turned away from the sun and even aligned in the direction of a cool breeze, to take heat away from its body.

Yet another argument suggests that dinosaurs could still have been as active as they were and been cold-blooded, because they lived in a much warmer climate than we do today. Because they were so enormous they would have kept their body heat much longer than smaller animals. So they could have remained lively when it was colder, even though they were cold-blooded.

The Komodo dragon is cold-blooded. Many scientists say that the fact that reptiles today are cold-blooded proves that dinosaurs probably were too.

Dinosaur Bones

Nothing about dinosaurs has survived quite as well as their bones. And bones tell tales in extraordinary detail. A complete skeleton will give a scientist a good idea of the likely size and appearance of a dinosaur. A skull will reveal what it probably ate, and features such as claws and armor plates will show how it attacked enemies or defended itself.

MAKING A DIFFERENCE

Not all the features of *Diplodocus* are common to all the giant sauropods. Other enormous plant eaters, such as *Brachiosaurus* and *Apatosaurus*, did not have a hollow bone structure, and were much heavier.

Its small skull meant less weight for its long neck to carry.

Long neck bones allowed it to reach the very tops of trees.

A single long tendon (shown here in red) stretched from neck to tail along a groove in the backbone, keeping both in balance.

Hollow vertebrae made its skeleton lighter.

Its thigh bone was very straight to give the legs maximum strength to support its heavy weight.

A single clawed toe on each foot was used for defense.

BUILT TO PLOD

Diplodocus dedicated its life to munching leaves off the tops of tall trees. Its body shape reveals how well it was designed to do this. *Diplodocus* was an enormous animal—at least 85 feet (26 meters) long. It weighed 10 tons (10 tonnes), surprisingly light for such a large sauropod. Its skeleton did not do all the work. Clever arrangements of muscles also supported its massive frame.

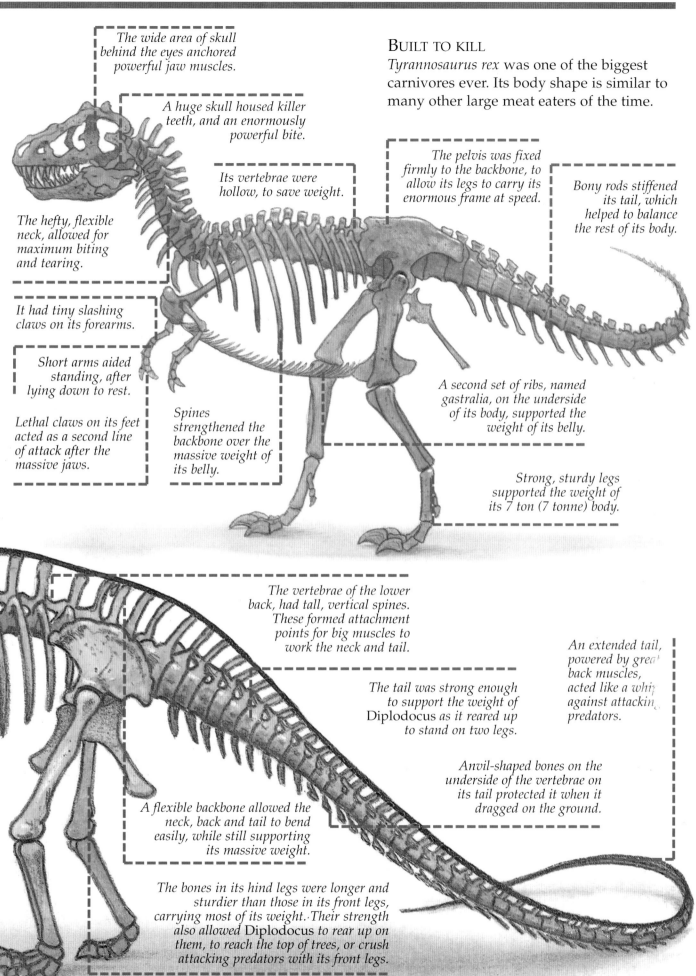

The wide area of skull behind the eyes anchored powerful jaw muscles.

A huge skull housed killer teeth, and an enormously powerful bite.

BUILT TO KILL
Tyrannosaurus rex was one of the biggest carnivores ever. Its body shape is similar to many other large meat eaters of the time.

Its vertebrae were hollow, to save weight.

The pelvis was fixed firmly to the backbone, to allow its legs to carry its enormous frame at speed.

Bony rods stiffened its tail, which helped to balance the rest of its body.

The hefty, flexible neck, allowed for maximum biting and tearing.

It had tiny slashing claws on its forearms.

Short arms aided standing, after lying down to rest.

Lethal claws on its feet acted as a second line of attack after the massive jaws.

Spines strengthened the backbone over the massive weight of its belly.

A second set of ribs, named gastralia, on the underside of its body, supported the weight of its belly.

Strong, sturdy legs supported the weight of its 7 ton (7 tonne) body.

The vertebrae of the lower back, had tall, vertical spines. These formed attachment points for big muscles to work the neck and tail.

An extended tail, powered by great back muscles, acted like a whip against attacking predators.

The tail was strong enough to support the weight of Diplodocus as it reared up to stand on two legs.

Anvil-shaped bones on the underside of the vertebrae on its tail protected it when it dragged on the ground.

A flexible backbone allowed the neck, back and tail to bend easily, while still supporting its massive weight.

The bones in its hind legs were longer and sturdier than those in its front legs, carrying most of its weight. Their strength also allowed Diplodocus to rear up on them, to reach the top of trees, or crush attacking predators with its front legs.

A to Z of
DINOSAURS

Albertosaurus

Albertosaurus comes from the same dinosaur family as its better-known and slightly larger relative, *Tyrannosaurus*. It lived before *Tyrannosaurus*, and the two creatures are similar in several ways—both had large heads and tiny front arms. A noticeable difference between *Albertosaurus* and its close cousin *Tyrannosaurus* is in the position of its eyes. While the eyes of *Tyrannosaurus* looked straight ahead, those of *Albertosaurus* were positioned at the sides of its head.

FAST FACTS

DESCRIPTION	A bipedal carnivore
ORDER	Saurischia ("lizard-hipped")
NAME MEANS	"Alberta lizard"
PERIOD	Late Cretaceous, about 70 million years ago
LOCATION	United States; Canada
LENGTH	30 feet (9 meters)
WEIGHT	2 tons (2 tonnes)

As a meat eater, or carnivore, *Albertosaurus* was a hunter. It was a "land shark" that preyed on slower-moving animals, such as duck-billed dinosaurs the size of modern rhinoceroses. Their only chance of escape from the kicks and blows of its powerful legs would have been to out-run it, or dive into thick vegetation for cover. In Canada, a group of *Albertosaurus* skeletons have been found close together in one place, and this suggests it lived in herds with its fellow dinosaurs.

Its body was balanced by a long, flexible tail.

DISCOVERY
In 1884 Joseph Tyrrell led an expedition from the Canadian Geological Survey to explore part of Alberta, a vast area in the west of Canada.

Where they lived

TIMELINE

Millions of years ago

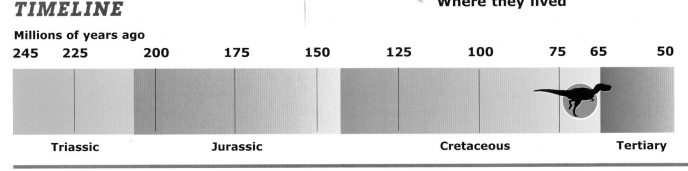

245	225	200	175	150	125	100	75	65	50

Triassic	Jurassic	Cretaceous	Tertiary

His team of scientists set out to make the first detailed maps of the region and to look for useful mineral deposits. But, as well as discovering vast deposits of coal, they found something totally unexpected. On June 9, in the valley of the Red Deer River, Tyrrell discovered fossilized bones belonging to a large meat-eating dinosaur. Although these were not the first dinosaur remains found in Canada (the first were found in 1874), they caused great excitement because they came from a previously unknown species. The new dinosaur was named *Albertosaurus* after the area in which it was found. Many other *Albertosaurus* fossils have since been found in Alberta, Canada, and in the western United States.

Two small, blunt horns near its eyes may have been used for display—to attract a mate or frighten an enemy.

Like Tyrannosaurus, Albertosaurus *had a large head.*

The eyes of Albertosaurus *were on the sides of its head. Because of this, it is thought that* Albertosaurus *could not see as well as* Tyrannosaurus. *Despite its poorer eyesight,* Albertosaurus *was still a fierce predator.*

Its tiny front arms ended in two small fingers.

Albertosaurus *walked on two strong, muscular back legs. It was probably a fast runner—up to 19 mph (30 kph).*

THE MOST COMPLETE CARNIVORE

The *Albertosaurus* specimen on display in the American Museum of Natural History in New York City, is one of the most complete fossils of a meat-eating dinosaur found in North America. It was discovered in 1917 by the fossil collector Charles Sternberg, and bought by the Museum in 1918 for $2,000.

Allosaurus

Allosaurus was one of the largest meat-eating dinosaurs of the Jurassic Period. Until tyrannosaurs such as *Albertosaurus* and *Tyrannosaurus* appeared some 50 million years later, *Allosaurus* was the largest predator on Earth.

Scientists used to think that the bulky body of *Allosaurus* was not built for high-speed chases. But this idea is now changing. The ribs of one *Allosaurus* are broken in several places and have healed, showing that the animal survived its injuries. It must have been moving at some speed, then fallen over and broken its bones. So, maybe *Allosaurus* was a chaser after all, able to run after its prey and throw itself at its victims.

DISCOVERY

A well-preserved *Allosaurus* skeleton was unearthed in the Como Bluff area of Wyoming, in 1879. It was packed up and sent to the American Museum of Natural History in New York City, where it remained in storage until 1903. Only then were the boxes unpacked and the identity of the dinosaur became known. By then other *Allosaurus* skeletons had been found, the most complete of which was discovered in 1883 by a fossil collector, M.P. Felch, at Canyon City, Colorado.

> *Its backbone was different from that of other dinosaurs of the time. This explains its name, the "different lizard."*

When attacking a prey animal larger than itself, such as a *Diplodocus*, *Allosaurus* may have hunted in packs. Perhaps the pack singled out a weak animal, separating it from the rest of the herd before going in for the kill. At other times, *Allosaurus* may have hunted alone, ambushing smaller animals, such as *Stegosaurus*.

Where they lived

TIMELINE

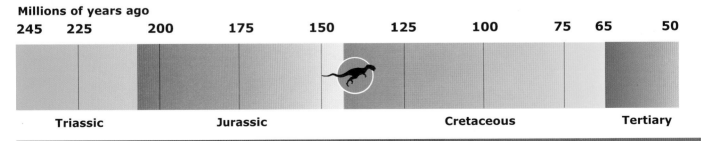

Millions of years ago

| 245 | 225 | 200 | 175 | 150 | 125 | 100 | 75 | 65 | 50 |

| Triassic | Jurassic | Cretaceous | Tertiary |

FAST FACTS

DESCRIPTION	A bipedal carnivore
ORDER	Saurischia ("lizard-hipped")
NAME MEANS	"Different lizard"
PERIOD	Late Jurassic, about 140 million years ago
LOCATION	North America
LENGTH	39 feet (12 meters)
WEIGHT	2—5 tons (2—5 tonnes)

Allosaurus had a thick, "S"-shaped neck.

Inside its jaws were many backward-pointing teeth, serrated like steak knives to slice easily through meat. Each tooth was up to 4 inches (10 centimeters) long. When an Allosaurus chewed into meat, it tossed its head from side to side, breaking off some of its fragile teeth in the process.

Its jaws were ideally suited for biting through flesh. They were controlled by powerful muscles—once they had hold of their prey they did not let it go.

Its arms were short and ended in hands that had three curved and pointed claws, each of which was up to 6 inches (15 centimeters) long.

It walked on two powerful back legs.

ALLOSAURUS GRAVEYARD

Since the 1920s more than 10,000 dinosaur bones have been excavated at a quarry in Utah. About 5,000 of the bones come from *Allosaurus* dinosaurs, the rest belong to plant eaters such as *Stegosaurus* and *Barosaurus*. In prehistoric times the area might have been a place where plant eaters came to feed. The plant eaters may have become trapped in marshy ground when the *Allosaurus* moved in to feed on them, but got stuck themselves and died.

Ankylosaurus

Ankylosaurus belongs to a family of dinosaurs known as the Ankylosauria. Their family name means "fused together lizards," because of the plates of bony armor that were joined together over their bodies. Ankylosaurs were four-legged, armor-plated dinosaurs with long, wide bodies. They ranged in length from the 3-foot- (1-meter-) long *Pinacosaurus* to the giant of the group, the 40-foot-(10-meter-) long *Ankylosaurus*. It was the last member of its family to evolve. It appeared in North America toward the very end of the Age of Dinosaurs. *Ankylosaurus* was a slow-moving animal, at risk of attack from meat eaters such as *Tyrannosaurus*. Its body armor protected it from bites and it swung its clubbed tail at an attacker. But, if *Ankylosaurus* was knocked over, its soft belly offered no protection against the bites, scratches, and kicks of a predator.

Where they lived

Two rows of spikes grew along its back, and horns poked from the back of its head.

Its head and face were sheathed in pads of protective armor, too, and when it blinked its eyes, armor-plated eyelids closed over them.

Its wide bill and small teeth were perfect for nipping off low-growing plants.

Large throat bones show that Ankylosaurus *had a big tongue, which probably pushed its food around inside its mouth before swallowing.*

Short legs kept Ankylosaurus *close to the ground.*

TIMELINE

Millions of years ago

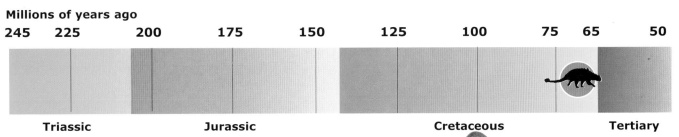

| 245 | 225 | 200 | 175 | 150 | 125 | 100 | 75 | 65 | 50 |

Triassic   Jurassic   Cretaceous   Tertiary

DISCOVERY

In 1908, Barnum Brown of the American Museum of Natural History in New York City described an entirely new dinosaur. Its fossilized remains had been unearthed in the State of Montana in the United States and in Alberta, Canada. Brown, who was one of the most famous dinosaur collectors of the twentieth century, named the dinosaur *Ankylosaurus*. It has become one of the world's best known dinosaurs.

THE BLUSHING DINOSAUR

It's difficult to say what color dinosaurs were, but some scientists believe that *Ankylosaurus* might have been pink! This is because its bony plates were filled with blood vessels. When blood rushed into them it could well have "blushed" pink.

Ankylosaurus grew to a little over 3 feet (1 meter) in height, but was almost twice as wide as this.

Thick oval plates of bony material, called scutes, covered the whole of its top side. The scutes ran in bands and were embedded in its leathery skin.

FAST FACTS

DESCRIPTION	A quadrupedal herbivore
ORDER	Saurischia ("lizard-hipped")
NAME MEANS	"Stiff lizard"
PERIOD	Late Cretaceous, about 70 million years ago
LOCATION	North America
LENGTH	33 feet (10 meters)
WEIGHT	5 tons (5 tonnes)

Its tail ended in a wide, bony club made from several plates of armor that locked together.

Apatosaurus

Apatosaurus is the best known of all the long-necked, plant-eating dinosaurs, but there is still much that remains a mystery about it. For example, it is not known for certain whether it lived alone or in herds. *Apatosaurus* was one of the largest creatures ever to have lived on Earth, measuring about 16 feet (5 meters) tall at the hips and over 66 feet (20 meters) from nose to tail. Much of its great length was taken up by its long, slender tail and neck.

DISCOVERY

Apatosaurus was given its name in 1877 after its bones were collected from near the town of Morrison, Colorado. Two years later, in 1879, bones from another dinosaur were found in a quarry at Como Bluff, Wyoming. At the time no one realized that these bones also came from an *Apatosaurus*. Instead, the experts of the day thought they belonged to a new type of dinosaur and so they gave it the name "*Brontosaurus*," meaning "thunder lizard." As more bones were found, scientists realized that a mistake had been made, and in 1903 the name "*Brontosaurus*" was dropped. According to the scientific rules, the animal had to be called by the name it was first given—it should only be known as *Apatosaurus*. But, in 1905, when a complete *Apatosaurus* skeleton went on display at the American Museum of Natural History, it was mistakenly labeled as "*Brontosaurus*." The name stuck, and for much of the twentieth century the so-called "thunder lizard" was the world's most famous long-necked dinosaur.

Its long tail may have been used to fend off attackers.

Where they lived

THE FIRST SAUROPOD ON SHOW

History was made in 1905 when the American Museum of Natural History in New York City unveiled its famous *Apatosaurus* skeleton. This was the first complete sauropod (long-necked, browsing dinosaur) skeleton to go on display anywhere in the world, and it aroused great public interest. In fact, the bones come from more than one *Apatosaurus*. Although most of the bones do come from one skeleton, to make it whole some missing bones have been added from other *Apatosaurus* skeletons in the Museum's collection.

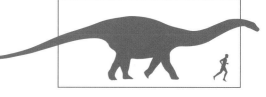

FAST FACTS

DESCRIPTION	A quadrupedal herbivore
ORDER	Ornithischia ("bird-hipped")
NAME MEANS	"Deceptive lizard"
PERIOD	Late Jurassic, about 150 million years ago
LOCATION	North America
LENGTH	69 feet (21 meters)
WEIGHT	30 tons (30 tonnes)

Its nostrils were on top of its head. Scientists once believed the animal was a water-dweller, wading through deep water with its head held high like a snorkel. But no fossils have ever been found near water.

For such a massive animal it had a surprisingly small head, inside which was a tiny brain and peg-shaped teeth.

Its great weight was carried along on its four towerlike legs. Its hind legs were longer than its front legs.

Each foot had short, stubby toes. On the front feet the toes were blunt, but the toes of the back feet ended in claws. Each massive footprint was up to 3 feet (1 meter) wide.

TIMELINE

Millions of years ago

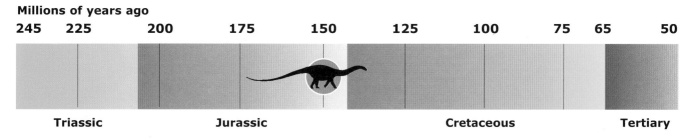

245	225	200	175	150	125	100	75	65	50

Triassic	Jurassic	Cretaceous	Tertiary

GETTING ENOUGH TO EAT

For such a giant, *Apatosaurus* only had small jaws. So how did it manage to get enough food inside its mouth to feed its enormous body? The answer might be that it searched for food for much of the day and night, stopping only for brief rest periods. But this is not the whole answer. The problem is that the main food plants available 150 million years ago were conifer trees. Even though *Apatosaurus* could easily reach up to them with its long neck, the leaves of conifers may not have been enough to fuel its enormous body. It would have needed to feed off other plants, too, such as low-growing horse-tails, club mosses, and ferns.

Gastroliths

STOMACH STONES

Smooth, round stones found in the stomach regions of some *Apatosaurus* skeletons are a clue to the eating habits of these creatures. The stones, which are called gastroliths, were deliberately eaten by the dinosaurs. As they tumbled around inside their stomachs the stones bashed against the tough vegetation the animals had swallowed. The stones worked like grinders, breaking food down into smaller and smaller pieces and making it easier for the animals to digest. In the grinding process, the rough edges of the stones were worn smooth. *Apatosaurus* probably did not chew its food—as soon as its peglike teeth had stripped the leaves off trees or pulled up ground plants they were swallowed whole. Once inside the creature's belly the stomach stones crushed the vegetation into a nutritious pulp.

Apatosaurus *had very strong back legs. Some scientists think this giant creature may have been able to rear up on its hind legs to warn off predators.*

Apatosaurus *was thought to keep its tail off the ground when walking. This would have prevented predators from grabbing the tail and attacking* Apatosaurus.

BUILT FOR DEFENSE

Apatosaurus lived at the same time and in the same place as the meat-eating predator *Allosaurus*. It is likely that *Allosaurus*—and other theropods, too—preyed on *Apatosaurus*, picking on the young, the old, and the weak. With its long neck at full stretch, the mighty *Apatosaurus* would have towered over an *Allosaurus*, and if it reared up on its hind legs, it might have been able to bring the full weight of its body crashing down on any attacker. It may have thrashed its long tail from side to side, using it like a whip to drive a predator away.

BIG ANIMALS LAY BIG EGGS

Baby *Apatosaurus* dinosaurs hatched out from enormous eggs that measured up to 12 inches (30 centimeters) across. Because no nests of eggs have been found, it is thought that these animals might have laid their eggs as they walked along.

A HEADLESS GIANT

Until the 1970s no one knew what the skull of an *Apatosaurus* looked like since no skeletons had been found with their heads in place. This was a problem for scientists who had to guess at what the creature's head had looked like by using skulls from other dinosaurs. For many years they believed that *Apatosaurus* had a head like *Camarasaurus*. But by careful detective work they were able to track down a real *Apatosaurus* skull that had been wrongly labeled as coming from a *Diplodocus*.

The bones of the neck and back had hollow areas, called pleurocoels, to make them lighter.

Apatosaurus skeleton

The "thumb" on each "hand" had a large claw.

Baryonyx

Baryonyx was a meat-eating dinosaur that walked on two legs. It gets its name from the long, curved claws on its thumbs. We know something about the kind of food *Baryonyx* ate because, incredibly, the fossilized remains of its last meal have been found inside its ribcage. Partly-digested fish bones and scales show that this dinosaur was a fish eater. Perhaps it waded into shallow water where it grabbed fish with its great thumb-claws, like bears do today. Or maybe it scooped up passing fish in its jaws, just as crocodiles do. But it is possible that *Baryonyx* was a scavenger, too, poking its narrow tooth-filled jaws into the bodies of dead animals.

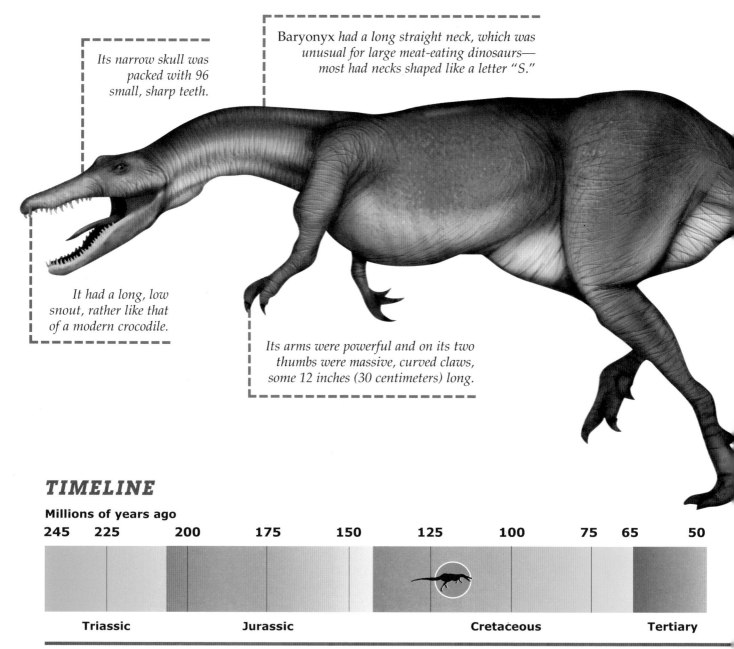

Its narrow skull was packed with 96 small, sharp teeth.

Baryonyx *had a long straight neck, which was unusual for large meat-eating dinosaurs— most had necks shaped like a letter "S."*

It had a long, low snout, rather like that of a modern crocodile.

Its arms were powerful and on its two thumbs were massive, curved claws, some 12 inches (30 centimeters) long.

TIMELINE

Millions of years ago

245	225	200	175	150	125	100	75	65	50

| Triassic | Jurassic | Cretaceous | Tertiary |

DISCOVERY

In January 1983, William Walker, an amateur fossil collector, visited a clay pit in Surrey, southern England. In the mud, Walker found a rock the size of a soccer ball. He saw that a small fragment of bone was sticking out from it, and with a blow from his hammer he shattered it to pieces. Out fell several fragments of an enormous claw bone.

When the claw was shown to scientists at the Natural History Museum in London, England, they realized that it was a major find. In the spring of 1983, a team of eight paleontologists from the museum spent three weeks searching for more remains of the "creature in the claypit." Eventually, almost three-quarters of the skeleton was found, and the work of learning about it began.

Where they lived

It had a long, straight tail.

FAST FACTS

DESCRIPTION	A bipedal carnivore
ORDER	Saurischia ("lizard-hipped")
NAME MEANS	"Heavy claw"
PERIOD	Early Cretaceous, about 120 million years ago
LOCATION	England
LENGTH	33 feet (10 meters)
WEIGHT	2 tons (2 tonnes)

THE FISH-EATING DINOSAUR

So far, *Baryonyx* is the only known dinosaur that ate fish. The fish remains found inside it come from a big fish known as *Lepidotes*. At 3 feet (1 meter) in length, the largest *Lepidotes* would have made a good-sized meal for *Baryonyx*.

Brachiosaurus

Brachiosaurus was the "giraffe" of the dinosaur world. With its long, graceful neck, it had a distinct advantage over other smaller leaf-eating dinosaurs. For them, tasty shoots, fruit, and leaves that grew high off the ground were beyond their reach, but for *Brachiosaurus* they were an important part of its food supply. At full stretch *Brachiosaurus* could graze foliage that grew up to 52 feet (16 meters) above the ground.

DISCOVERY

Fossil bones from *Brachiosaurus* were first found in Colorado, in 1900. Even though the massive skeleton was not complete, it was clear that this was a new kind of dinosaur. A world-wide search began to track down more examples. Between 1909 and 1912, *Brachiosaurus* specimens were uncovered in Tanzania, East Africa. They were found by German paleontologist Werner Janensch who used hundreds of local workers to dig for the buried bones. For three years his workers labored in sweltering heat to unearth thousands of dinosaur bones.

FAST FACTS

DESCRIPTION	A quadrupedal herbivore
ORDER	Saurischia ("lizard-hipped")
NAME MEANS	"Arm lizard"
PERIOD	Late Jurassic, about 150 million years ago
LOCATION	North America; Africa
LENGTH	82 feet (25 meters)
WEIGHT	30—49 tons (30—50 tonnes)

Brachiosaurus walked on four legs. Unlike most other dinosaurs, its front legs were longer than its hind legs. This meant that its body sloped down toward its short tail.

Its nostrils were on top of its head, almost between its eyes. Its large nasal openings suggest that Brachiosaurus had a good sense of smell. Its sense of smell may have been better than its eyesight, allowing it to smell food and the scent of other animals before seeing them.

For such a huge creature its head was small in proportion to the rest of its body, and its brain was tiny.

Its 52 chisellike teeth were perfect for tugging and nipping away at soft vegetation.

Its long, giraffelike neck allowed Brachiosaurus *to stretch up to the highest green leaves.*

Where they lived

Once uncovered, each bone was carefully packed. Then, the whole collection was carried on foot, cross-country, to a port on the east coast of Africa. From there the bones were shipped to Germany, where the dinosaur skeleton was assembled and put on display at the Humboldt Museum in Berlin. The skeleton stood as high as a three-storey building and is the tallest complete dinosaur skeleton on display anywhere in the world.

LOOK, NO ARMS!

"Arm lizard" might seem like a strange name to give to a creature with four legs. It was given this name because its long front legs grew from its shoulders, as if they were arms.

TIMELINE

Millions of years ago

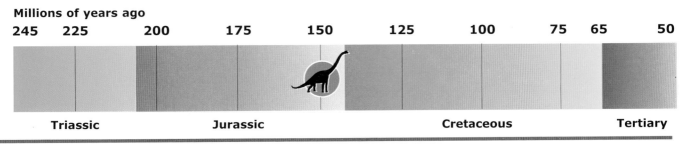

245	225	200	175	150	125	100	75	65	50

Triassic	Jurassic	Cretaceous	Tertiary

Brachiosaurus skull

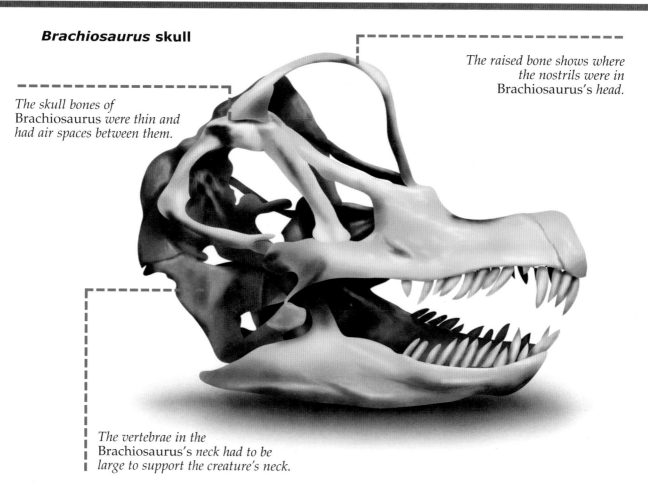

The skull bones of
Brachiosaurus *were thin and
had air spaces between them.*

*The raised bone shows where
the nostrils were in
Brachiosaurus's head.*

*The vertebrae in the
Brachiosaurus's neck had to be
large to support the creature's neck.*

LIFE IN THE HERD

Brachiosaurus probably spent most of its waking hours feeding—an animal so large would have needed a massive daily intake of food simply to stay alive. A fully-grown adult may have needed to eat about 440 pounds (200 kilograms) of plant food each day.

As a herbivore *Brachiosaurus* may have lived with others in small herds. A herd would have been made up of a range of animals of all ages, living side by side. They moved slowly. Fossilized footprints have been found, and by taking measurements between each one it is possible to work out how slow they were—plodding along at perhaps no more than about 2 mph (3 kph), which is less than half the walking speed of an adult human.

*The long tail of
Brachiosaurus helped to
balance its enormous body.*

A POWERFUL HEART

Beating away inside this giant's body was a powerful heart. It needed to be strong in order to pump blood along the miles of arteries, veins, and capillaries that twisted around inside it. The pressure inside its blood vessels was high —imagine how much force must have been needed to keep all that blood constantly circulating throughout its body.

Positioned at the end of its long neck, the head of a 40-feet- (12-meter-) tall adult *Brachiosaurus* was some 25 feet (7.5 meters) above its heart. The pressure needed to circulate blood upward through such a distance would have placed a great strain on its heart. Because of this fact, scientists believe that *Brachiosaurus* (and all other dinosaurs, too) had a form of "double-pump" circulation, as mammals and birds do today. In this type of circulation, the heart is separated into left and right halves. The halves share the work of pumping blood around the body, placing less strain on the heart.

Muscle structure of Brachiosaurus

Brachiosaurus *was not an agile dinosaur. It was heavy and slow-moving because of its enormous size.*

STAY OUT OF THE WATER!

When *Brachiosaurus* was first studied, its nose puzzled paleontologists. Because it was on top of its head they wondered if the dinosaur lived under water, stretching its neck to the surface where it could breathe through its nostrils like a snorkel. No one takes this idea seriously any longer. *Brachiosaurus* could not have lived underwater because the water pressure on its massive body would have crushed its lungs, making breathing almost impossible.

Experts once believed that Brachiosaurus *must have had many hearts to have been able to pump blood around the large body.*

Camarasaurus

Camarasaurus was a long-necked, long-tailed dinosaur that walked on all fours. It was one of the giant plant eaters of the late Jurassic Period. Scientists believe that while other plant eaters grazed on the soft, juicy parts of plants, *Camarasaurus* was able to eat the parts they did not, such as twigs and branches. When a *Camarasaurus* tooth from an adult is examined under a microscope, tiny scratches can be seen on its surface. The scratches show that this dinosaur must have had rough material in its mouth, which is why paleontologists believe it ate coarse vegetation. However, young *Camarasaurus* dinosaurs did not have scratches on their teeth. This suggests they ate softer vegetation than their parents, just like other herbivores.

As a large, slow-moving dinosaur, *Camarasaurus* was vulnerable to attack from predators. It is likely that *Camarasaurus* lived in herds. Faced with an attack on a herd member, the others could come to its aid to drive the predator away.

DISCOVERY

The "First Great Dinosaur Rush" began in 1877, when fossil hunters set about uncovering the remains of many previously unknown prehistoric creatures buried in the western region of North America. One of the most active researchers at that time was the American paleontologist Edward Drinker Cope. In 1877, Oramel Lucas, a teacher, sent Cope some dinosaur bones that he had found near Canyon City, Colorado. Cope examined the bones, and realized that they came from a new species. He named the creature *Camarasaurus*.

TIMELINE

Millions of years ago

245	225	200	175	150	125	100	75	65	50

Triassic	Jurassic	Cretaceous	Tertiary

FAST FACTS

DESCRIPTION	A quadrupedal herbivore
ORDER	Saurischia ("lizard-hipped")
NAME MEANS	"Chambered lizard"
PERIOD	Late Jurassic, about 150 million years ago
LOCATION	North America; Europe
LENGTH	59 feet (18 meters)
WEIGHT	19 tons (20 tonnes)

It had a small, long head with a blunt, round snout. Its nostrils were on the top of its head.

Its strong jaws were packed with large spoon-shaped teeth that could cut through tough vegetation.

Its front legs were about the same length as its hind legs, so it stood with its back level to the ground.

Where they lived

HOLLOW BONES

The vertebrae of *Camarasaurus* were not made of solid bone. Instead, they contained hollow chambers, and it is because of these that it was named "chambered lizard." The spaces inside its backbone helped to make the animal's skeleton lighter.

Coelophysis

It had a long narrow head, large eyes and a mouth filled with sharp teeth.

Its front legs were small and were probably used for clawing and grasping at food.

Coelophysis was a small dinosaur, built for speed and agility. Standing about 6.5 feet (2 meters) tall, its powerful hind legs and long, thin body made it a fast and deadly predator. Paleontologists believe that *Coelophysis* was a pack animal, living and hunting in groups. Some of the adult skeletons found contained the bones of baby *Coelophysis* inside their rib cages. At first, this was thought to be proof that they gave birth to live young rather than laying eggs like other dinosaurs. But now scientists think that *Coelophysis* was a cannibal that occasionally ate its own young. However, its main source of food was probably meat from other animals, including fish.

Unlike other dinosaurs, the leg bones of Coelophysis *were nearly hollow, and it is from these that it gets the name "hollow form." The hollow bones kept its weight down —a great help to any animal that relied on speed of attack to chase after and catch its prey.*

TIMELINE

Millions of years ago

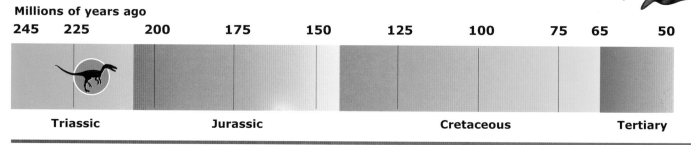

245	225	200	175	150	125	100	75	65	50

Triassic   **Jurassic**   **Cretaceous**   **Tertiary**

DISCOVERY

Coelophysis is one of the oldest dinosaurs from North America. Despite being 220 million years old, some remarkable fossils have been found, making it one of the world's best-known dinosaurs. In 1889, American paleontologist Edward Drinker Cope announced the discovery of a new dinosaur, which he named *Coelophysis*. Cope's studies were based on the bones from an incomplete skeleton. It was not until 1947 that the first complete *Coelophysis* skeleton was found— and what a find it was. That year, Edwin Colbert and a team from the American Museum of Natural History, New York, discovered hundreds of complete and partial *Coelophysis* skeletons at Ghost Ranch, New Mexico. They may have perished there in a great flood.

Where they lived

Its hind legs were very powerful, allowing it to run quickly.

THE FIRST DINOSAUR IN SPACE

A 220 million-year-old *Coelophysis* skull from the Carnegie Museum of Natural History, Pittsburgh, Pennsylvania, made history when it was taken to the Russian Space Station *Mir*, in January 1998. The 8-inch- (20-centimeter-) long skull traveled on board the space shuttle Endeavour, and so became the first dinosaur in space. The skull traveled some 4 million miles (6.5 million kilometers) around the Earth. This unusual journey came about when the museum was given the chance to send an object into space —and the oldest dinosaur in the United States was chosen.

FAST FACTS

DESCRIPTION	A bipedal carnivore
ORDER	Saurischia ("lizard-hipped")
NAME MEANS	"Hollow form"
PERIOD	Late Triassic, about 220 million years ago
LOCATION	North America
LENGTH	10 feet (3 meters)
WEIGHT	88 pounds (40 kilograms)

Compsognathus

Compsognathus was one of the smallest known dinosaurs. A small, delicate creature, it was a fast-running predator that traveled on its hind legs.

Very few examples of *Compsognathus* have ever been found. Because it occurs in the same locality, and in the same limestone deposits as the first known bird, *Archaeopteryx*, it has sometimes been confused with it. The two animals have similar skeletons and are roughly the same size—but while *Archaeopteryx* had feathers, as far as is known *Compsognathus* did not. However, their other similarities are clues to the theory that birds and dinosaurs are related.

DISCOVERY

Compsognathus was discovered in Bavaria, southern Germany by Dr. Oberndorfer in the late 1850s. It was a remarkable find, since the animal's skeleton was almost all there, preserved in limestone. Only the tip of its long tail was missing. In 1861, German paleontologist Andreas Wagner described the new creature and named it *Compsognathus*. Wagner did not think it was a dinosaur because at that time people thought all dinosaurs were huge animals. Since *Compsognathus* was not much bigger than a turkey, Wagner thought it was far too small to be a dinosaur. Today we know that dinosaurs came in all sizes.

> Its long flexible tail took up more than half its length and helped *Compsognathus* to keep its balance.

BEST FIND

The tiny *Compsognathus* specimen found in Germany by Dr. Oberndorfer in the 1850s was that of a young animal, not a fully grown adult. It was the first complete dinosaur skeleton found anywhere in the world.

TIMELINE

Millions of years ago

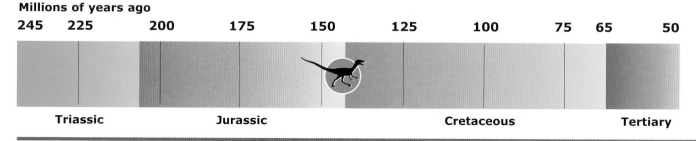

245	225	200	175	150	125	100	75	65	50

Triassic   Jurassic   Cretaceous   Tertiary

FAST FACTS

DESCRIPTION	A bipedal carnivore
ORDER	Saurischia ("lizard-hipped")
NAME MEANS	"Elegant jaw"
PERIOD	Late Jurassic, about 145 million years ago
LOCATION	Europe
LENGTH	3 feet (1 meter)
WEIGHT	6.5 pounds (3 kilograms)

Inside its large skull there were many sharp, curved teeth. Its teeth were small and spaced apart from each other. They are the type of teeth that could do little damage to a large animal, but which were perfect for nipping at small reptiles, insects, and mammals.

It had short arms that may have had two clawed fingers on each hand.

It had powerful hind legs.

FOOD FOR THOUGHT

In 1881, American paleontologist Othniel Marsh noticed that the tiny *Compsognathus* skeleton found in Germany by Dr. Oberndorfer had something in its stomach. For many years scientists argued over whether it was a baby *Compsognathus* or the remains of a meal. The mystery was cleared up in 1978 when American paleontologist John Ostrom identified it as the chewed-up skeleton of a lizard named *Bavarisaurus*. On the day that this particular *Compsognathus* had died, this small reptile had had the misfortune to be seen, caught, and eaten.

Where they lived

89

Corythosaurus

Corythosaurus was a large, plant-eating dinosaur that walked on two legs. *Corythosaurus* was a swamp-dweller that lived along the edges of forests during the Cretaceous Period. It lived in herds near water, and was probably able to swim, as it had webbed hands and feet. *Corythosaurus* grazed on low-growing plants, such as palm leaves, pine needles, and fruits. It had a long, flat bill, which marked it out as one of the duck-billed dinosaurs, or hadrosaurs.

DISCOVERY

In 1912, the fossil hunter Barnum Brown was searching for fossils along the Red Deer River in Alberta, Canada, when he found the first example of *Corythosaurus*. It was a remarkable discovery, not only because the skeleton was almost complete, but because much of the creature's skin had survived as a fossil too.

THE HEAD CREST

It is still not clear what the head crest was for. Like other crested duck-billed dinosaurs, it was filled with nasal passages, so perhaps it functioned as a sounding device.

The booming, low sounds it made might have been used to warn others of danger, or to attract a mate. But maybe it acted as a nose—which increased the creature's sense of smell. Some scientists believe it may have been brightly colored. Like special sounds, the use of color could have been used in a courtship display to attract a mate. Only adult males had a fully developed head crest. The crests of females and young were much smaller.

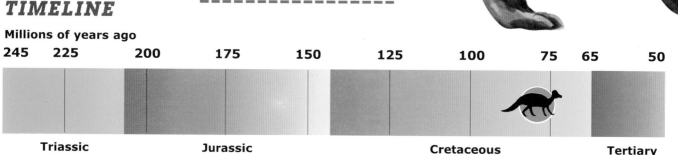

Its tail was flat, and its hands and feet were wide and paddlelike. They appear to have been webbed.

TIMELINE

Millions of years ago

245	225	200	175	150	125	100	75	65	50

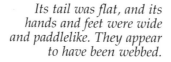

Triassic	Jurassic	Cretaceous	Tertiary

Where they lived

FAST FACTS

Description	A bipedal herbivore
Order	Ornithischia ("bird-hipped")
Name means	"Helmet lizard"
Period	Late Cretaceous, about 80 million years ago
Location	North America
Length	33 feet (10 meters)
Weight	3.9 tons (4 tonnes)

Its name—"helmet lizard"—was given to it because of the distinctive bony crest on top of its head, which resembled a flattened helmet.

It had a long flat bill, which it used to graze on plants that were close to the ground.

It had no teeth in its bill, but hundreds of small, sharp teeth grew behind it inside its jaws. As Corythosaurus chewed on its food, its teeth wore down. When they fell out, new ones grew in their place.

Its skin was covered in tiny, pebbly scales that did not overlap, as in many reptiles.

SUNK WITHOUT TRACE

In 1916, the British ship *Mount Temple* was crossing the Atlantic Ocean on its way from the United States to Britain. Amongst its cargo were two specimens of *Corythosaurus*. The journey was made during World War I, when trans-Atlantic crossings were hazardous. A German U-boat torpedoed the *Mount Temple*, sending it and its 80-million-year-old cargo to the bottom of the ocean, where they rest to this day.

Deinonychus

At about 6.5 feet (2 meters) tall, *Deinonychus* was taller than an adult human is today. Compared with other dinosaurs it was small. But being small was not a disadvantage, for *Deinonychus* was the perfect chase-and-kill predator of its time. It moved swiftly along on two powerful hind legs. Each foot had three toes, and it was here that its most distinctive feature was to be found—a long and deadly claw.

There was little movement in its back and tail, which were held stiff and straight by powerful ligaments and bony rods. As it ran at speed it held its tail straight out behind it, helping it to keep its balance.

THE NAME THAT GOT AWAY

Barnum Brown knew that the bones he found in 1931 came from a new type of small, meat-eating dinosaur. It needed a name, and so he called it "*Daptosaurus*," meaning "active lizard." But, according to the rules of naming dinosaurs, a new dinosaur has to be described in writing before its name can be officially accepted. Unfortunately for Brown he never did write about "*Daptosaurus*," which meant that this name could not be used. The name we use today, *Deinonychus*, was given to this dinosaur by John Ostrom, in 1969.

DISCOVERY

It was the great American fossil hunter Barnum Brown who uncovered the first remains of *Deinonychus*. In 1931 he found the skull, limbs, and backbone of a small, meat-eating dinosaur, in southern Montana. Even though it was recognized as a new dinosaur right from the start, more than 30 years passed before the creature really made the news. In 1964, American paleontologist John Ostrom discovered several nearly complete *Deinonychus* skeletons in the same area as Brown. It became clear that this little dinosaur with the terrible claws was one of the fiercest dinosaurs that ever lived.

TIMELINE

Millions of years ago

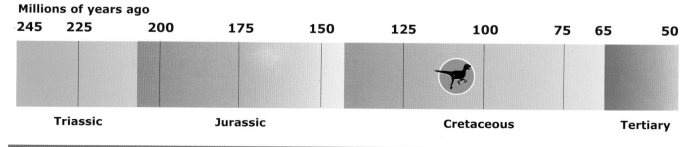

| 245 | 225 | 200 | 175 | 150 | 125 | 100 | 75 | 65 | 50 |

| Triassic | Jurassic | Cretaceous | Tertiary |

It had the large eyes of a hunter, suggesting that its eyesight was good.

FAST FACTS

DESCRIPTION	A bipedal carnivore
ORDER	Saurischia ("lizard-hipped")
NAME MEANS	"Terrible claw"
PERIOD	Early Cretaceous, about 110 million years ago
LOCATION	North America
LENGTH	10 feet (3 meters)
WEIGHT	176 pounds (80 kilograms)

The slender neck was curved and flexible, which gave the head a wide range of movement.

Deinonychus had a large head and jaws. The skull was lightly built, and its jaws were packed with sharp teeth that had serrated edges and which curved backward inside its mouth. Powerful jaw muscles gave the animal a fearsome, snapping bite.

Its arms were long and its three-fingered hands were very large with powerful, sharply curved talons.

On the second toe of the foot was a long, curved claw—a deadly weapon.

Where they lived

TERRIBLE CLAWS

Each foot had a large, curved claw. When fully grown the claws were 5 inches (13 centimeters) long, and were extremely sharp. It is from these claws that the creature was named—"terrible claw." Studies have shown that when *Deinonychus* walked or ran, it kept these claws raised up off the ground. There was a good reason for this. If the claws had been used for walking, they would have come into contact with the ground and would have worn down, making them blunt.

The bones and claws of a well-armed *Deinonychus* foot

As if the "terrible claw" was not enough of a killing machine, *Deinonychus* was also equipped with an extra-strong jaw to grip onto the flesh of its prey, and razor-sharp teeth to pull off big lumps of meat.

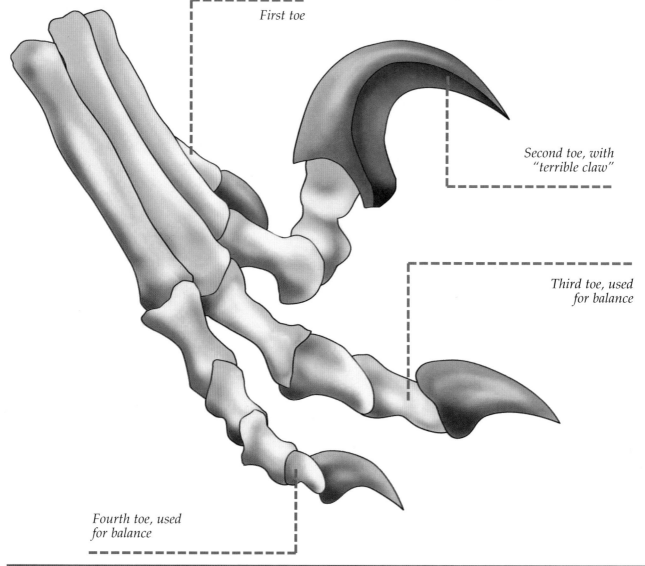

First toe

Second toe, with "terrible claw"

Third toe, used for balance

Fourth toe, used for balance

How *Deinonychus* used its "terrible claw"

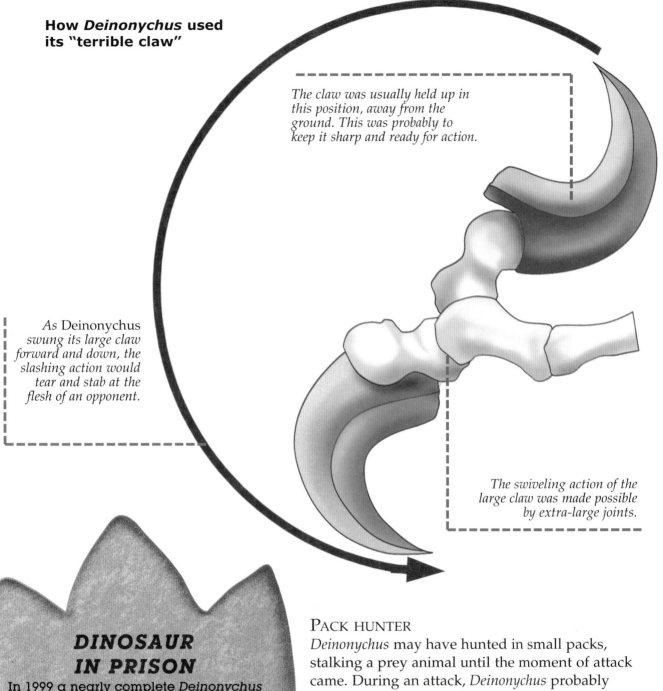

The claw was usually held up in this position, away from the ground. This was probably to keep it sharp and ready for action.

As Deinonychus swung its large claw forward and down, the slashing action would tear and stab at the flesh of an opponent.

The swiveling action of the large claw was made possible by extra-large joints.

DINOSAUR IN PRISON

In 1999 a nearly complete *Deinonychus* skeleton was discovered in the grounds of a prison near the town of Farris, Oklahoma. This latest find is one of the best *Deinonychus* fossils ever found. With it were the remains of the plant-eating dinosaur *Tenontosaurus*—a rare example of hunter and prey being found together.

PACK HUNTER

Deinonychus may have hunted in small packs, stalking a prey animal until the moment of attack came. During an attack, *Deinonychus* probably grabbed its prey with its jaws and hands. As it balanced on one leg, it kicked at the soft underbelly of its victim with the flesh-slicing claw on its other foot. Amid this kicking frenzy, its teeth bit down hard into another part of the animal, and with a backward thrust of its neck a chunk of meat was torn from it.

Several *Deinonychus* specimens have been found next to the remains of a plant-eating dinosaur named *Tenontosaurus*, and it is likely that this much larger animal was its prey. Paleontologists believe that *Deinonychus* was a pack hunter, since a lone predator might not have been able to kill a creature several times its own size.

Diplodocus

Diplodocus is one of the longest land animals that has ever lived on Earth. As it moved slowly on its four trunklike legs, it searched the landscape for food. This massive herbivore must have needed to eat a vast amount of vegetation every day to survive. When eating, *Diplodocus* clamped its peglike teeth around conifers, gingkoes, ferns, cycads, club mosses, and horse-tails. Then, as it pulled its head backward, its teeth tugged on the foliage and combed their way through it, stripping off a mouthful of food, which it swallowed whole. Once inside its stomach, gastroliths (stomach stones) rolled around and knocked against the food, crushing it to a pulp and making it easier to digest. *Diplodocus* may have lived in herds, traveling from one feeding place to the next.

DISCOVERY

The first *Diplodocus* bones were found in 1877 in Colorado, by fossil hunter Samuel Williston. The skeleton was not complete, but enough of it had survived to show that it was a new dinosaur. In 1878 the great American paleontologist Othniel Marsh named it *Diplodocus*. He gave it this name —meaning "double beam"—because some of its tail bones reminded him of the shape of a beam. The first complete skeleton was found in 1899, in Wyoming. Since then, *Diplodocus* has become one of the world's best-known dinosaurs.

The long tail was up to 45 feet (14 meters) long. There were between 70—80 vertebrae (backbones) in it. If attacked, Diplodocus may have used its tail like a whip, thrashing it through the air to frighten a predator away.

In the past it was thought that when Diplodocus walked it dragged its tail along the ground. But because no drag marks have been found alongside its fossilized footprints, it is now believed that the tail was held high off the ground..

The hind legs were longer than the front legs. There were five toes on each foot, and the first three toes had claws.

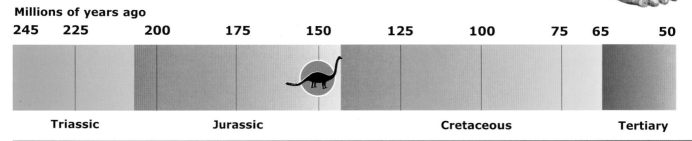

TIMELINE

Millions of years ago

245	225	200	175	150	125	100	75	65	50

Triassic	Jurassic	Cretaceous	Tertiary

For a giant, Diplodocus had a tiny head, only about 2 feet (0.5 meter) long.

Where they lived

Its long neck stretched out in front of its body for 26 feet (8 meters).

Inside its mouth were many peglike teeth. They were in the front of its jaws. There were no teeth in the back of its mouth.

FAST FACTS

DESCRIPTION	A quadrupedal herbivore
ORDER	Saurischia ("lizard-hipped")
NAME MEANS	"Double-beam lizard"
PERIOD	Late Jurassic, about 150 million years ago
LOCATION	North America
LENGTH	88 feet (27 meters)
WEIGHT	12 tons (12 tonnes)

FAME AT LAST

In 1905, the Carnegie Museum of Natural History, Pittsburgh, Pennsylvania, began to send copies of its famous *Diplodocus* skeleton (known as "Dippy") to museums in London, Paris, Berlin, Vienna, St Petersburg, Mexico City, La Plata (Argentina), and Munich. Wherever the giant skeleton went on display, it caused great excitement, and for many years afterward *Diplodocus* was the most famous dinosaur in the world—that is, until *Tyrannosaurus* was discovered.

Edmontosaurus

Edmontosaurus was a large, duck-billed herbivore that probably lived in herds, with others of its kind. It walked on two legs, but when feeding on low-growing plants it probably moved slowly on all fours. Its bill nipped and tugged at flowering plants and the tough leaves of conifer trees. *Edmontosaurus* ate bark and pine cones, too. Once inside its mouth, its tongue pushed food into the cheek pouches that lay along either side of its jaw. Rows of tiny interlocking teeth then began to chew on the food, grinding it down until it was ready to swallow.

Edmontosaurus herds may have migrated, or traveled, over thousands of miles each year, since large numbers of their skeletons have been found in two separate places—one in Alaska, the other in Alberta, Canada. Perhaps the animals followed a trail between these places that led them to food at different seasons of the year.

DISCOVERY

Edmontosaurus lived at the very end of the Age of Dinosaurs, in parts of western Canada and the United States. It is named after Edmonton, Canada, near where many of its fossils were originally found. At first, this dinosaur was called "*Claosaurus*," and for many years museums used this name when they put specimens on display. But in 1917, the paleontologist Lawrence Lambe studied this duck-billed creature in greater detail than anyone had before, and as a result it was renamed *Edmontosaurus*.

Edmontosaurus *had a long, pointed tail.*

TIMELINE

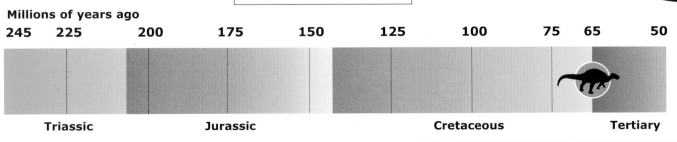

Millions of years ago

245	225	200	175	150	125	100	75	65	50

Triassic   **Jurassic**   **Cretaceous**   **Tertiary**

FAST FACTS

DESCRIPTION	A bipedal/quadrupedal herbivore
ORDER	Ornithischia ("bird-hipped")
NAME MEANS	"Lizard from Edmonton"
PERIOD	Late Cretaceous, about 65 million years ago
LOCATION	North America
LENGTH	43 feet (13 meters)
WEIGHT	4 tons (4 tonnes)

DINOSAUR MUMMY

In 1908, Charles Sternberg and his three sons made one of the most incredible of all dinosaur discoveries—a 65-million-year-old mummified *Edmontosaurus*. They were searching for bones in the Lance Creek area of Wyoming, when they came across the remains of an *Edmontosaurus* lying on its back. As they uncovered the creature, the shrunken remains of its fossilized skin were found, still stretched over the animal's body. It was a truly unbelievable find.

Its head had a broad snout, like a duck's bill, long jaws with cheek pouches, and large eyes. At the tip of its snout was a horny covering.

It had large nostrils, covered with folds of skin.

There were as many as 1,000 tiny teeth—named a dental battery—set toward the back of its jaws. They could be locked together in a grinding pattern. As old teeth fell out, new ones grew in their place.

It had short arms.

Each foot had three toes.

Where they lived

NOISY NOSE

Because the nostrils of *Edmontosaurus* were large and hollow, paleontologists wonder if its nose was covered in folds of loose skin. When it inflated these folds, by blowing air through its nostrils, the effect might have been to create a "sound chamber," which made loud, bellowing noises.

99

Euoplocephalus

Some paleontologists think that *Euoplocephalus* lived in herds, while others believe it wandered alone through its forest home. It was a plant eater, using its toothless bill to tug and chop at whatever low-lying vegetation it could reach. It pushed food into its cheek pouches, where tiny teeth chewed and grated it until it was ready to be swallowed.

Its armor-clad body was protected by bony plates named scutes. This gives us a clue to the dangers it may have faced. For some meat-eating animals, such as *Tyrannosaurus*, *Euoplocephalus* must have made a tasty meal. To protect itself from the teeth and claws of predators, *Euoplocephalus* had evolved its tough outer coat. But it was not protected with bony armor all over. Its underbelly was soft. An intelligent attacker would have tried to flip *Euoplocephalus* on to its back—and then lunged at the defenseless creature's fleshy underside.

DISCOVERY

Euoplocephalus lived in parts of western Canada and the United States. Over the years, fossil hunters have found many more than 40 specimens, particularly in Alberta, Canada, and Montana. The most striking feature of this dinosaur is its armor, which covered its body from head to toe. When paleontologists first studied it at the beginning of the twentieth century, they were amazed to find how well armored its head was. From this came its name, "well-armored head," given to it in 1910 by Lawrence Lambe.

Spines ran down its back.

The large, bony club at the end of its tail was probably swung from side to side to warn a predator to keep away.

FASTER THAN YOU THINK

Considering that this dinosaur was so heavily built, it seems that it was not a sluggish giant. Paleontologists have found numerous lines of fossilized footprints, which were probably made by armored dinosaurs. By measuring the distance between the prints and linking them to the length of the animal's legs, they believe that *Euoplocephalus* could jog along at speed.

Where they lived

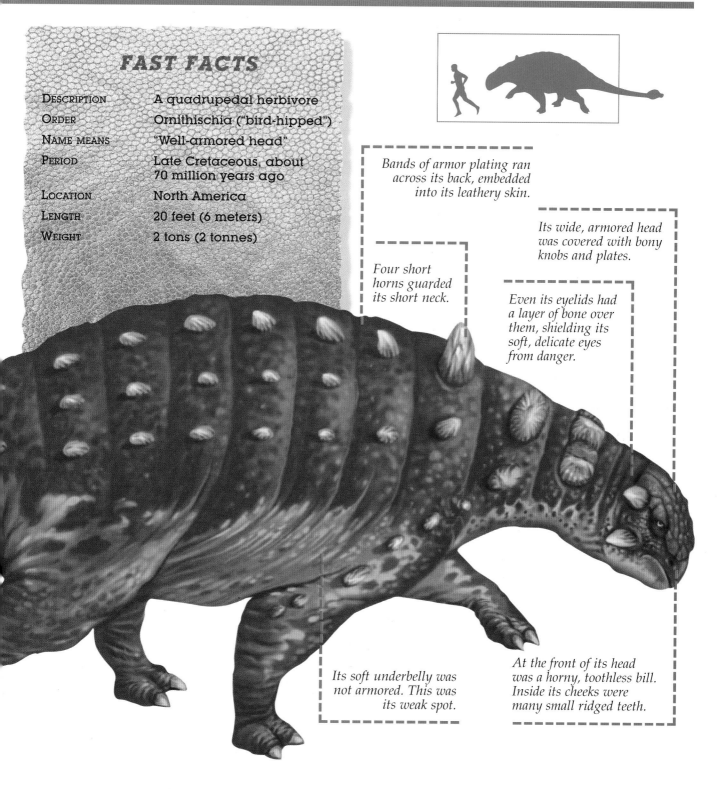

FAST FACTS

DESCRIPTION	A quadrupedal herbivore
ORDER	Ornithischia ("bird-hipped")
NAME MEANS	"Well-armored head"
PERIOD	Late Cretaceous, about 70 million years ago
LOCATION	North America
LENGTH	20 feet (6 meters)
WEIGHT	2 tons (2 tonnes)

Bands of armor plating ran across its back, embedded into its leathery skin.

Its wide, armored head was covered with bony knobs and plates.

Four short horns guarded its short neck.

Even its eyelids had a layer of bone over them, shielding its soft, delicate eyes from danger.

Its soft underbelly was not armored. This was its weak spot.

At the front of its head was a horny, toothless bill. Inside its cheeks were many small ridged teeth.

TIMELINE

Millions of years ago

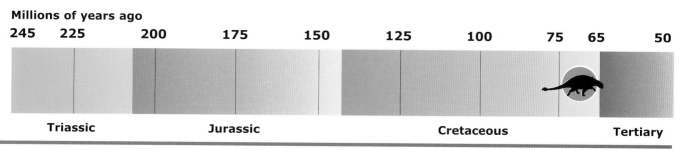

245 225 200 175 150 125 100 75 65 50

Triassic   Jurassic   Cretaceous   Tertiary

101

Gallimimus

One of the ways that paleontologists reconstruct the life styles of extinct animals is by using evidence from similar creatures that are alive today. *Gallimimus* has been compared with today's ostriches—but only more research will confirm whether the beliefs of the scientists are true. One of the main similarities is to be seen in the legs of *Gallimimus*. Its long, slender limbs are extremely birdlike, and it is likely that this dinosaur was a fast runner—perhaps the fastest of them all. If it could run as fast as an ostrich, for example, then it may have reached speeds of 43 mph (70 kph).

When *Gallimimus* was first studied, scientists thought that it was a herbivore. This idea has changed, and now it is believed it was an omnivore—it may have eaten small animals, insects, and eggs, as well as plants. Its long fingers and sharp claws seem to have been the perfect tools for scratching around on the ground, as well as for holding food.

It had large eyes, and its sight may have been good.

It had a long, mobile neck.

It had a long and flat, toothless, horny bill on its small head.

There were three spindly fingers on each hand, tipped with pointed claws.

Gallimimus had a short and compact body.

Where they lived

TIMELINE

Millions of years ago

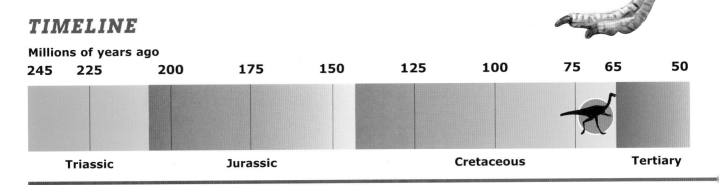

245	225	200	175	150	125	100	75	65	50

| Triassic | Jurassic | Cretaceous | Tertiary |

FAST FACTS

DESCRIPTION	A bipedal omnivore
ORDER	Saurischia ("lizard-hipped")
NAME MEANS	"Chicken mimic"
PERIOD	Late Cretaceous, about 70 million years ago
LOCATION	Asia
LENGTH	20 feet (6 meters)
WEIGHT	1,103 pounds (500 kilograms)

DISCOVERY

The first evidence of *Gallimimus* came in the late 1960s and early 1970s, when an expedition of Polish and Mongolian paleontologists uncovered its fossilized remains in the Gobi Desert, Mongolia. Scientists already knew that some dinosaurs had looked like, or mimicked, present-day ostriches. *Gallimimus* turned out to be the largest member of this group. After careful study, it was given its name in 1972. For a creature so big, it might seem odd that it was named "chicken mimic," but as other dinosaurs had already been named as "ostrich mimic" and "emu mimic," there were not many flightless birds left that it could be named after!

Its long tail was held out straight behind it for balance as it ran, acting as a stabilizer during fast turns.

Long, slim legs, each with three clawed toes.

WHY SO FAST?

In the animal kingdom, speed has always been used for both attack and defense. For *Gallimimus*, its ability to run fast would have taken it quickly to safety, away from an approaching predator. And, in the hunt for food, a speedy animal usually gets its prey.

Gigantosaurus

Very few *Gigantosaurus* specimens have been found, so its life style and habits are still a bit of a mystery. The ideas that paleontologists have about it are mainly based on the habits of other, better-known meat eaters, such as *Allosaurus* and *Tyrannosaurus*. *Gigantosaurus* lived in a moist, tropical environment. It was a hunter, probably stalking its prey alone—although it may have occasionally joined up with others to hunt in packs. Its eyesight may have been good, and its large nostrils suggest that it had a good sense of smell.

Where they lived

Its slender, pointed tail, which may have acted as a counterbalance, kept Gigantosaurus *upright as it ran.*

At the same fossil site where the bones of *Giganotosaurus* were first found, the remains of a massive plant-eating dinosaur were also discovered. It measured 72 feet (22 meters) in length—a lot longer than *Gigantosaurus*. Perhaps this creature was hunted by *Gigantosaurus*. We can imagine how the hunter might have charged at the herbivore, rushing toward it at anything up to 20 mph (32 kph). Maybe it sank its knifelike teeth into its victim's body, biting into and tugging at its flesh. Or perhaps it clamped its huge jaws around the creature's neck, cutting off its air supply and suffocating it.

DISCOVERY

For many years, scientists believed that *Tyrannosaurus rex* was the largest meat-eating dinosaur that had ever roamed the planet—but all that changed in 1994, when an even bigger carnivore was found. That year, Rubén Carolini, an amateur fossil hunter, discovered the almost complete skeleton of a huge meat eater in Patagonia, a region in southern Argentina, South America. The new dinosaur was named *Gigantosaurus*, meaning "giant southern lizard." It is the largest meat-eating dinosaur found—so far.

TIMELINE

Millions of years ago

245	225	200	175	150	125	100	75	65	50

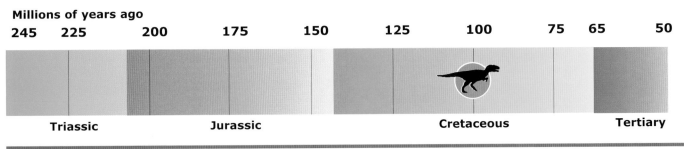

Triassic   Jurassic   Cretaceous   Tertiary

FAST FACTS

DESCRIPTION	A bipedal carnivore
ORDER	Saurischia ("lizard-hipped")
NAME MEANS	"Giant southern lizard"
PERIOD	Late Cretaceous, about 100 million years ago
LOCATION	South America
LENGTH	52 feet (16 meters)
WEIGHT	8 tons (8 tonnes)

Gigantosaurus had a huge skull, 6 feet (1.8 meters) long, with a small banana-shaped brain.

Its eyes stared straight ahead, like those of an eagle.

Inside its large, powerful jaws were many narrow teeth, pointed like arrowheads and serrated along their edges. The largest were 5 inches (20 centimeters) long.

It had short arms with three fingers on each hand.

NO RELATION

At first sight, *Gigantosaurus* and *Tyrannosaurus* seem to have many things in common. But paleontologists who have studied *Gigantosaurus* now know that the two were not related to each other. They were entirely different animals, separated by huge distances and a time span of about 30 million years.

Hypsilophodon

Hypsilophodon was a fast-moving dinosaur that moved quickly on its two long hind legs. Scientists have good evidence for it living in herds, since many skeletons have been found together in one place on the Isle of Wight, an island off the south coast of Britain.

The landscape that *Hypsilophodon* lived in was covered by ferns and horse-tails, which may have been its main source of food. As a grazing animal it would have nipped off the soft parts of plants with its tough, horny bill, passing them to the sides of its mouth where food was held in its cheek pouches. It was here that the sharp, high-ridged teeth after which it is named crushed and ground up the food into a soft pulp. Constant chewing eventually wore its teeth down, and as old ones fell out, sharp new ones grew in their place.

DISCOVERY

Hypsilophodon was first found in 1849, on the Isle of Wight. The *Hypsilophodon* fossil was examined by the leading researchers of the day, including Sir Richard Owen. At that time the study of dinosaurs was a new science, and no one could have known what we do today—that there were thousands of different species. At first *Hypsilophodon* was identified as a young *Iguanodon*. But as more fossils were found over the following 20 years, scientists realized that a mistake had been made. In 1869, English paleontologist Thomas Huxley declared that the creature was, in fact, a new dinosaur, which he named *Hypsilophodon* after its distinctive teeth.

Its tail, stiffened by bony tendons, was held straight out behind it to balance the front of its body.

Hypsilophodon *had long, slender hind legs for speed and agility. Each foot had four long toes.*

TIMELINE

Millions of years ago

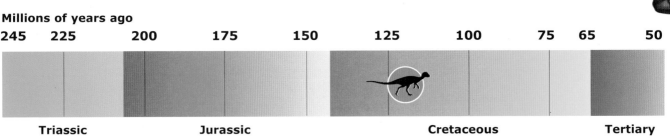

245	225	200	175	150	125	100	75	65	50

Triassic	Jurassic	Cretaceous	Tertiary

Where they lived

FAST FACTS

DESCRIPTION	A bipedal herbivore
ORDER	Ornithischia ("bird-hipped")
NAME MEANS	"High ridge tooth"
PERIOD	Early Cretaceous, about 120 million years ago
LOCATION	Europe; North America
LENGTH	8 feet (2.3 meters)
WEIGHT	154 pounds (70 kilograms)

Two rows of bony studs may have run down its back.

It has a small skull with a horny bill, cheek pouches, and large eyes. Inside its mouth were about 30 chisellike teeth.

It had short arms with five-fingered hands. Each finger was tipped with a sharp claw.

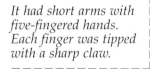

A GENTLE DINOSAUR

Remains of *Hypsilophodon* nests have been found, where they laid their eggs. Scientists believe *Hypsilophodon* parents cared for their young, as fossilized eggs have been found in carefully arranged patterns, suggesting that *Hypsilophodon* was a loving, caring animal.

Iguanodon

Iguanodon is one of the world's best-known dinosaurs. It was a large plant eater. Able to walk on its two hind legs as well as on all fours, it could reach a speed of up to 12 mph (20 kph). *Iguanodon* may have been a herd animal, as shown by the discovery in Belgium and Germany of bone beds containing the remains of many *Iguanodon* that had died together at the same time. With its tough bill it cropped vegetation which its tongue would then push into its cheek pouches. Long, sharp teeth chewed on the plants, crushing and grinding them until they could be swallowed.

DISCOVERY

Iguanodon was the second dinosaur ever to be named. In 1822, Dr. Gideon Mantell and his wife, Mary Ann Mantell, were visiting a patient near the small town of Cuckfield, Sussex, in England. While Dr. Mantell was treating his patient, Mary Ann went for a walk. In a pile of stones used for road repairs, she saw a fossil tooth. The Mantells knew a lot about fossils, but neither of them had ever seen such a tooth before. They found that it had been dug up at a nearby quarry, from where they were able to find more teeth belonging to the mysterious creature. While visiting the Royal College of Surgeons, London, England, Dr. Mantell was

Its snout ended in a blunt, toothless bill, covered in horn. Its teeth—2 inches (50mm) long— were at the back of its mouth, tightly packed into its cheeks.

Each hand had four fingers, and a large spiked thumb.

Iguanodon *had three-toed feet with hooves, like today's cows and horses.*

TIMELINE

Millions of years ago

245	225	200	175	150	125	100	75	65	50

Triassic   Jurassic   Cretaceous   Tertiary

shown the tooth from a present-day iguana. It was similar to the fossil tooth found by his wife, except that it was much smaller. In 1825, Dr. Mantell named the ancient creature *Iguanodon*, meaning "iguana tooth."

FAST FACTS

DESCRIPTION	A bipedal/quadrupedal herbivore
ORDER	Ornithischia ("bird-hipped")
NAME MEANS	"Iguana tooth"
PERIOD	Early Cretaceous, about 130 million years ago
LOCATION	Europe; North America
LENGTH	33 feet (10 meters)
WEIGHT	5 tons (5 tonnes)

SPIKED THUMB

Iguanodon's large spiked thumb on each hand may have been used for defense. If attacked, its thumb—like a dagger—could stab into the body of its enemy. It might also have been used in contests between rival animals, where two *Iguanodon* reared up against each other until one backed away. There may have been fights between rivals over territory, food, and mates.

Its long tail was stiffened by bony tendons.

Where they lived

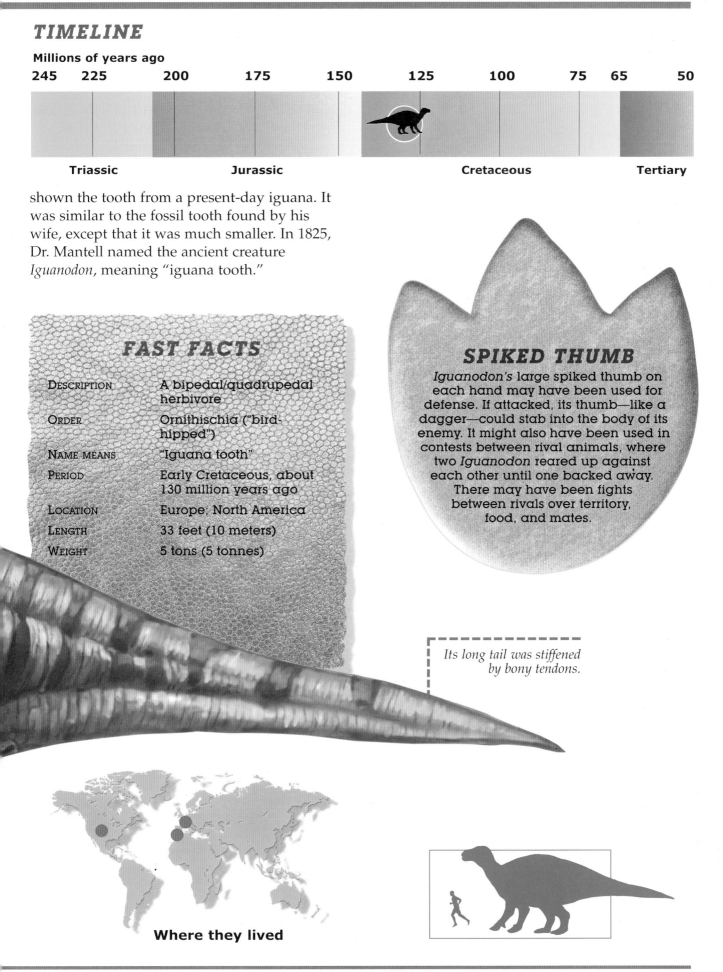

Janenschia

So little is known about *Janenschia* that it is difficult to describe the life style it may have led. The reason for this difficulty is because so far only some parts of one *Janenschia* dinosaur have ever been found. The skull was missing, so nothing is known about its head.

Despite there being so few fossils of *Janenschia*, it is clear that it was a giant herbivore that walked on four pillarlike legs. Like other giant plant eaters, such as *Brachiosaurus*, it may have swallowed leaves whole, without chewing them. The job of crushing its food was left to the stomach stones, or gastroliths, that rolled around inside its belly. Only when the vegetation had been broken down by the movement of the stones and the action of stomach juices and bacteria, could the plant material be fully digested.

Given its great size, and its long giraffelike neck, *Janenschia* might have eaten leaves from the tops of tall trees, leaving lower-growing plants to smaller herbivores. Because only one *Janenschia* has been found, no one can say whether it lived in herds or on its own. Further work is needed to find more fossils, which might provide answers to the many questions that are asked about this Jurassic giant.

KNOBBLY SKIN?

For many years, paleontologists thought that sauropods—long-necked, four-legged giant herbivores—did not have any armor plating on their bodies. But, discoveries in the 1980s revealed that at least one sauropod, *Saltasaurus*, from South America, probably had rows of bony plates set into the skin on its back. And if one *sauropod* was armored, then maybe others, such as *Janenschia*, were too.

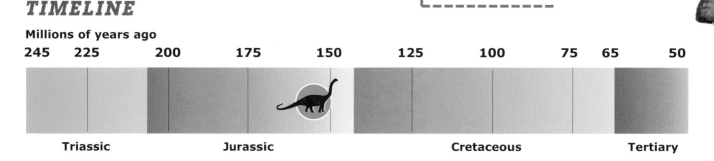

Its long tail was thick and muscular.

TIMELINE

Millions of years ago

245	225	200	175	150	125	100	75	65	50

Triassic	Jurassic	Cretaceous	Tertiary

DISCOVERY

Janenschia was discovered in Tanzania, East Africa, and was named in 1991 by German paleontologist Rupert Wild. He named it in honor of a fellow German, Werner Janensch, who had worked in the same part of Africa some 80 years earlier and had uncovered several *Brachiosaurus* fossils.

Where they lived

Janenschia *had a long, flexible neck.*

Armored plates (called scutes) may have been embedded in the leathery skin of its back.

It had stumpy, pillarlike legs. The hind legs had long claws on the toes.

FAST FACTS

DESCRIPTION	A quadrupedal herbivore
ORDER	Saurischia ("lizard-hipped")
NAME MEANS	"Janensch"
PERIOD	Late Jurassic, about 155 million years ago
LOCATION	Africa
LENGTH	79 feet (24 meters)
WEIGHT	Unknown

Kentrosaurus

Kentrosaurus lived near river mouths. A plant eater, it spent its life wandering slowly across the river's flood plain, possibly in a herd. It walked with its small head close to the ground, grazing on low-growing vegetation. As its hind legs were much longer than its front legs, it may have been able to rear up, balancing on its tail, to reach for plants that grew a little higher up.

The most distinctive features of *Kentrosaurus* are its plates and spines. They were not attached to its bones, so no one can be entirely certain where they were located on its body. The most likely reason for this body armor is for self-defense. Its tail was flexible and was not made stiff by bony tendons. If attacked, *Kentrosaurus* may have flicked its tail from side to side, aiming the sharp, pointed spines at a

Two rows of bony plates were embedded into the skin of its back. They were arranged in pairs and ran from its neck to half-way down its body.

Pairs of long spines ran from its midsection to the tip of its tail.

Scientists are not sure if this spine protected the hip or the shoulder.

Kentrosaurus *had a small, narrow head inside which was a tiny brain— no bigger than a walnut.*

It had large nasal passages and may have had a good sense of smell.

Its snout ended in a toothless bill and many small, weak teeth were packed inside its cheeks.

The hind legs were twice as long as the front legs.

There were hooflike claws on its toes.

TIMELINE

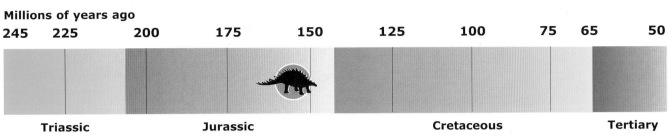

| 245 | 225 | 200 | 175 | 150 | 125 | 100 | 75 | 65 | 50 |

| Triassic | Jurassic | Cretaceous | Tertiary |

predator. But if an attacker managed to avoid the spines, its target may well have been the soft underbelly of *Kentrosaurus*, which was unprotected because its bony plates only shielded its back from attack.

DISCOVERY

In the early 1900s, many spectacular dinosaur discoveries were made at Tendaguru, in Tanzania, East Africa. It was a remote place, four days' march inland from the nearest port. But in 1907, several gigantic fossil bones were found weathering out of the ground. Between 1909—1912, German paleontologist Werner Janensch led an expedition to the fossil site. A work-force of 500 laborers dug enormous pits, unearthing the fossilized bones of many extinct creatures. More than 250 tons of bones were carted to the coast and shipped to Germany to be studied. Among the fossils excavated at Tendaguru was a creature whose back was covered with huge bony plates and long, sharp spikes. In 1915 it was given the name *Kentrosaurus*, meaning "spiked lizard."

FAST FACTS

DESCRIPTION	A quadrupedal herbivore
ORDER	Ornithischia ("bird-hipped")
NAME MEANS	"Spiked lizard"
PERIOD	Late Jurassic, about 155 million years ago
LOCATION	Africa
LENGTH	16 feet (5 meters)
WEIGHT	about 1 ton (1 tonne)

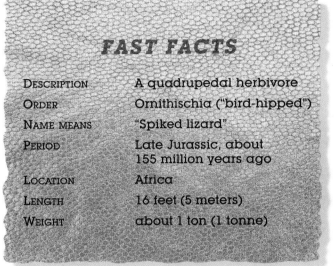

Where they lived

THE DINOSAUR WITH TWO BRAINS

Scientists once thought that *Kentrosaurus*, along with other members of the stegosaur family, had two brains. There was a small brain inside its skull, but a much larger "brain" appeared to be located between two of its hip vertebrae (bones of the spine). However, on closer inspection the so called "second brain" has turned out to be a large bundle of nerve fibres. It was not a brain at all.

Lesothosaurus

Lesothosaurus is one of the oldest African dinosaurs. It was a small lizardlike herbivore, about the size of a fox. It had a lightweight body, built for speed. It probably lived in packs, running swiftly across the hot, dry plains of its homeland. As a herbivore it mostly ate low-growing plants, chewing on them with its sharp teeth. Some scientists think it may also have eaten the occasional insect, or even carrion (meat from a dead animal) that it came across as it scratched on the ground. If *Lesothosaurus* sensed danger, it may have been able to signal to the rest of the pack by making a warning noise—and then, quick as a flash, they would have scurried away quickly to safety. A sudden burst of great speed was the main means of defense for this tiny dinosaur.

DISCOVERY
When a small fragment of jaw with three teeth in it was found in Lesotho, South Africa, in the early 1960s, paleontologists identified it as belonging to an entirely new dinosaur species. In 1964, in honor of its French discoverer, a geologist named Fabre, the new creature was named *Fabrosaurus*, meaning "Fabre's lizard."

Then, when more fossilized bones were found in the same part of Lesotho, scientists thought they had found yet another type of dinosaur, and in 1978 this other "new" creature was named *Lesothosaurus*. But, many scientists now think that *Fabrosaurus* and *Lesothosaurus* are the same dinosaur. If this is true, then according to the rules of naming an animal it will have to be called by the name it was first given—*Fabrosaurus*. But until that happens, most people, including paleontologists, are happy to use the name *Lesothosaurus*.

Lesothosaurus had a long, pointed tail.

Where they lived

TIMELINE

Millions of years ago

245	225	200	175	150	125	100	75	65	50

Triassic	Jurassic	Cretaceous	Tertiary

It had a flexible neck and a small triangular head with large eyes.

FAST FACTS

DESCRIPTION	A bipedal herbivore
ORDER	Ornithischia ("bird-hipped")
NAME MEANS	"Lizard from Lesotho"
PERIOD	Early Jurassic, about 200 million years ago
LOCATION	Africa
LENGTH	3 feet (1 meter)
WEIGHT	66 pounds (30 kilograms)

It had sharp, pointed incisors (front teeth) and cheek teeth in the shape of arrowheads.

Short arms, with five fingers on each hand suitable for grabbing and seizing at things.

Its long hind legs made it a fast runner—a sprinter among the dinosaurs.

DID IT HIBERNATE?

The skeletons of a pair of *Lesothosaurus* were found curled up together. Paleontologists think that these two dinosaurs had gone into a burrow under the ground to hibernate, but for some unknown reason they had died in their sleep.

Each foot had four toes.

Maiasaura

Maiasaura was a duck-billed dinosaur. It was a plant eater that lived on high ground overlooking the sea. It seems it lived in huge herds—some of which may have contained as many as 10,000 animals. With so many mouths to feed, the search for food was a continual process, and scientists believe that the *Maiasaura* herds migrated along well-known routes throughout the seasons of the year, always knowing where the best places were to find adequate supplies of food. It has been calculated that an adult *Maiasaura* needed to eat about 200 pounds (90 kilograms) of vegetation every day. If attacked by a predator, such as the meat-eating *Albertosaurus*, the main means of defense for *Maiasaura* was to run. It had no bony armor to protect its body and no big teeth or claws with which to fight back. Instead, it might have reared up on to its two hind legs and run for cover. And if one *Maiasaura* ran, then panic might sweep through the herd—and soon thousands would be on the move, heading away from danger.

DISCOVERY

The first fossils of *Maiasaura* were discovered quite by chance in 1978, in Montana. American paleontologists Robert Makela and John Horner were in a rock shop in the small town of Bynum, Montana. Lying among the minerals and common fossils on sale in the shop, they came across a totally unexpected find—the bones of a baby dinosaur. The scientists knew they had to find out where the tiny bones had come from, as dinosaur babies are extremely rare. It turned out they came from a range of hills that lay just outside of Bynum.

It had a long, flexible tail, useful for balancing the upper body when the creature ran.

Makela and Horner visited the site, where they found not only baby dinosaurs, but eggs and nests. In 1979, the first full-scale fieldwork began at the site. Work continues to this day, revealing more clues into the life of *Maiasaura*—the "good mother lizard" from 80 million years ago.

TIMELINE

Millions of years ago

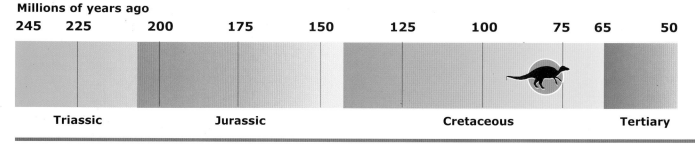

245	225	200	175	150	125	100	75	65	50

| Triassic | Jurassic | Cretaceous | Tertiary |

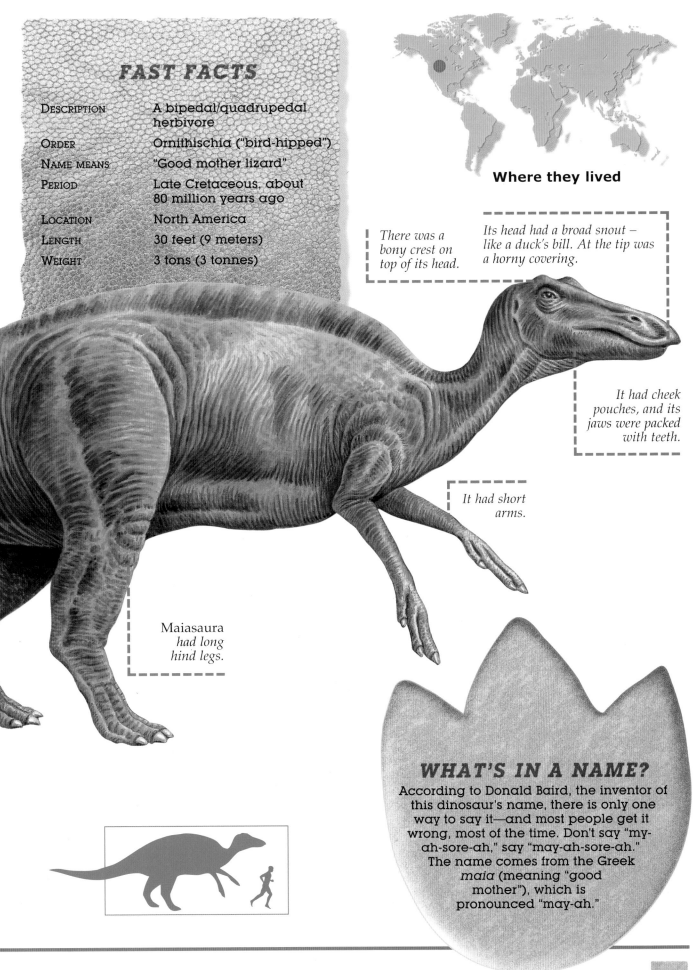

FAST FACTS

DESCRIPTION	A bipedal/quadrupedal herbivore
ORDER	Ornithischia ("bird-hipped")
NAME MEANS	"Good mother lizard"
PERIOD	Late Cretaceous, about 80 million years ago
LOCATION	North America
LENGTH	30 feet (9 meters)
WEIGHT	3 tons (3 tonnes)

Where they lived

There was a bony crest on top of its head.

Its head had a broad snout – like a duck's bill. At the tip was a horny covering.

It had cheek pouches, and its jaws were packed with teeth.

It had short arms.

Maiasaura *had long hind legs.*

WHAT'S IN A NAME?

According to Donald Baird, the inventor of this dinosaur's name, there is only one way to say it—and most people get it wrong, most of the time. Don't say "my-ah-sore-ah," say "may-ah-sore-ah." The name comes from the Greek *maia* (meaning "good mother"), which is pronounced "may-ah."

117

Maiasaura nests

Maiasaura was given the name "good mother" because of the evidence found at the nest site in Montana. Nests were large—about 7 feet (2 meters) across. They were scooped out of the soil to make a hollow in the ground. Vegetation was placed inside the hollow to make a soft lining. As many as 25 oval eggs, each about the size of a grapefruit, were laid in the nest, arranged in circles. Each egg was separate from its neighbor. This made sure that they did not get damaged by rolling into each other. *Maiasaura* did not sit on the nest—to do so might have damaged the precious eggs inside. Instead, the nest was covered with a thick layer of plants. As the piled-up vegetation rotted down, heat was produced, which kept the eggs warm. Inside their "incubator," the eggs developed. While this was happening, *Maiasaura* probably stayed close by, guarding the nest from egg thieves—and from other *Maiasaura* who might have trampled on it.

Maiasaura young

Newly hatched *Maiasaura* babies were about 1 foot (30 centimeters) long. Their leg bones and joints were not fully formed, and it was not until they had grown to five times their size at birth that they were ready to leave the nest. Until then they were brought food by their parents—but whether it was both parents or just one is not yet known. Perhaps the feeding parent spat out partly digested food for its young to eat, just as some birds do. Once the young were able to leave the nest, the adults must have had some way of recognizing their own children among the many others at the nest site. Perhaps they did this by smell, or by special sounds. Or maybe the young had distinctive markings on their skins that only their parents could recognize.

A *Maiasaura* mother and her hatchlings

At the age of one year, a young *Maiasaura* was about 8 feet (2.5 meters) long—about five times smaller than an adult. Most paleontologists think that the young stayed with their parents for several years before becoming fully independent and able to fend for themselves. Between 10 and 12 years old, a *Maiasaura* reached adulthood, and was able to begin a family of its own.

HOMING INSTINCT

Just like many wild animals do today, *Maiasaura* herds returned to the same nesting grounds year after year. It is possible that the animals returned to their old nests, cleaning them out and repairing them ready for that year's clutch of eggs to be laid.

Mamenchisaurus

Mamenchisaurus
had a small head.

*Its skull was box-shaped,
and it had strong spoon-
shaped teeth.*

*It had a very long neck that
measured about 46 feet (14
meters), making it one of the
longest of all dinosaur necks.
There were 19 vertebrae
(neck bones) in its neck – a
giraffe only has seven neck
bones. Each of its neck bones
was supported by two
overlapping, rodlike ribs,
making its neck quite stiff.*

Mamenchisaurus was a gigantic, long-necked,
long-tailed, plant-eating dinosaur that walked
slowly on all four legs. It may have lived in herds,
like other giant herbivores. The Late Jurassic landscape
through which it roamed was covered with a vast forest
of tall sequoia trees, but even their high-growing leaves
came within reach of a browsing *Mamenchisaurus* at full
stretch. When feeding, the animal was probably able to crop
vegetation from over a wide area without having to move its
enormous body—it simply reached out with its neck to strip off
the next mouthful of leaves with its blunt, spoonlike teeth. Leaves,
ferns, horse-tails, stems, twigs, seeds and fruits were swallowed
whole, passing down its long neck and into its stomach. Gastroliths
(stomach stones), digestive juices, and bacteria got to work on the
vegetation, crushing it into a digestible, semiliquid mush.

DISCOVERY

In China, dinosaurs have been linked with dragons for a very long
time. For years, so-called "dragon's bones" had been dug up in
Sichuan, a province in central China. The old bones were ground into
powder and used in traditional Chinese medicines. In the 1950s,
Chinese paleontologists took an interest in the place where the bones
were being found. The site was at Mamenchi, and what the scientists
found turned out to be the fossilized bones of a massive dinosaur. In
1954, Young Chung Chien, a Chinese paleontologist, named the new
dinosaur *Mamenchisaurus*, meaning "Maman Brook lizard" ("*chi*"
means brook, and "*Mamen*" was the name of the brook).

TIMELINE

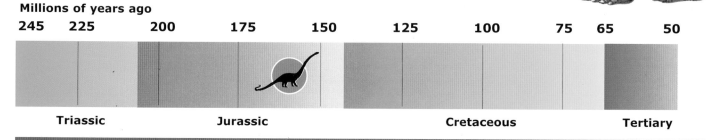

Millions of years ago

245	225	200	175	150	125	100	75	65	50

Triassic	Jurassic	Cretaceous	Tertiary

FAST FACTS

DESCRIPTION	A quadrupedal herbivore
ORDER	Saurischia ("lizard-hipped")
NAME MEANS	"Mamen Brook lizard"
PERIOD	Late Jurassic, about 160 million years ago
LOCATION	Asia
LENGTH	82 feet (25 meters)
WEIGHT	27 tons (27 tonnes)

Where they lived

GET A HEAD!

When *Mamenchisaurus* was first discovered, the giant's skeleton was missing one vital piece of evidence—its skull. Scientists guessed that its head probably looked like that of a *Diplodocus*. Thirty years passed before the first skull bones were found, in the 1980s. Only then could scientists work out what the head of *Mamenchisaurus* was really like. They had been correct all along, and in many ways it actually was like the head of a *Diplodocus*, except that its snout was a little blunter and its teeth were more spoon-shaped.

Its hind legs were longer than its front legs.

Megalosaurus

Despite *Megalosaurus* being the first named dinosaur, very little is still known about it. No complete skeletons have ever been found and scientists have tried to work out its life style from that of other meat eaters. We know that it lived about 170 million years ago, at a time when the Earth's weather was mild. The world's plants were large and plentiful, as in a rainforest today. There were forest trees such as conifers, cycads and ginkgoes, and ferns and horse-tails grew on the ground. This scene would have been home to *Megalosaurus*, a predatory dinosaur that stalked through the vegetation in search of prey, such as *Iguanodon*. But perhaps it was a scavenger, too, eating flesh from an animal that was already dead. Like a lion, it may have stayed close to a kill for several days, returning to feed on the carcass.

Megalosaurus had a short neck, and a large head.

Its jaws were packed with sharp, serrated teeth, which curved backward into its mouth. They were ideal for cutting through meat.

Its arms were short and it had three-fingered hands with sharp claws.

There were sharp claws on the toes of its feet.

TIMELINE

Millions of years ago

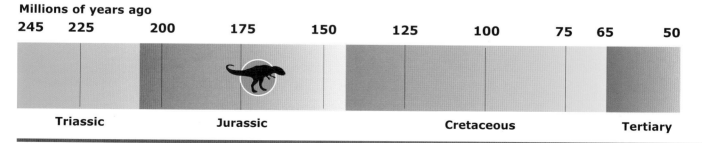

245	225	200	175	150	125	100	75	65	50

Triassic	Jurassic	Cretaceous	Tertiary

FAST FACTS

DESCRIPTION	A bipedal carnivore
ORDER	Saurischia ("lizard-hipped")
Name means	"Great lizard"
PERIOD	Middle Jurassic, about 170 million years ago
LOCATION	Europe
LENGTH	30 feet (9 meters)
WEIGHT	About 1 ton (1 tonne)

Where they lived

It had a heavy tail and a bulky body.

It walked on two strong legs.

DISCOVERY

Megalosaurus was not the biggest meat eater that walked on Earth, yet its name, "great lizard," marks it out as being, in some way, special. In the story of dinosaur discoveries, this was the animal whose prehistoric remains, found in the south of England, were first thought to belong to a giant reptile. As early as 1676, a bone from *Megalosaurus* had caused scientists in England to wonder what kind of animals had once lived. One scientist said that the bone belonged to a giant elephant, brought to England by the Romans. Another believed it was from the skeleton of a giant human! No one came up with a better idea until 1822, when James Parkinson examined a collection of fossil bones and teeth found at a slate quarry near Oxford in England. He correctly identified them as coming from a giant reptile, a lizard, which he named *Megalosaurus*. This was the first time a dinosaur had been described and named—though the world would have to wait another 20 years before the word "dinosaur" was invented.

DINOSAUR WASTE BASKET

We know that *Megalosaurus* was not the only meat eater that lived in what is now Europe. But things have not always been this way. In the early years of dinosaur studies, scientists thought that all bones from large meat eaters came from the same species of dinosaur. They were all labeled as *Megalosaurus* bones. *Megalosaurus* became a "waste basket" name into which lots of different species were placed by mistake. These old mistakes are now being corrected and the bones are being correctly identified with the right dinosaurs.

Minmi

Minmi was a small, armored dinosaur, a member of the ankylosaur family. It was a plant eater that grazed on low-growing vegetation, such as cycads, ferns, and horse-tails, which it nipped off with its bill. Its most distinctive feature was its heavily armored skin—every part of which seems to have been covered in a variety of different-shaped bony plates. All this armor increased its body weight, but far from being a slow-moving giant, this particular creature seems to have been able to move quite fast. The evidence for this comes from two facts. First, it had longish legs, suggesting it was able to break into a trot when necessary. Second, its backbone was especially strong and may have evolved like this to take the strain of its great weight as *Minmi* thundered across the ground. But if a predator caught up with it, even its tough belly skin would not have been able to resist the bites, kicks, and tears from a determined meat eater.

Even its underside was protected by small bony plates, embedded in its skin. Most other armored dinosaurs did not have any bony protection on their bellies.

DISCOVERY

Minmi—or *Minmi paravertebra* to give it its full scientific name—was discovered in 1964 by Alan Bartholomai, in Queensland, northeastern Australia. It was the first time that an armor-plated, "bird-hipped" dinosaur had been found in the Southern Hemisphere. It was described by Ralph Molnar in 1980, and it was he who gave it its name, naming it *Minmi* after the site at Minmi Crossing, near the small town of Roma, where it was found. A second, almost complete *Minmi* skeleton was discovered in 1990, at Marathon Station, also in Queensland.

Its legs were quite long for an armored dinosaur, and its hind legs were longer than the front pair.

TIMELINE

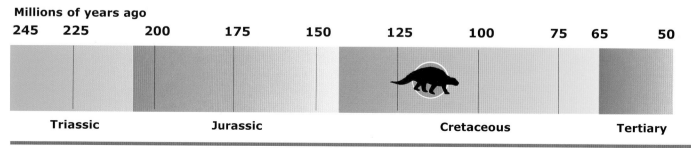

Millions of years ago

245	225	200	175	150	125	100	75	65	50

Triassic　　　　Jurassic　　　　Cretaceous　　　　Tertiary

Where they lived

STRONG BACK

Extending out from the vertebrae (backbones) were bones named paravertebrae. No other dinosaur is known to have had such bones. Some scientists believe they helped to reinforce the back of *Minmi*, making it strong enough to carry the weight of its armor, especially if it ran.

Minmi had a short neck and a turtle-shaped head, inside which was a tiny brain and many small, leaf-shaped teeth.

Its body was covered in bony plates, named scutes. There were plates around the neck, across the back and along the tail.

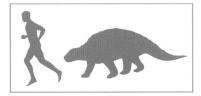

FAST FACTS

DESCRIPTION	A quadrupedal herbivore
ORDER	Ornithischia ("bird-hipped")
NAME MEANS	"From Minmi Crossing"
PERIOD	Early Cretaceous, about 115 million years ago
LOCATION	Australia
LENGTH	10 feet (3 meters)
WEIGHT	About 1 ton (1 tonne)

Notoceratops

Very little is known about this dinosaur. Scientists are in debate about what kind of dinosaur it was. If *Notoceratops* was a horned dinosaur, then that puts it in the same family as the better-known *Triceratops* and *Styracosaurus*. If this is the case, then its life style can be worked out based on what is known about its relatives. *Notoceratops* would probably have been a herd animal, like other ceratopsians. It was a herbivore that grazed on low-growing vegetation, such as cycads. Its horns might have been used to pull down on leafy branches, bringing them within biting range of its snapping bill.

NECK FRILL AND HEAD HORNS

Of all the dinosaurs, the ceratopsians had the most distinctive headgear. But why did they grow neck frills and head horns? The most likely idea is that these devices evolved so that they could be used in acts of display and defense. Just as today's stags lock their antlers together in a test of strength, perhaps the ceratopsians pushed each other around with their horns. And the neck frill might have been highly patterned, sending out colorful signals to attract mates—or to frighten attackers away. Birds and insects, such as butterflies and moths, use colors in just this way today.

As a ceratopsian, it would have had a long, low snout that ended in a horny bill, like that of a parrot. There would have been many cheek teeth packed into the back of its mouth.

If it was a ceratopsian dinosaur, then it would have had a bony frill at the back of its head, and horns projecting from the front.

TIMELINE

Millions of years ago

245	225	200	175	150	125	100	75	65	50

Triassic	Jurassic	Cretaceous	Tertiary

Where they lived

MISSING BONE

Since the naming of *Notoceratops* in 1918, the jawbone that led to its identification has been lost. This is a problem. Paleontologists today are not so sure that *Notoceratops* really was a horned dinosaur, and because the original bone is missing, it is impossible now to check the facts. Only when another *Notoceratops* fossil is found will its true appearance really be known. Until then there is a big question mark hanging over its identification.

Size unknown

Notoceratops
walked on four
short legs.

FAST FACTS

DESCRIPTION	A quadrupedal herbivore
ORDER	Ornithischia ("bird-hipped")
NAME MEANS	"Southern horned face"
PERIOD	Late Cretaceous, about 80 million years ago
LOCATION	South America
LENGTH	unknown
WEIGHT	unknown

DISCOVERY

When part of a fossilized jawbone was found in the early 1900s, in Chubut province, Argentina, the scientists of the day decided it was from a new species of dinosaur. They compared it with bones found elsewhere in the world, and said it belonged to a creature from the ceratopsian family of dinosaurs. These dinosaurs were noted for their parrotlike bills and horned and frilled heads. In 1918, Argentinian paleontologist Augusto Tapia gave the animal its name—*Notoceratops*, meaning "southern horned face." He called it "southern" because it was from the continent of South America. But not all today's paleontologists are convinced that *Notoceratops* was a horned dinosaur.

Ornithomimus

Ornithomimus belongs to a family of dinosaurs called the ornithomimids. These were ostrichlike dinosaurs whose toothless bills, graceful bodies, and clawed feet give them the appearance of an ostrich. *Ornithomimus* was one of the fastest animals alive in its time. It used its long legs to run at speeds of up to 43 mph (70 kph) over short distances. This is the speed an ostrich reaches today. Speed was this dinosaurs best defense—it was far better for it to run to safety than to try and fight off a predator.

As it sprinted across the land, the three toes on its hind feet dug into the ground like the spikes on running shoes. With its long arms it could reach up into trees to pull branches toward its mouth, nipping off leaves, seeds, buds, and fruit with the tip and sides of its bony bill. There were no teeth inside its mouth. Instead, it used its scissorlike bill to chop its food into smaller and smaller pieces, ready to be swallowed.

It had a long tail, which it held out straight behind it for balance as it ran.

FAST FACTS

DESCRIPTION	A bipedal omnivore
ORDER	Saurischia ("lizard-hipped")
NAME MEANS	"Bird mimic"
PERIOD	Late Cretaceous, about 70 million years ago
LOCATION	North America
LENGTH	11 feet (3.5 meters)
WEIGHT	331 pounds (150 kilograms)

It had long, slim legs, each with three clawed toes.

TIMELINE

Millions of years ago

245	225	200	175	150	125	100	75	65	50

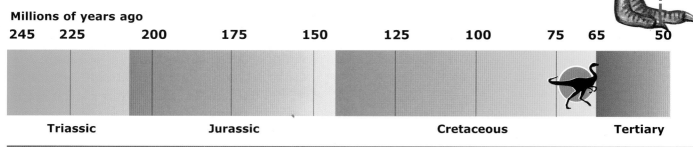

Triassic	Jurassic	Cretaceous	Tertiary

DISCOVERY

The first fossilized *Ornithomimus* bones were found in Colorado and Montana in the late 1880s. None of the skeletons were complete—one was made up of just a part of a foot and hind leg—but they were enough for the American paleontologist Othniel Marsh to recognize that a new dinosaur species had been discovered. He named it the following year. It was not until 1917 that the first reasonably complete *Ornithomimus* skeleton was described.

It had a long, toothless, horny bill.

Its small head had large eyes and a big brain.

Where they lived

Its short arms ended in hands with three spindly fingers that were tipped with pointed claws.

Ornithomimus *had a short and compact body.*

HARD TO CHEW

Many scientists believe that *Ornithomimus* was an omnivore—a creature that ate both plants and meat. If so, then it may have lived on a diet of insects, small lizards, and mammals, fruit, eggs, and leaves. But not everyone agrees with this. Some scientists think it was a herbivore, living only on a diet of plants. They say that for it to eat meat, it would have needed teeth—which it did not have.

Oviraptor

It had a short lump of horn on its nose.

It had a short bill without any teeth.

Oviraptor belonged to the dinosaur family *Oviraptoridae*, to which it gave its name. It was the same size as the *Velociraptor,* which was made famous in the film *Jurassic Park* (although *Velociraptor* came from a different dinosaur family). *Oviraptor* was not as well armed as *Velociraptor*. It had three main toes on its feet, but lacked the long, curved blade on its second toe that *Velociraptor* and *Deinonychus* used for attack. *Oviraptor* had three prey-holding fingers on each hand with long nails about 3 inches (8 centimeters) long.

Powerful jaw muscles allowed Oviraptor to crush hard objects, such as bones.

DISCOVERY

Oviraptor was discovered in Mongolia by members of a 1924 expedition from the American Museum of Natural History. They had originally gone to Asia to look for the remains of early humans, but instead made many fascinating dinosaur discoveries. Among these was the first ever find of dinosaur eggs, which had belonged to *Protoceratops*.

When the scientists first found *Oviraptor*, its remains were lying on a batch of eggs that were thought to belong to a *Protoceratops*. This is what gave *Oviraptor* its name, which means "egg thief." In fact, modern scientific techniques have been used to examine the embryo inside the eggs. *Oviraptor* is now known to have been lying on its own unhatched young.

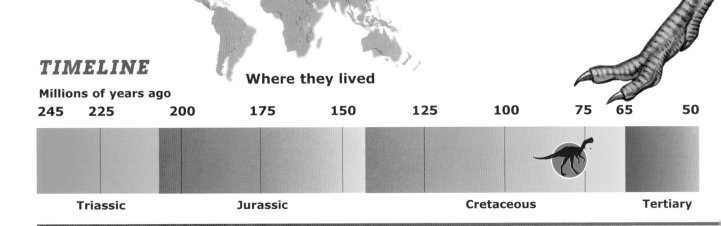

Its long fingers and nails were used for grasping on to prey.

Where they lived

TIMELINE

Millions of years ago

245	225	200	175	150	125	100	75	65	50

Triassic	Jurassic	Cretaceous	Tertiary

POWERFUL HUNTER

Oviraptor had an unusually shaped skull. Its head had a short bill almost like a parrot's, but with no teeth. Above the snout was a small lump like the beginnings of a rhinoceros horn. The muscles that worked *Oviraptor*'s jaw were extremely powerful, and its bill could easily have bitten through an arm bone.

   Oviraptor's tail was not used as a weapon, but the predator could not have hunted without it. As the dinosaur ran forward its tail would have been held straight out behind as a counterbalance to its head and body, and while actually attacking its prey its tail was again crucial for balance.

FAST FACTS

DESCRIPTION	A bipedal carnivore
ORDER	Saurischia ("lizard-hipped")
NAME MEANS	"Egg thief"
PERIOD	Late Cretaceous
LOCATION	Asia (what is now Mongolia)
LENGTH	6 feet (1.8 meters)
WEIGHT	44 pounds (20 kilograms)

Its slender, powerful leg muscles were ideal for high-speed pursuit.

Its long tail was used for balance when attacking prey and when running.

It had three-toed feet with claws.

THE MYSTERY OF THE EGGS

Several *Oviraptors* have been unearthed lying on their own eggs. Very few other dinosaurs have been found in this position, which makes *Oviraptor* a bit of a mystery. Perhaps it often died giving birth to its young, or defending the nest against predators. Another theory is that the original find in Mongolia had been covered over by a sandstorm, and the female *Oviraptor* had refused to leave her eggs.

Pachycephalosaurus

Imagine the scene: Two billy goats are facing each other in a contest to decide which is the strongest. Suddenly they charge, full speed, straight at each other; their heads and horns crash together with a shocking bang. The goats stagger away dazed, before turning to face each other and butt heads again.

Now meet the king of the headbutters: *Pachycephalosaurus*. This dinosaur was the largest of a group sometimes called "thick-headed lizards," which had specially thick skulls that were used for head-butting contests. Some of the dinosaurs in this group had fringes of bone, knobs, and spikes around the sides of their heads, which made them look a little like bald old men. *Pachycephalosaurus* itself had one of these fringes at the back of its head, as well as small spikes on its nose.

Its skull was topped by 10 inches (25 centimeters) of solid bone capable of withstanding massive impacts.

It had an enormous skull 2 feet (60 centimeters) long—far bigger than any of Pachycephalosaurus's known relatives.

Its teeth were small and serrated. They curved backward a little and were excellent at shredding plant material.

It had small arms with five fingers.

Where they lived

TIMELINE

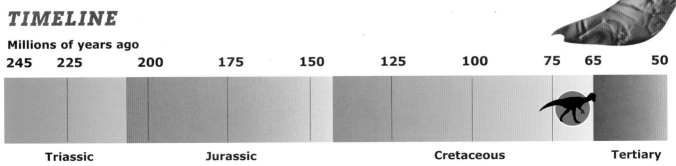

Millions of years ago

245	225	200	175	150	125	100	75	65	50

Triassic	Jurassic	Cretaceous	Tertiary

FAST FACTS

DESCRIPTION	A bipedal herbivore
ORDER	Ornithiscia ("bird-hipped")
NAME MEANS	"Thick-headed lizard"
PERIOD	Late Cretaceous, about 70 million years ago
LOCATION	North America
LENGTH	15 feet (4.6 meters)
WEIGHT	660 pounds (300 kilograms)

SOCIABLE HEADBUTTER

Most scientists think that *Pachycephalosaurus* must have lived in herds, like today's mountain goats. Only constant contact with other males would have led to such regular competitions that the super-thick skull would have evolved.

It used its tail for balance.

It had long legs with three toes. The third toe was tiny and useless, and the other two carried Pachycephalosaurus's *weight as it walked.*

BONE HEAD

Pachycephalosaurus's skull was topped by a huge dome of bone that was 10 inches (25 centimeters) thick. The whole dinosaur was probably about 15 feet (4.6 meters) long, but it is only known from its skull, which was first unearthed in 1943 by two dinosaur hunters named Brown and Schaikjer. The rest of *Pachycephalosaurus*'s dimensions have been worked out by scaling it up in proportion to other dinosaurs from the same family, such as *Stegoceras*.

Males would have competed with one another for females and leadership by running as fast as they could at their opponent. Long, powerful legs would have driven them forward with their heads lowered. *Pachycephalosaurus* would have held its tail straight out behind for balance as it raced ahead, before all the force crashed into the collision of heads.

Pachycephalosaurus was the largest dinosaur in its family by far, and as a species it was the longest lasting. It only disappeared when all its meat-eating and plant-eating relatives were wiped out, too, at the end of the Cretaceous Period. Not bad for such a bonehead!

Parasaurolophus

The forests of Late Cretaceous North America must have been very noisy places. They were full of a kind of dinosaur named hadrosaurs, or duck-bills. All duck-bills had a crest on top of their head: Some crests were hollow, others solid. The dinosaurs with solid crests made a loud honking noise using their nasal sacs. But the most spectacular noise came from the hollow-crested duck-bills, which trumpeted by blowing air through their crests. One of the greatest trumpeters of all was *Parasaurolophus*.

Its tail may have been brightly colored to attract females or for herd visibility in the forest.

Parasaurolophus shared with its relatives a mouth that was broad and flat, which made it look like a duck's bill. Its most noticeable feature, though, was the crest that swept back from the top of its head. On adult males this could be as long as 6 feet (1.8 meters)—big enough for a tall (but very thin) man to hide inside.

The dinosaur's backbone had an unusual feature, which was a notch just between its shoulders. This was placed just where the tip of its crest would have rested. No one is quite sure what the purpose of this notch was, but one theory is that *Parasaurolophus* used it while traveling through thick undergrowth. Anchored into the notch, the crest would have acted like an ice-breaker on the front of a ship, parting the foliage and making it easier for the dinosaur to get through.

THE BILLBOARD DINOSAUR

Parasaurolophus had a tall, narrow tail: Much taller than most of its relatives. A bright tail could have been very useful. It may have been used like a big advertising billboard to attract females: The bigger its tail, the more females it could attract. Another use might have been as a signal, so that the herd could keep sight of one another more easily as they traveled through the dense forests.

TIMELINE

Millions of years ago

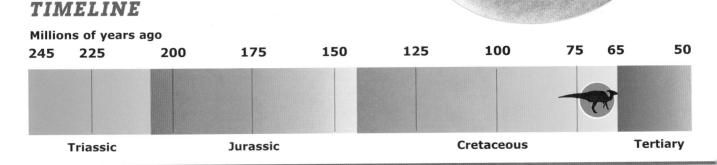

| 245 | 225 | 200 | 175 | 150 | 125 | 100 | 75 | 65 | 50 |

| Triassic | Jurassic | Cretaceous | Tertiary |

Parasaurolophus's tail was unusual, because it was much bigger from top to bottom than from side to side. The tail may also have been colorful or patterned. Some dinosaur experts have suggested that *Parasaurolophus* may have been even more brightly colored than this; the dinosaur's head crest may have been joined to the back of its neck by a loose, brightly colored flap of skin.

Where they lived

A notch in the backbone gave the crest a resting place and may have been part of an "ice-breaker" system for traveling through undergrowth.

Its long head crest contained nasal passages that doubled back on themselves before blowing air out in a great trumpeting noise.

Oversized pelvic bones allowed it to rear up on its hind legs to reach higher food and to run away from predators.

Parasaurolophus *spent much of its time on all four legs, so it needed to have muscular shoulders.*

FAST FACTS

DESCRIPTION	Four-legged plant eater that often walked on two legs
ORDER	Ornithiscia ("bird-hipped")
NAME MEANS	"Beside Saurolophus" (Saurolophus was a dinosaur whose name means "the ridged lizard.")
PERIOD	Late Cretaceous, about 70 million years ago
LOCATION	North America
LENGTH	33 feet (10 meters)
WEIGHT	7700 pounds (3500 kilograms)

Plateosaurus

Plateosaurus was a smaller relative of one of the most famous dinosaurs, *Apatosaurus*, although it lived much earlier. It was a large dinosaur with a long tail, which probably made up almost half its total length. *Plateosaurus* would have moved around looking for food on all four legs, but would sometimes have stood up on its back legs to stretch up to the higher branches.

This dinosaur almost certainly ate only plants, including the foliage of trees. We know this because of the shape of its jaw and teeth, which are similar to those of some plant-eating animals today. Coniferous trees were common in Europe in the Late Triassic Period, and *Plateosaurus* would have been able to reach up to the top branches of these when standing on its back legs.

A lot of *Plateosaurus* fossils have been found close together, buried in the sandstones of Europe. This has made many scientists think that *Plateosaurus* must have lived in herds, which traveled together through the landscape of Europe looking for feeding grounds.

ONE WORLD

The fossils of plant-eating dinosaurs that were very like *Plateosaurus* have been found in other parts of the world. Most are smaller than *Plateosaurus*: *Lufengosaurus* was 20 feet (6 meters) long and lived in southern China, while *Coloradia* lived in South America and was 13 feet (4 meters) long. But these similar-looking dinosaurs, which lived in almost exactly the same way and had almost the same body shapes, support the idea that at one time all the world's continents were joined together.

It is also possible that *Plateosaurus* looked for food alone, in the dry upland areas of the European semi desert. Even today flash floods are common in places like this. When they died, the bodies of lone *Plateosauruses* might have washed together into the flood channels at the edges of the upland areas.

Its long tail allowed Plateosaurus *to balance while standing up on hind legs and feeding in upper branches.*

TIMELINE

Millions of years ago

245	225	200	175	150	125	100	75	65	50

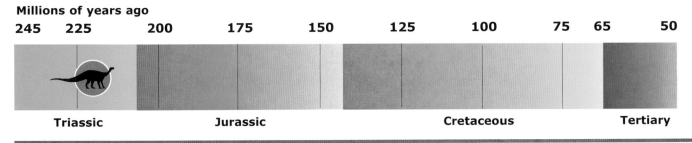

Triassic	Jurassic	Cretaceous	Tertiary

DISCOVERY

Plateosaurus was first uncovered by Hermann von Meyer in Germany in 1837. One of the best finds ever, though, was by Reinhold Seemann in the Trossingen region of Germany. The skeleton he found was so complete that it is still used to check other fossils against today, to see if they are also those of a *Plateosaurus*.

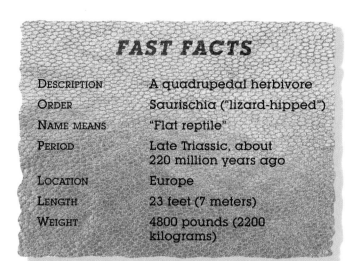

FAST FACTS

DESCRIPTION	A quadrupedal herbivore
ORDER	Saurischia ("lizard-hipped")
NAME MEANS	"Flat reptile"
PERIOD	Late Triassic, about 220 million years ago
LOCATION	Europe
LENGTH	23 feet (7 meters)
WEIGHT	4800 pounds (2200 kilograms)

Where they lived

It had a stronger head than most prosauropods.

Its low-slung lower jaw hinge allowed the jaw muscles greater leverage.

It had small, leaf-shaped teeth for munching plants.

Its long neck allowed it to reach food in a wide range of places.

Protoceratops

Protoceratops came from a dinosaur family that we now think was descended from the parrot dinosaurs: *Protoceratops* had a similar bill-like mouth. It could almost certainly run upright if it needed to, just as the parrot dinosaurs had millions of years earlier to escape from predators. But *Protoceratops* probably spent most of its time on all four legs.

The dinosaur's most distinctive feature was a wide neck frill that grew out of its big, heavy skull. This would have anchored the powerful jaw muscles that helped *Protoceratops* chew its food, as well as making it harder for predators to attack its neck. The jaws ended in a bill. Powerful muscles drove its jaws, and *Protoceratops* was able to bite through thick branches if required.

Unlike later dinosaurs, such as *Triceratops*, *Protoceratops* did not have any horns. Its only weapon apart from its jaws was a bump that stuck out halfway along its snout. This bump seems to have been bigger in older males who would have competed for females, so it is possible that *Protoceratops* entered headbutting contests of strength. These would have established which was the biggest, toughest male and who had the right to mate with the females.

The bump on its snout may have been used by males in head-butting contests.

The bony neck frill anchored its jaw muscles and provided some defense against predators.

It had clawed feet.

The billed jaws were powerful enough to bite through thick vegetation.

It had shorter front legs with five toes.

TIMELINE

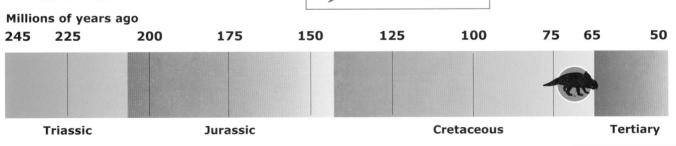

Millions of years ago

245	225	200	175	150	125	100	75	65	50

Triassic	Jurassic	Cretaceous	Tertiary

Where they lived

HOW PROTOCERATOPS GOT ITS NAME

When dinosaur hunters first discovered *Protoceratops*, they already knew about the later horned dinosaurs from the family called *Ceratopsidae*. (*Triceratops*, for example, had been discovered 34 years earlier, in 1889.) They thought that the new dinosaur looked as though it might have been an early version of the ceratopsians, so they called it "first horned face."

It had longer back legs, which were more powerful. Protoceratops *probably escaped from predators by standing on its hind legs and running.*

FAST FACTS

DESCRIPTION	A quadrupedal herbivore
ORDER	Ornithiscia ("bird-hipped")
NAME MEANS	"First horned face"
PERIOD	Late Cretaceous, about 70 million years ago
LOCATION	Asia (what is now Mongolia)
LENGTH	9 feet (2.7 meters)
WEIGHT	400 pounds (180 kilograms)

DID DINOSAURS LAY EGGS?

It was *Protoceratops* that finally answered the question of whether or not dinosaurs laid eggs. The first fossilized eggs ever found were discovered in 1923 in Mongolia, by a team of dinosaur hunters from the American Museum of Natural History. The eggs were unearthed at the foot of a red sandstone cliff. They were sausage-shaped and about the size of a large baked potato. The thin, wrinkly shells were less than ¼ inch (a few centimeters) thick, and had been laid in neat spirals.

The American team eventually found about 70 eggs in the area—some of the nests had as many as 18 eggs in them. The most amazing thing was that some of the eggs were intact. They were found to contain the tiny bones of fossilized *Protoceratops* embryos. It is possible that so many nests were found together because they were buried by a sandstorm, which would have been fairly common in Mongolia during the Late Cretaceous Period.

Psittacosaurus

Psittacosaurus is the best-known dinosaur from a family called *Psittacosauridae*, or "parrot" dinosaurs. These were almost certainly the ancestors of the famous horned dinosaurs or ceratopsians, such as *Triceratops*. All the dinosaurs in the psittacosaurid family were light, long-tailed animals that could escape from predators by racing away on two legs. Their only real defense against attack was speed.

DISCOVERY

The first *Psittacosaurus* was discovered in Mongolia by the 1922 expedition of the American Museum of Natural History. Two almost complete skeletons were found. The most striking thing about them was their square skulls and curved bills, which gave the dinosaur its name, "parrot lizard."

FOOD AND FEEDING

Psittacosaurus's bill was made of horn and was toothless, but had a powerful bite. The lower jaw was joined to a ridge of bone at the back of the skull by strong muscles, which meant that *Psittacosaurus* could bite through thick vegetation. The dinosaur's cheek bones stuck out like horns. These almost certainly evolved into the great horns that grew out of the head shield of ceratopsian dinosaurs of the Late Cretaceous Period.

Reaching up into the higher branches was made easier for *Psittacosaurus* by its ability to stretch up on two legs. It also had a long, flexible neck that would have allowed it to graze across a wider area, and four clawed fingers on each hand could have been used for pulling branches to its mouth or, more likely, for balance. *Psittacosaurus*'s long tail also helped it to balance.

Its long tail helped Psittacosaurus balance.

TIMELINE

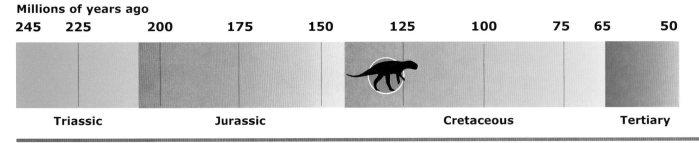

Millions of years ago

245	225	200	175	150	125	100	75	65	50

| Triassic | Jurassic | Cretaceous | Tertiary |

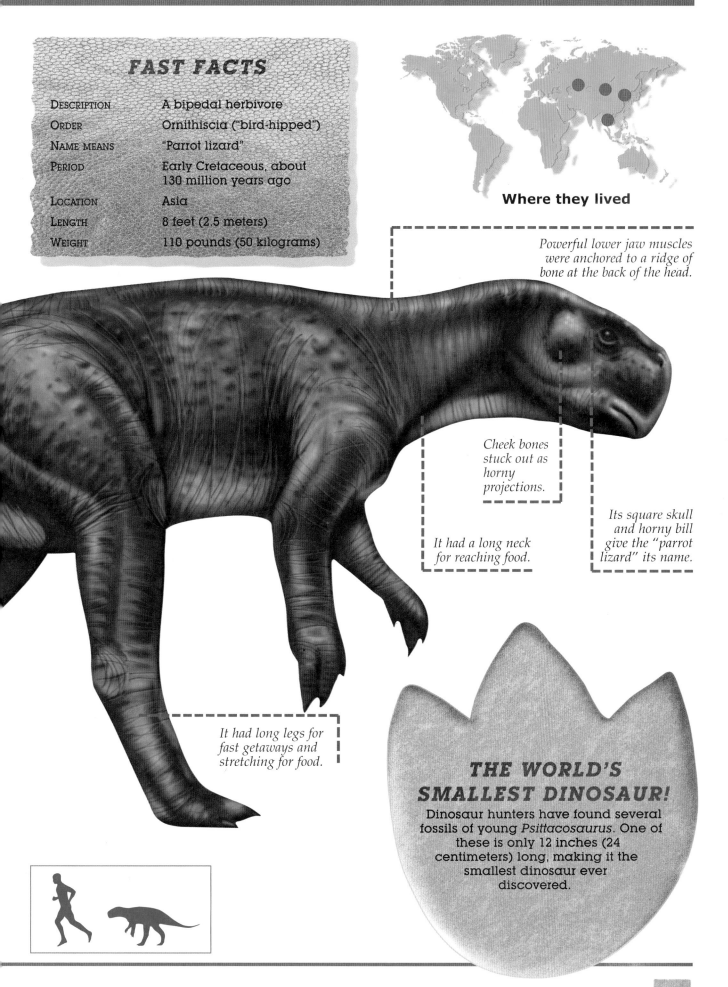

FAST FACTS

DESCRIPTION	A bipedal herbivore
ORDER	Ornithiscia ("bird-hipped")
NAME MEANS	"Parrot lizard"
PERIOD	Early Cretaceous, about 130 million years ago
LOCATION	Asia
LENGTH	8 feet (2.5 meters)
WEIGHT	110 pounds (50 kilograms)

Where they lived

Powerful lower jaw muscles were anchored to a ridge of bone at the back of the head.

Cheek bones stuck out as horny projections.

It had a long neck for reaching food.

Its square skull and horny bill give the "parrot lizard" its name.

It had long legs for fast getaways and stretching for food.

THE WORLD'S SMALLEST DINOSAUR!

Dinosaur hunters have found several fossils of young *Psittacosaurus*. One of these is only 12 inches (24 centimeters) long, making it the smallest dinosaur ever discovered.

Riojasaurus

Riojasaurus was a massive, four-legged herbivore. It may have lived in herds, wandering across an ancient marshy landscape full of ferns, horse-tails, gingko, and conifer trees. With its long neck it could reach high into the foliage, feeding off the parts that were too high for other dinosaurs. Its teeth combed leaves from the branches, and its strong tongue pushed them to the back of its throat. They were gulped down whole and disappeared into its enormous stomach. Here they were crushed by stomach stones (gastroliths), which crushed the plants into a watery, digestible pulp. *Riojasaurus* may have been one of the first dinosaurs to evolve a long neck, millions of years before the giraffe-necked giants of the Jurassic Period, such as *Brachiosaurus* and *Diplodocus*.

Where they lived

Its long, slender tail could be flicked from side to side.

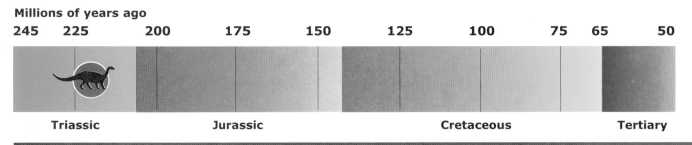

Scientists used to think that *Riojasaurus* and others like it were meat eaters, not plant eaters. This idea came about because sharp teeth were found among their fossilized bones, which paleontologists identified as belonging to meat-eating dinosaurs. They thought these meat-slicing teeth came from *Riojasaurus*, but the truth is that they had probably fallen from the mouths of carnivores as they fed on the meat of the dead herbivores.

Discovery

In the Valley of the Moon, a remote place in northwestern Argentina, the skeleton of a gigantic herbivore was discovered in the 1960s. The windswept valley lies in the province of La Rioja, after which the new dinosaur was named. In 1969, José Bonaparte, an Argentinian paleontologist, named the dinosaur *Riojasaurus*—the "lizard from Rioja."

TIMELINE

Millions of years ago

245	225	200	175	150	125	100	75	65	50

Triassic	Jurassic	Cretaceous	Tertiary

STEALING THE PAST

In Argentina it has been illegal to buy and sell dinosaur fossils since 1913. The country values its great wealth of dinosaur sites and knows that the trade in illegally excavated remains means that scientists will not find out about new discoveries. Despite the law, people still plunder Argentina's treasure trove of buried fossils—and even museums are raided. In January 1994, a 200-million-year-old *Riojasaurus* backbone mysteriously disappeared from the Institute of Anthropology at the University of La Rioja.

It had a long neck and a small head. Inside its mouth were many leaf-shaped, serrated teeth.

Riojasaurus had a long, heavy body with elephantlike legs and clawed feet. Its front legs were almost as long as its hind legs. Its leg bones were massive and solidly formed.

FAST FACTS

DESCRIPTION	A quadrupedal herbivore
ORDER	Saurischia ("lizard-hipped")
NAME MEANS	"Lizard from Rioja"
PERIOD	Late Triassic, about 220 million years ago
LOCATION	South America
LENGTH	33 feet (10 meters)
WEIGHT	(just under 1 ton) 1 tonne

Seismosaurus

Seismosaurus was, without doubt, one of the largest animals ever to have lived on land. It may have lived in herds—but until more evidence is found, such as fossilized footprints or several skeletons in the same place, this is a guess. So far, paleontologists have only found one *Seismosaurus* skeleton, but already a lot has been learned from it. Luckily, the skeleton was more or less complete. It is certain that *Seismosaurus* swallowed stones to help it digest its food. When the scientists uncovered the remains of the creature's stomach area they came across a pile of about 250 stomach stones, or gastroliths. These small stones, which were about 2 inches (5 centimeters) in diameter, had rolled around inside the giant's stomach, crushing plant food into a pulp. Scientists had known about dinosaur stomach stones for many years—but until the discovery of the *Seismosaurus,* no one knew how many stones a big animal held in its belly. The main food eaten by *Seismosaurus* was probably conifers and gingkoes. With its long reach it could stretch high into the trees to strip them of their leaves with its peglike teeth. Other food sources were probably ferns, cycads, club mosses, and horse-tails.

Its nostrils were on top of its head.

Seismosaurus was a long-necked dinosaur, bigger even than its close relative, Diplodocus. *It had a small head, and peglike teeth filled the front of its jaws.*

DISCOVERY

Some of the world's most important dinosaur discoveries have been made by chance. When two hikers stumbled across the fossilized bones of a dinosaur in New Mexico, in 1979, they could hardly have known just how big a find it would turn out to be. American paleontologist David Gillette visited the site and with a team of workers began the long process of excavating the bones. He uncovered the partial remains of an enormous dinosaur—so big that it is the longest dinosaur known so far. Because of its enormous size, in 1991, Gillette gave the new dinosaur its name—*Seismosaurus,* which means "earth-shaking lizard."

TIMELINE

Millions of years ago

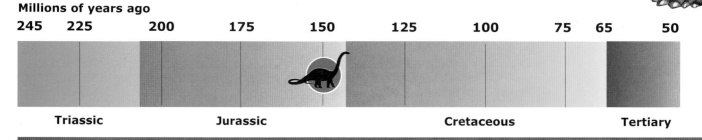

245	225	200	175	150	125	100	75	65	50

Triassic	Jurassic	Cretaceous	Tertiary

MODEL MONSTER

A full-size *Seismosaurus* model was made in 1999, at a cost of $350,000. The largest dinosaur model ever made, it went on show outside the Wyoming Dinosaur Center before beginning a tour to museums across the United States. To keep the weight of the model down, it was made from lightweight Styrofoam.

FAST FACTS

DESCRIPTION	A quadrupedal herbivore
ORDER	Saurischia ("lizard-hipped")
NAME MEANS	"Earth-shaking lizard"
PERIOD	Late Jurassic, about 150 million years ago
LOCATION	North America
LENGTH	131 feet (40 meters)
WEIGHT	30 tons (30 tonnes)

Where they lived

It had a long whiplike tail, which it might have used to lash out at a predator with.

It had short front legs and longer hind legs. Its feet had five toes—one on each foot had a thumb claw.

Spinosaurus

Spinosaurus was one of the most spectacular-looking dinosaurs of all. It was a huge, meat-eating creature that was probably a very successful predator because of the special adaptations to its body. The most noticeable thing about *Spinosaurus* was the amazing "sail" that grew out of its back. This sail was made up of spike-shaped spines of bone that extended from its backbone, joined together by a layer of skin.

DISCOVERY

As fossils, the giant spines look almost like giant thorns, which is how *Spinosaurus* got the name "thorn lizard" when it was discovered by a dinosaur hunter named Stromer in 1915. The sail of a fully grown male *Spinosaurus* would have been well over 6 feet (2 meters) long, which is taller than a big man. And that's just the sail—the rest of the dinosaur measured 40 feet (12 meters)! Such a heavy body part must have had an important purpose.

The weight of this enormous structure means that *Spinosaurus* is one of the heaviest meat-eating dinosaurs ever. It weighed just a little less than the largest meat eater to live on our planet at any time, *Tyrannosaurus*.

FAST FACTS

DESCRIPTION	A bipedal carnivore
ORDER	Saurischia ("lizard-hipped")
NAME MEANS	"Thorn lizard"
PERIOD	Late Cretaceous, about 70 million years ago
LOCATION	Africa
LENGTH	40 feet (12 meters)
WEIGHT	7 tons (7 tonnes)

Powerful jaws held teeth that were straight, rather than curved like most other meat-eating dinosaurs.

Having longer arms than most other two-legged meat eaters suggests that Spinosaurus *may have spent some time walking on all fours.*

TIMELINE

Millions of years ago

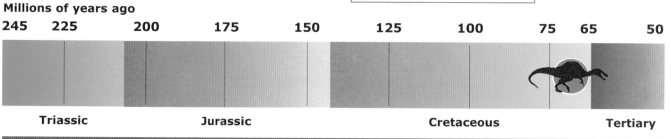

245	225	200	175	150	125	100	75	65	50

Triassic	Jurassic	Cretaceous	Tertiary

Where they lived

Its spines were up to 6.5 feet (2 meters) long, projecting from the backbone.

The spines were linked by a layer of skin, which probably carried many blood vessels and helped Spinosaurus warm up.

EUROPEAN RELATIVES

A new African dinosaur from the same family as *Spinosaurus*, named *Suchomimus*, has been discovered. It has a long snout like a crocodile, which is very similar to that of the European dinosaur *Baryonyx*. Perhaps *Spinosaurus* had distant relatives living in Europe.

The skin of Spinosaurus's sail may have been brightly colored for display, as a way of attracting females.

WHAT WAS THE SAIL FOR?

There are lots of theories about the use of *Spinosaurus*'s sail. The most popular is that it was used to control the dinosaur's body temperature. Early in the morning *Spinosaurus* would have turned its sail toward the sun, which would have warmed the blood as it passed through the sail. This is part of the reason for *Spinosaurus* being such a great hunter: Because it warmed up more quickly than the cold-blooded reptiles on which it fed, it was faster moving than they were in the morning. *Spinosaurus* must have eaten lunch early every day!

Another theory is that *Spinosaurus*'s sail could have been brightly colored. As well as being used to control its body temperature, it would have been used by males to attract females, in the same way as peacocks use their fans. The males might also have used their sails to compete with each other when trying to decide which of them was the toughest dinosaur in the neighborhood.

Stegoceras

Stegoceras was one of the bone-headed dinosaurs—a pachycephalosaur from the same family as *Pachycephalosaurus* and *Wannanosaurus*. It was a two-legged plant eater, and like the other members of its family its characteristic feature was its thick, bony skull. It was probably a herd animal, living in a group with others of its kind along a coastal region of what became North America.

DISCOVERY

Canadian paleontologist Lawrence Lamb worked for his country's Geographical Survey. He discovered several new species of dinosaurs, including *Stegoceras*, which he described and named in 1902, from fossils discovered in Alberta, Canada. Lamb even had a dinosaur named after him—*Lambeosaurus*.

Stegoceras had an 8-inch- (20-centimeter-) long dome-shaped skull with a very thick, knobbly-looking front region. The thickest part of the skull, above the brain, was 2 inches (6 centimeters) thick. On the back of the skull cap was a ridge (a skull shelf) covered with wartlike knobs and bumps.

It had large eyes.

It had short arms with five fingers on the hands.

Where they lived

TIMELINE

Millions of years ago

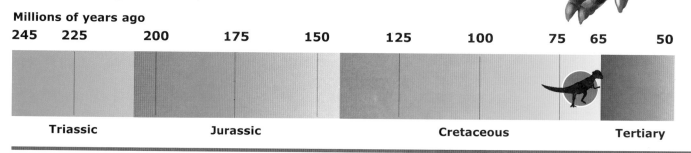

| 245 | 225 | 200 | 175 | 150 | 125 | 100 | 75 | 65 | 50 |

Triassic   Jurassic   Cretaceous   Tertiary

FAST FACTS

DESCRIPTION	A bipedal herbivore
ORDER	Ornithischia ("bird-hipped")
NAME MEANS	"Horny roof"
PERIOD	Late Cretaceous, about 70 million years ago
LOCATION	North America
LENGTH	6 feet (2 meters)
WEIGHT	121 pounds (55 kilograms)

WHY SUCH A THICK SKULL?

One of the biggest questions about *Stegoceras*, and the other bone heads, too, is what was the purpose of the reinforced skull? Beginning in 1955, scientists believed that these dinosaurs charged at each other, as bighorn sheep do today, cracking heads together in a contest to settle disagreements about territory, food, and mates. But now, ideas have changed. Because their skulls were so solidly built, they have survived far better than most other parts of the skeleton, and with many specimens to examine, paleontologists have come up with another answer to the big question. *Stegoceras* skulls have been looked at under microscopes, and no signs of headbutting damage have been found. There are no battle scars or injuries. The skull bone is solid—there are no spaces inside the bone that would have acted like an air bag to absorb the shock of a hard knock. So, some scientists believe that *Stegocerases* did not smash their skulls together. Instead, they might have put their heads together and pushed each other around like bulls.

It had a long tail.

Stegoceras had long four-toed hind legs.

MALE OR FEMALE?

Two styles of *Stegoceras* skull have been found—ones with thick, heavy domes and ones with thinner, lighter domes. It is thought that the heavy domes belonged to males and the lighter ones to females.

Stegosaurus

Stegosaurus was the largest dinosaur in the plant-eating family named *Stegosauridae*. For such a large animal it had a remarkably tiny brain, which was about the size of a walnut. *Stegosaurus* was not very well adapted to eating a variety of different plant foods. It had only a toothless bill at the front of its mouth and weak, small teeth in its cheeks. Because of this, *Stegosaurus* probably had to swallow stones to help it digest its food. Once in its stomach the stones (named gastroliths) would have moved about and helped break up whatever the dinosaur had eaten.

DISCOVERY

Stegosaurus was discovered in 1877 by Professor Othniel C. Marsh. When the dinosaur's back was uncovered he found that it had large, bony plates on its back, which reminded him of roof tiles. This is how *Stegosaurus* came by its name, which means "roofed lizard." Some of the bony plates were over 3 feet (1 meter) high, but no one is quite certain how they were positioned or what they were for. The most popular idea is that they projected almost straight into the air and acted as a defense against predators.

Its small head contained a tiny brain the size of a table tennis ball.

Its bill-like mouth contained small cheek teeth.

TIMELINE

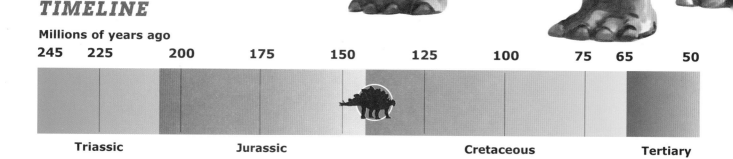

Millions of years ago

245	225	200	175	150	125	100	75	65	50

Triassic	Jurassic	Cretaceous	Tertiary

Where they lived

FAST FACTS

DESCRIPTION	A quadrupedal herbvore
ORDER	Ornithiscia ("bird-hipped")
NAME MEANS	"Roofed lizard"
PERIOD	Early Cretaceous, about 140 million years ago
LOCATION	Upland forests of North America
LENGTH	Up to 30 feet (9 meters)
WEIGHT	2 tons (2 tonnes)

Its bony plates may have been flat, arranged in pairs or on alternating sides.

It had a horned tail for defense against predators.

Its rear legs were twice as long as its front legs. Stegosaurus was able to stand on its hind legs to reach food in lower branches.

AIR-CONDITIONED DINOSAUR?

One alternative theory about the plates on *Stegosaurus*'s spine is that they might have lain flat on the dinosaur's back and shielded it from attack. The most interesting theory, though, is that the plates might have acted as a kind of temperature control. Covered in blood vessels close to the surface, they could have quickly warmed up a dinosaur pointing its plates at the sun. If it got too hot, it had only to turn away or go into the shade to cool down.

DINOSAUR SICK DAYS

Several species of dinosaur, including *Stegosaurus*, are thought to have swallowed stones to help them digest their food. The rough edges would have broken down tough plant matter that had been missed by the crude bills. But what happened to the stones after their rough edges had been worn smooth? Were the Late Cretaceous forests full of the noise of dinosaurs being sick, as they vomited stones that were no longer any use?

TWO (TINY) BRAINS?

Paleontologists have also discovered that *Stegosaurus* had a large space in its hips, just where the spine would have been. This has made them think that *Stegosaurus* might have had a "second brain" (which would really have been a large bundle of nerve endings) just above the tops of its legs.

Another possibility is that the opening held a special energy-boosting substance, which *Stegosaurus* released when it was under threat to give it more power.

Stegosaurus may have turned side-on to the morning sun in order to warm up the blood flowing through its back plates.

DEFENSE AGAINST PREDATORS

Because *Stegosaurus* was four-legged and heavy, it was also slow-moving. Instead of running away it had to stay in one place and defend itself against attackers. Its best weapon was its powerful tail, which was heavily muscled and armed with bony spikes at the end. Some species had two pairs of spikes, while others had four pairs. An attacking predator, such as an *Allosaurus*, might well have been badly wounded or even killed by a blow from this tail. One big problem for *Stegosaurus* when it was trying to defend itself, though, was its tiny brain. It is doubtful whether the dinosaur could have coordinated its movements very well with so little brain power. *Stegosaurus* was unlikely to have been able to do more than just thrash its tail about wildly.

SPECIAL ADAPTATIONS

Stegosaurus has often been seen as a stupid dinosaur that was poorly adapted and walked in a peculiar way. In fact, this may not be the whole truth. *Stegosaurus* had tall spines that grew up from its backbone around the hips and the base of its tail. These anchored strong muscles around its rear legs, which would have helped the dinosaur when it reached up to the lower branches of trees.

Certainly *Stegosaurus* would have looked odd as it shambled through the undergrowth of a Late Cretaceous forest on all fours, its long hind legs forcing its hindquarters up in the air. But once it spotted a tasty bit of food in the branches overhead, it would have taken just a slight push of its short forelegs to tilt back and reach up to the tops of shrubs or the bottom branches of trees.

The mechanism for this movement onto two legs would have been like a mixture of a modern crane and a suspension bridge. *Stegosaurus*'s high hindquarters were like the pillar of a suspension bridge, holding its body in balance and tension. When it wanted to stand up, the rear muscles would have pulled like the cables of a crane, and the front of the body would have lifted up with a slight push.

So, while *Stegosaurus* was not very well designed for walking, it was better designed for feeding from higher branches.

Stegosaurus

Styracosaurus

Styracosaurus was one of the *Ceratopsidae* dinosaur family, which all have horns and neck frills. Like other ceratopsians, *Styracosaurus* lived in herds, which grazed their way through the great forests that covered much of North America at the end of the Late Cretaceous Period.

The two main groups of ceratopsians were those with short neck frills and those with long ones. *Styracosaurus* was among the short-frilled group but is still most famous for its amazing neck frill. This had six main spikes around the top, some of them as long as *Styracosaurus*'s nose horn, as well as other smaller spikes. These must have been an effective defense against predators that were trying to attack *Styracosaurus*'s neck. The neck frill, which grew out of the dinosaur's rear skull plates, had skin-covered holes in it. These were much lighter than solid bone. Without these holes, it would have been impossible for *Styracosaurus* to support the heavy spikes on its neck frill.

Many of today's animals try to frighten off attackers by making themselves look bigger than they actually are. *Styracosuarus* must have used its enormous neck frills in the same way—facing a predator straight on, it would have looked like a difficult meal.

Styracosaurus had another weapon for defending itself—an enormous horn that grew straight out of its snout. This nose horn could be a deadly weapon. Any *Albertosaurus* that attacked a herd of *Styracosaurus* would have risked being charged by one of the males and gouged in its soft stomach by its long horn.

DINO-GRAVEYARD

The Red Deer River Valley in Alberta, Canada, where *Styracosaurus* was discovered in 1915, was the graveyard for several other dinosaurs as well. Between 1910—1917 several new kinds of dinosaurs were discovered, among them the duck-billed dinosaur *Corythosaurus* and the tyrannosaur *Albertosaurus*.

TIMELINE

Millions of years ago

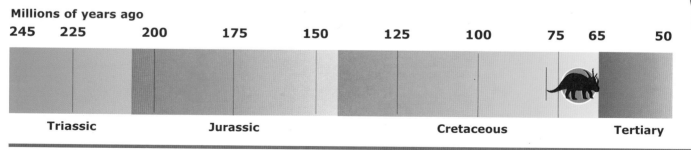

245	225	200	175	150	125	100	75	65	50

Triassic	Jurassic	Cretaceous	Tertiary

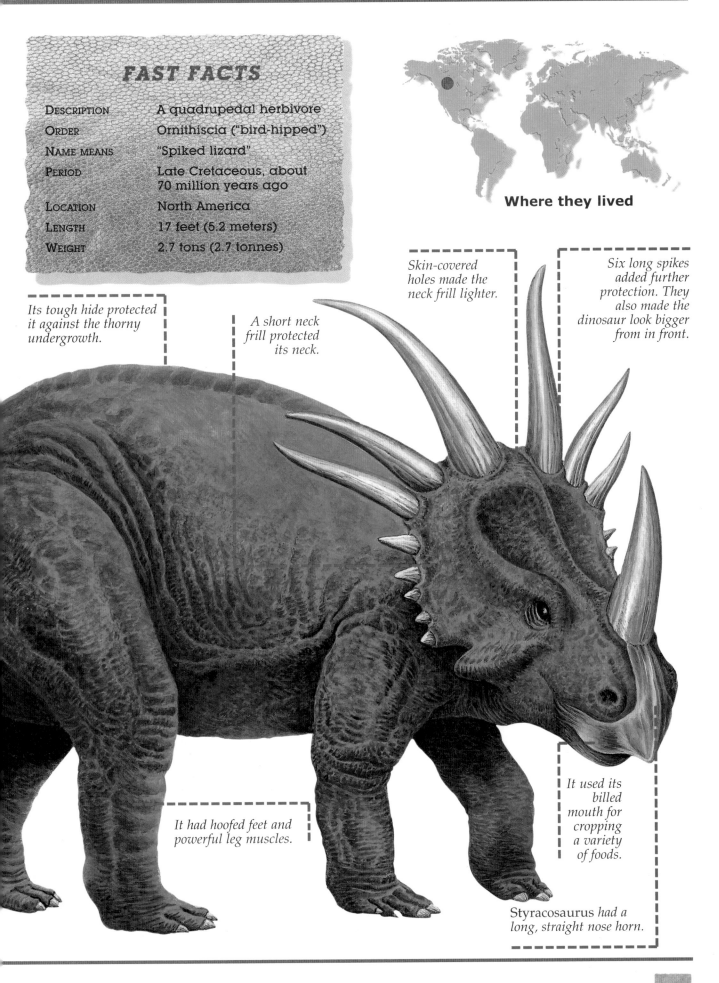

FAST FACTS

DESCRIPTION	A quadrupedal herbivore
ORDER	Ornithiscia ("bird-hipped")
NAME MEANS	"Spiked lizard"
PERIOD	Late Cretaceous, about 70 million years ago
LOCATION	North America
LENGTH	17 feet (5.2 meters)
WEIGHT	2.7 tons (2.7 tonnes)

Where they lived

Skin-covered holes made the neck frill lighter.

Six long spikes added further protection. They also made the dinosaur look bigger from in front.

Its tough hide protected it against the thorny undergrowth.

A short neck frill protected its neck.

It used its billed mouth for cropping a variety of foods.

It had hoofed feet and powerful leg muscles.

Styracosaurus *had a long, straight nose horn.*

155

Triceratops

The name *Triceratops* means "three-horned face" (it was named by the famous American dinosaur hunter Othniel C. Marsh, in 1889). *Triceratops* was a herbivore, which grazed in large herds throughout western North America at the very end of the Late Cretaceous Period. It was the largest and heaviest member of the dinosaur family called *Ceratopsidae*, which were four-legged dinosaurs with sharp horns growing from massive heads. Ceratopsians grew bony frills from the base of the skull to guard their neck from attack. A fully grown male *Triceratops* would have weighed more than one of the largest of today's African elephants.

Triceratops had to be able to defend itself from attack by the large two-legged predators that hunted in North America during the Late Cretaceous Period, such as *Tyrannosaurus* and *Albertosaurus*. *Triceratops*'s best weapons were its long brow horns, which could be at least 3 feet (1 meter) long. Using its powerful neck muscles and thick, pillarlike legs to thrust with these horns, *Triceratops* would have been able to cause a lot of damage to an attacker. Its third, shorter horn was thicker than the brow horns and placed toward the end of its nose.

Its thick hide protected Triceratops against thorns and undergrowth, as well as attack.

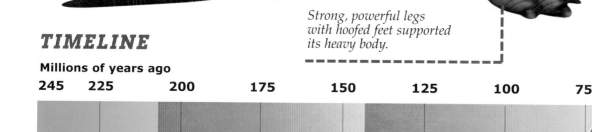

Strong, powerful legs with hoofed feet supported its heavy body.

TIMELINE

Millions of years ago

245	225	200	175	150	125	100	75	65	50

| Triassic | Jurassic | Cretaceous | Tertiary |

FAST FACTS

DESCRIPTION	A quadrupedal herbivore
ORDER	Ornithiscia ("bird-hipped")
NAME MEANS	"Three-horned face"
PERIOD	Late Cretaceous, about 70 million years ago
LOCATION	Upland forests of North America
LENGTH	30 feet (9 meters)
WEIGHT	5 tons (5 tonnes)

THICK SKULLS

The enormous, thick bones of a *Triceratops* skull meant that it was far more likely to survive fossilization than the thinner skulls of most other dinosaurs. Hundreds of skulls have been found over the years since the first was uncovered in 1889. The famous American dinosaur hunter Barnum Brown is supposed to have collected over 50 skulls at the end of the 1800s.

A solid bone neck frill grew out of the rear skull bones and was a useful defense against attack.

Knobs on the neck frill of some species offered further protection.

It had long brow horns made of solid bone that could be used as defensive weapons.

Its shorter, wider nose horn was also used for defense.

It had a sharp, parrotlike bill and powerful jaws that it used for chomping even the toughest food.

DISCOVERY

Triceratops was first discovered in 1889 by a dinosaur hunter named Marsh. Many of the fossilized heads of *Triceratops* that have been found since then are scarred and damaged in some way. Part of this damage could have been done by attackers, but it is also possible that *Triceratops* competed with each other. This would have been done by locking horns and pushing with the head shield, which would explain the scarring on the fossilized remains. *Triceratops* would have used this contest of strength to decide which was the most powerful dinosaur in the group, without needing to fight to the death.

Where they lived

157

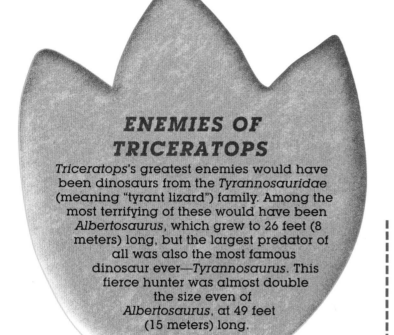

The neck frill was edged with pieces of bone.

The shoulders were protected by the wide neck frill.

ENEMIES OF TRICERATOPS

Triceratops's greatest enemies would have been dinosaurs from the *Tyrannosauridae* (meaning "tyrant lizard") family. Among the most terrifying of these would have been *Albertosaurus*, which grew to 26 feet (8 meters) long, but the largest predator of all was also the most famous dinosaur ever—*Tyrannosaurus*. This fierce hunter was almost double the size even of *Albertosaurus*, at 49 feet (15 meters) long.

HOW DID TRICERATOPS DEFEND ITSELF?

On average *Triceratops* probably weighed about 5 tons (5 tonnes), but a fully grown adult male could have weighed a good deal more than this. The biggest males would have weighed almost as much as a *Tyrannosaurus*. It is unlikely that even this, one of the largest land predators ever, would have been able to stand up to a straight-on charge from a large male *Triceratops*.

The main function of *Triceratops*'s neck frill was probably defense. The neck frill was made of solid bone with no openings in it. The frill would have made it hard for an attacker to get hold of a *Triceratops*'s neck in an attack, even in a *Tyrannosaurus*-style ambush. Some species of *Triceratops* had pointed knobs all around the edge of their neck frill, which would have given even better defenses.

THE DINOSAUR WARS

Triceratops was one of the dinosaurs discovered in Wyoming, Colorado, and Montana toward the end of the 1800s. This was a great age in American dinosaur hunting, when many important fossil discoveries were made. The number of expeditions that took place was mainly due to the bitter rivalry between two wealthy experts. This competition has become known as The Dinosaur Wars. Othniel C. Marsh of Yale University and Edward Drinker Cope of the Academy of Natural Science in Philedelphia both led numerous expeditions in search of new dinosaurs, often spending their own money on the hunt and trying to out-do each other in the process.

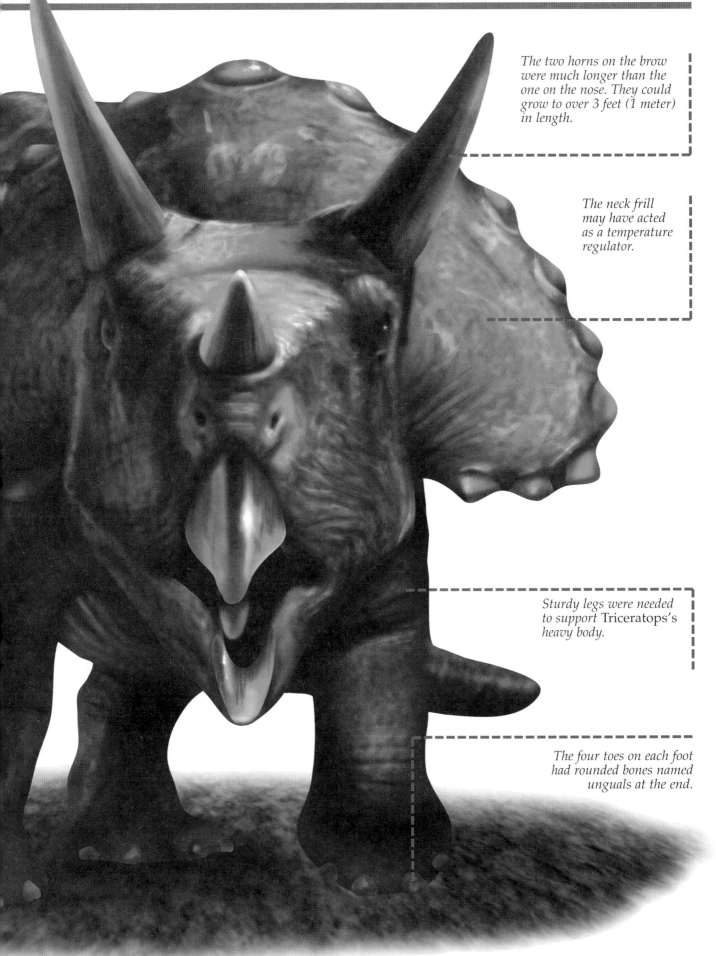

The two horns on the brow were much longer than the one on the nose. They could grow to over 3 feet (1 meter) in length.

The neck frill may have acted as a temperature regulator.

Sturdy legs were needed to support Triceratops's heavy body.

The four toes on each foot had rounded bones named unguals at the end.

Tröodon

Its tail helped it to balance while running and attacking.

Where they lived

Tröodon came from a dinosaur family named *Sauronithididae*, or "bird lizards." These were fast-moving and relatively intelligent dinosaurs, with excellent vision and a sickle-shaped claw on each foot, which they used for attacking prey.

Tröodon itself has led to important discoveries among dinosaur hunters. In 1982 scientists in Alberta, Canada, uncovered the fossilized brain case of *Tröodon*. When they examined it, it showed that the dinosaur was very similar in its basic physical structure to modern birds. This could mean that the small carnivorous dinosaurs and modern birds are closely related.

Tröodon may have been able to hunt at night, and it must have been a very effective predator. *Tröodon* had one of the largest brains in comparison to the size of its body of any dinosaur. It was lightly built but agile, could run faster than most other dinosaurs of the time, and had excellent co-ordination and vision. Its eyes were large: About 2 inches (50 millimeters) across, and it may well have had telescopic vision, which would have allowed it to spot prey easily.

On top of all this, *Tröodon* was armed with a vicious-looking claw on the second toe of each foot, with which it would have ripped at its prey. This claw was lifted back and off the ground when the dinosaur was chasing its victims, to stop it from catching on vegetation. As soon as *Tröodon* caught its prey, the claw would have been brought forward into attack mode, where it could catch on the prey's flesh.

Tröodon may well also have been a cunning scavenger. At a place known as Egg Mountain, in Montana, many dinosaur eggs have been discovered. In among them have been *Tröodon* teeth, so *Tröodon* may well have fed on the eggs of other dinosaurs. Its more usual prey would have been young dinosaurs that had only recently hatched, which may be why its fossilized teeth have been found in the same area as so many eggs.

TIMELINE

Millions of years ago

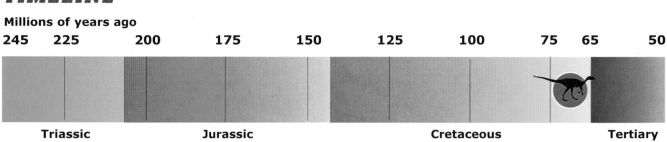

245	225	200	175	150	125	100	75	65	50

Triassic   **Jurassic**   **Cretaceous**   **Tertiary**

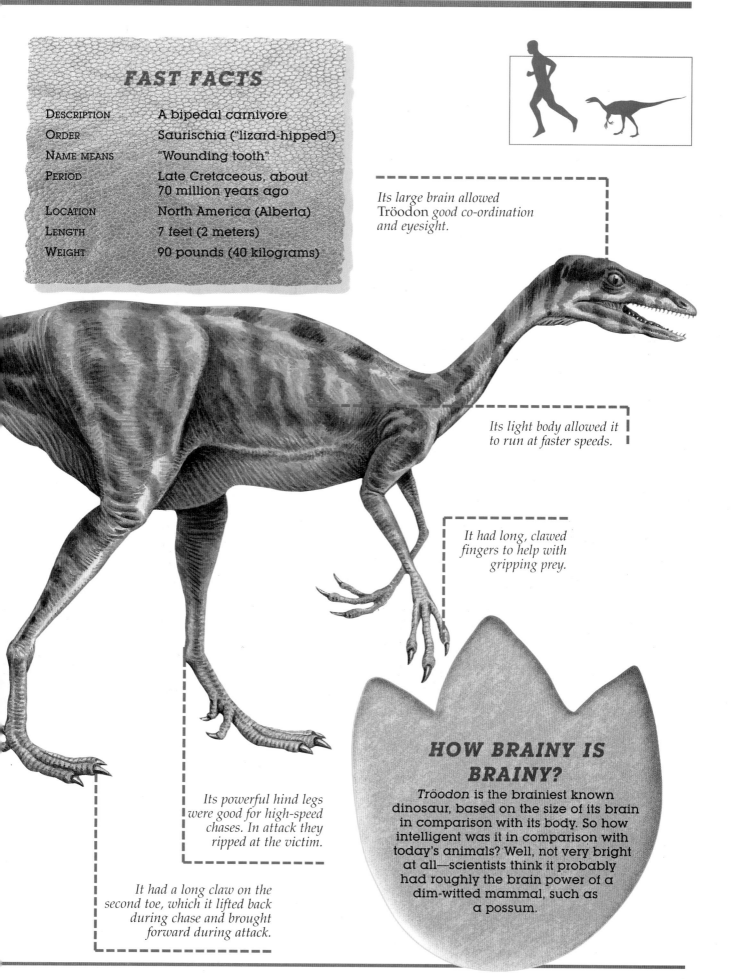

FAST FACTS

DESCRIPTION	A bipedal carnivore
ORDER	Saurischia ("lizard-hipped")
NAME MEANS	"Wounding tooth"
PERIOD	Late Cretaceous, about 70 million years ago
LOCATION	North America (Alberta)
LENGTH	7 feet (2 meters)
WEIGHT	90 pounds (40 kilograms)

Its large brain allowed Tröodon *good co-ordination and eyesight.*

Its light body allowed it to run at faster speeds.

It had long, clawed fingers to help with gripping prey.

Its powerful hind legs were good for high-speed chases. In attack they ripped at the victim.

It had a long claw on the second toe, which it lifted back during chase and brought forward during attack.

HOW BRAINY IS BRAINY?

Tröodon is the brainiest known dinosaur, based on the size of its brain in comparison with its body. So how intelligent was it in comparison with today's animals? Well, not very bright at all—scientists think it probably had roughly the brain power of a dim-witted mammal, such as a possum.

Tyrannosaurus Rex

It had enormous teeth with sawlike edges for biting, gripping, and ripping prey.

Powerful jaw muscles anchored to the skull behind the eyes gave Tyrannosaurus a ferocious bite, easily capable of going through a thick leg bone.

Its large brain had big areas devoted to sight and smell, and helped with hunting and co-ordination.

Its strong, flexible neck allowed Tyrannosaurus to adjust the angle of its attack.

It had puny arms.

It had powerful hind legs.

People used to think that dinosaurs were small, creeping animals, like snakes or lizards. Then an English scientist named Richard Owen showed that they were probably far bigger than people had imagined. In 1842 he named these long-dead animals "Dinosauria," which means "terrible lizard," and this name has been with us ever since.

The first real proof that Owen had been right about how terrible the lizards were came in 1908, when dinosaur hunters in Montana found the skull of a new dinosaur. It came from an animal that would have been able to look into a second-floor window, weighed more than a garbage truck, and had a mouth full of 8-inch- (20-centimeter-) long teeth like carving knives. Its head alone was over 4 feet (1.25 meters) long. The dinosaur hunters had found *Tyrannosaurus*, the largest predator ever to walk the Earth. *Tyrannosaurus* probably hunted mainly hadrosaurs, supplementing its diet with the odd *Triceratops* (although these would have been harder to kill as they were far better able to defend themselves). Its powerful hind legs would have allowed it to race from cover and quickly bite its prey, although *Tyrannosaurus* was too heavy to be able to run quickly over long distances.

TIMELINE

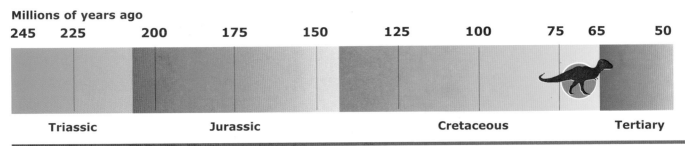

Millions of years ago

245	225	200	175	150	125	100	75	65	50

| Triassic | Jurassic | Cretaceous | Tertiary |

Fossil finds show that *Tyrannosaurus* was probably extremely well equipped as a hunter:
• It had large areas of its brain devoted to vision and smell. *Tyrannosaurus* may well have had telescopic vision and been able to smell prey from long distances.
• *Tyrannosaurus* had extremely powerful jaw muscles anchored to a wide area of the skull behind the eyes.
• Its mouth was lined with long, saw-edged teeth.
• It had a flexible neck that allowed it to change the direction of its attack at the last minute.

DINOSAUR AUCTIONS

There cannot be many dinosaurs that have been auctioned by Sothebys of New York City. In October 1997 a female *Tyrannosaurus* called Sue broke all the records. She had been unearthed in South Dakota in August 1990, and was one of the most complete skeletons ever found. After a long legal battle to decide who owned her, she was sold for an amazing $8,362,500.

The tail helped Tyrannosaurus to balance.

Where they lived

FAST FACTS

DESCRIPTION	A bipedal carnivore
ORDER	Saurischia ("lizard-hipped")
NAME MEANS	"Tyrant lizard"
PERIOD	Late Cretaceous, about 70 million years ago
LOCATION	North America and Asia (Mongolia)
LENGTH	40 feet (12 meters) long
WEIGHT	8 tons (8 tonnes)

A WEAKLING EGG-THIEF?

Some scientists have suggested that *Tyrannosaurus* was mainly a scavenger, stealing free meals by forcing other, smaller predators away from their kills. This is based mainly on two ideas. The first is that the dinosaur's weak forearms would not have allowed it to hunt properly, and it must therefore have found its food in some other way. The second is that it was too slow-moving to be able to hunt well.

It is possible that scavenging made up part of *Tyrannosaurus*'s diet, but the structure of its body makes it more likely that it hunted like a modern lion. Lions do use their front legs in hunting, to bring down prey, but their main technique is to chase and bite, and keep on biting until their prey is unable to escape. *Tyrannosaurus* would have been well equipped to hunt in this way, charging out of its hiding place and seizing its prey in its enormous jaws. The weight and size of its enormous, heavy head would have made an added impact.

Although *Tyrannosaurus* may not have been a fast-moving dinosaur, its body was probably better adapted for speed than other large Late Cretaceous dinosaurs such as hadrosaurs, ceratopsians, or ankylosaurs. It would almost certainly have had enough short-burst speed to catch such dinosaurs, especially from an ambush.

When two Tyrannosaurus *met there would be loud roaring and posturing. If neither decided to back off and avoid the risk of being injured, a bloody battle would follow.*

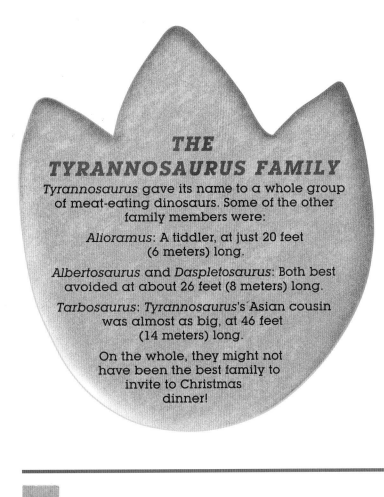

Each leg had thick leg-bones to support its huge weight. The three forward-pointing toes on each foot had sharp claws.

THE TYRANNOSAURUS FAMILY

Tyrannosaurus gave its name to a whole group of meat-eating dinosaurs. Some of the other family members were:

Alioramus: A tiddler, at just 20 feet (6 meters) long.

Albertosaurus and *Daspletosaurus*: Both best avoided at about 26 feet (8 meters) long.

Tarbosaurus: *Tyrannosaurus*'s Asian cousin was almost as big, at 46 feet (14 meters) long.

On the whole, they might not have been the best family to invite to Christmas dinner!

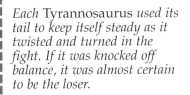

Each Tyrannosaurus *used its tail to keep itself steady as it twisted and turned in the fight. If it was knocked off balance, it was almost certain to be the loser.*

Tyrannosaurus *lunged at prey or rivals with it jaws wide open and teeth bared.*

The muscular legs *enabled Tyrannosaurus to sprint at 20 mph (32 kph) when chasing prey over short distances.*

CANNIBAL TYRANNOSAURUS

Recent fossil discoveries have shown that individual *Tyrannosaurus* regularly fought against each other, in battles over breeding and territory. In the last 20 years, fossils have been discovered with tooth fragments from other *Tyrannosaurus* embedded in their bones, as well as large bites that can only have come from another *Tyrannosaurus* on other parts of their bodies.

One of the most amazing discoveries was the fossilized remains of a dinosaur now known as Steven. Parts of his backbone had been bitten in half, and others are missing. The missing bones come from the places where the biggest, best bits of meat would have been. The only animal around at that time that could have bitten through a *Tyrannosaurus*'s backbone was ... another *Tyrannosaurus*.

Velociraptor

*Velociraptor*s were part of the family of carnivorous dinosaurs named *Dromaeosauridae*. These had large brains and were clever enough to hunt in packs, and were fearsome predators. Like all dromaeosaurs, *Velociraptor*s had a long, curved blade of a claw on the second toe of each foot, as well as clawed hands and sharp teeth. They had four toes on each foot: The first was useless, and all the weight of *Velociraptor* was carried by its third and fourth toes. This left the second toe and its scythelike claw free for attack. *Velociraptor*s had larger heads and longer jaws than the other dromaeosaurs, but their front claws were smaller.

Where they lived

Once a pack of *Velociraptor*s had prey in their sights, it must have been almost impossible to escape. As well as being well armed they were fast moving, with powerful hind legs and light bodies, and could catch slower-moving and heavier dinosaurs with ease. *Velociraptor*s had two main methods of attack. The first was to grab their prey with their front claws and use their powerful hind legs and long rear claws to rip it to shreds. The second was to stand on one leg and rip at their prey with the other.

Its long tail was held straight out while running. Used for balance while running and attacking, the tail was held rigid by strong muscles and specially adapted bones.

It had longer hind legs with powerful muscles for pursuit and attack.

The third and fourth toes were used to bear weight.

TIMELINE

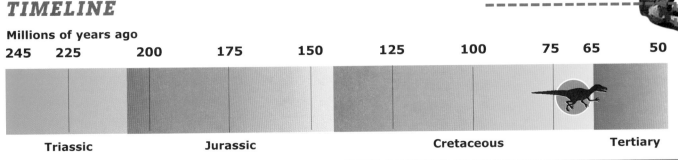

Millions of years ago

245	225	200	175	150	125	100	75	65	50

Triassic	Jurassic	Cretaceous	Tertiary

DINOSAUR FILM STARS

The credits for the blockbuster movie *Jurassic Park* listed human stars, but that didn't fool anyone. The real stars of the film were the dinosaurs, and the most popular and terrifying of these were the *Velociraptors*.

The *Velociraptors* were the villains, escaping and then picking off the humans until it seemed unlikely that anyone would survive. At the end all seemed lost, until *Tyrannosaurus* finished off the nasty "raptors."

DISCOVERY

Velociraptor was discovered in 1924 by an expedition to Mongolia by dinosaur hunters from the American Museum of Natural History in New York City. In 1972 dinosaur hunters in Mongolia made a great find: the fossils of a *Velociraptor* that was locked in battle with a *Protoceratops*. Although roughly the same length as a *Velociraptor*, the *Protoceratops* was much heavier than the predator and able to defend itself with its horned bill and powerful neck. Nonetheless the *Velociraptor* attacked, and even as it died of a crushed chest it was holding on to the neck frill of *Protoceratops* and ripping open its belly. The attack was typical of this fierce predator.

It had a large head and brain cavity. The large brain allows complicated co-ordinated movements, as well as giving Velociraptor *the ability to hunt in packs.*

Its long jaws allowed Velociraptor *to get its mouth right inside carcasses to eat.*

Its sharp teeth were for ripping flesh when attacking prey or feeding.

Its shorter front legs with three claws were used mainly for gripping prey.

The second toe had a long, sharp, curved claw used for ripping prey. This toe was lifted back while running.

FAST FACTS

DESCRIPTION	A bipedal carnivore
ORDER	Saurischia ("lizard-hipped")
NAME MEANS	"Quick plunderer"
PERIOD	Late Cretaceous, about 70 million years ago
LOCATION	Asia (what is now Mongolia and China)
LENGTH	6 feet (1.8 meters)
WEIGHT	55 pounds (25 kilograms)

Wannanosaurus

Wannanosaurus is one of the smallest known dinosaurs—smaller even than *Compsognathus*. It was a pachycephalosaur—a group of dinosaurs noted for their bony skulls.

Wannanosaurus was probably a herbivore, grazing on low-growing plants and other vegetation in a small herd. No one knows for certain, but it may have crouched down on all fours to tug at plants with its strong mouth parts. But if disturbed, it would rear up on its two powerful hind legs and move away at a steady trot. It is not thought to have been a fast-moving creature.

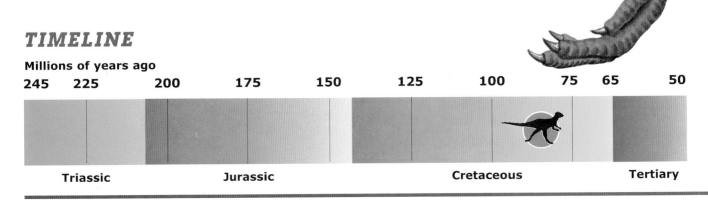

Where they lived

Wannanosaurus *had a heavy tail held stiffly behind its solidly built body.*

Its most distinctive feature was its bony skull cap. As with other pachycephalosaurs, scientists think it used its reinforced skull as a battering ram. It may have used it in a fight with another *Wannanosaurus*, to settle a dispute over territory, food, or mates. Rather than running headlong into each other, which may have injured both animals, scientists think that they rubbed and pushed their heads together. The weaker of the two was pushed backward and lost the contest. Or perhaps the bony cap was for self-defense and was used to headbutt an attacker. It could also have been used to ram into plants, knocking them to the ground where they were easy to eat.

DISCOVERY

Many dinosaur remains have been found on the vast continent of Asia, and none more so than in China, whose people call themselves the "descendants of the dragon." About 100 different species of dinosaur have been found in China so far, including *Wannanosaurus*, which was named in 1977. It was found in the province of Wannan, from which came its name.

TIMELINE

Millions of years ago

245	225	200	175	150	125	100	75	65	50

Triassic	Jurassic	Cretaceous	Tertiary

FAST FACTS

DESCRIPTION	A bipedal herbivore
ORDER	Ornithischia ("bird-hipped")
NAME MEANS	"Wannan lizard"
PERIOD	Late Cretaceous, about 85 million years ago
LOCATION	Asia
LENGTH	24 inches (60 centimeters)
WEIGHT	unknown

Wannanosaurus had a small flat head with a thick bony skull and tiny brain, similar to that of Pachycephalosaurus and Stegoceras. There were many sharp teeth inside its mouth.

It had short arms with clawed fingers.

It had strong hind legs with three-toed clawed feet.

MISSING BONES

Wannanosaurus is the most primitive bone-headed dinosaur yet found. It is known from just one specimen—and all that was discovered was part of its skull and jaw bone. Hopefully, more bones will come to light in the future, so that this dinosaur can be studied in more detail.

Xiaosaurus

Xiaosaurus is a mysterious dinosaur, about which little is known. Scientists in China are hoping to find better-preserved fossils, from which they will be able to put together a complete skeleton.

eyes, which would have been good for spotting signs of approaching danger. *Xiaosaurus* was probably hunted by many large predators, but at the first sign of trouble it would have raced away to safety, easily out-running a predator in a chase.

It had a stiff, pointed tail.

Only then will they be able to tell what it was like, and what kind of life it might have led. One thing that is known is the age of this dinosaur. The rocks in which it was found are about 165 million years old, which means that *Xiaosaurus* lived at the beginning of the Age of Dinosaurs. It is because of this fact that paleontologists named it the "dawn lizard."

Xiaosaurus was a small two-legged herbivore. It was a lizardlike dinosaur which may have had a lightweight body built for speed. It is thought to have been similar in appearance to *Lesothosaurus*, a dinosaur from Africa. If it did resemble *Lesothosaurus*, then perhaps its life style was similar, too. In this case, *Xiaosaurus* may have lived in a pack, grazing on low-growing plants, chewing on them with its cheek teeth. It is thought to have had large

DONG ZHIMING

Xiaosaurus is not the only Chinese dinosaur to have been named by Dong Zhiming. He is one of China's leading paleontologists, working at the Academia Sinica, in Beijing. He has named about 25 dinosaurs new to science.

TIMELINE

Millions of years ago

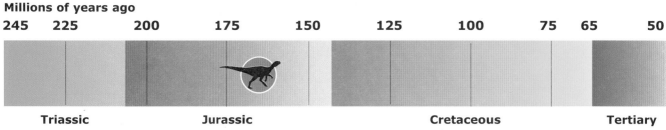

| 245 | 225 | 200 | 175 | 150 | 125 | 100 | 75 | 65 | 50 |

| Triassic | Jurassic | Cretaceous | Tertiary |

DISCOVERY

Xiaosaurus is known from only a single incomplete specimen. Parts of the skeleton were found in the early 1980s, in China. Although only a few teeth and part of the skull were found, they were enough to identify the creature as a new species of dinosaur. Chinese paleontologists Dong Zhiming and Tang Zilu gave it the name *Xiaosaurus* in 1983.

Where they lived

It probably had large eyes.

Its long hind legs may have made it an agile creature that was a fast runner. Each foot had four toes.

Its cheek teeth were shaped like leaves.

Xiaosaurus had a flexible neck.

It had short arms, with five fingers on each hand suitable for grabbing and seizing plants to eat.

Because so little of the Xiaosaurus *skeleton was found, it is difficult to know what this dinosaur really looked like. However, as its teeth were similar to those of* Lesothosaurus, Xiaosaurus *might have looked like this small lizard-like dinosaur.*

FAST FACTS

DESCRIPTION	A bipedal herbivore
ORDER	Ornithischia ("bird-hipped")
NAME MEANS	"Dawn lizard"
PERIOD	Middle Jurassic, about 165 million years ago
LOCATION	Asia
LENGTH	5 feet (1.5 meters)
WEIGHT	88 pounds (40 kilograms)

Yangchuanosaurus

There were miniature horns just in front of its eyes.

It had a strong, short neck, and a large head with powerful jaws packed with long, serrated teeth.

A low crest ran along the front of its snout from its nose to just in front of its eyes. The crest may have had a horny covering and could well have been brightly colored.

Yangchuanosaurus was a big, strongly built meat eater with large, sharp teeth. It was fully capable of taking on plant eaters that shared its habitat, such as sauropods and stegosaurs. Like its North American cousins, Yangchuanosaurus was born to hunt—either alone or in packs. It might have been a scavenger, too. Maybe it waited for another dinosaur to do all the tiring, hard work of hunting. Then, when the kill had been made, Yangchuanosaurus might have chased the first predator away, and moved in for the easy pickings of a free lunch.

Its arms were short, and it had three clawed fingers on each hand.

DISCOVERY
Until the 1970s, very little was known about the carnivorous dinosaurs of China. While the likes of Allosaurus and Tyrannosaurus rex were well-known meat eaters from North America, their Chinese relatives were slow to show themselves.

Its feet had three toes, each with a large claw.

TIMELINE

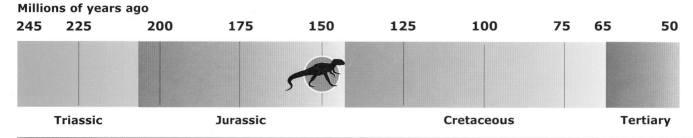

Millions of years ago

245	225	200	175	150	125	100	75	65	50

| Triassic | Jurassic | Cretaceous | Tertiary |

Where they lived

FAST FACTS

DESCRIPTION	A bipedal carnivore
ORDER	Saurischia ("lizard-hipped")
NAME MEANS	"Yangchuan lizard"
PERIOD	Late Jurassic, about 150 million years ago
LOCATION	Asia
LENGTH	33 feet (10 meters)
WEIGHT	about 1—3 tons (1—3 tonnes)

Its tail was long—about half of the dinosaur's total length.

Yangchuanosaurus *walked on two strong, muscular legs.*

BRIGHT CREST

The crest on the snout of *Yangchuanosaurus* is a feature it shares with many other predatory dinosaurs. But what was it for? Scientists think it could well have been colorful, in contrast to the rest of its drab reptilian skin. Maybe it was used to attract a mate, or as a warning to frighten away unwelcome visitors.

But all this changed in 1976, when a construction worker at the site of the Shangyou Dam, in the east of China, found the nearly complete skeleton of a large meat eater. It was China's answer to *Allosaurus*, and was given the name *Yangchuanosaurus*—the "Yangchuan lizard"—by Chinese paleontologist Dong Zhiming in 1978.

Zigongosaurus

Like many other sauropods from China, *Zigongosaurus* had an extremely long neck. It probably evolved like this so that it could stretch up to vegetation that grew high up in the forest canopy. Its teeth tugged away on vegetation like a rake being pulled through grass. As it moved its head backward, its teeth stripped leaves and twigs from the branches, and with a great gulp they were swallowed whole. Inside its stomach, many gastroliths (stomach stones) rolled around, knocking into the food and crushing it into smaller and smaller pieces.

This great creature may have lived and traveled in herds, moving slowly along from one feeding place to the next. It was a defenseless animal, and would have made a soft target for an attacking predatory meat eater. But perhaps its great size was more than enough to make a meat eater think twice before getting too close—a swipe from the tail of *Zigongosaurus* might have been more than enough to knock a predator down. But an old or young *Zigongosaurus*, or one that was injured, would have been far easier to attack than a healthy adult. Maybe it was these weaker animals that fell prey to the bites and kicks of predators.

DISCOVERY

Chinese paleontologists discovered the almost complete skeleton of a giant plant-eating dinosaur in the 1970s. After studying it they decided it was a new species, though not everyone agrees with them. In 1976, they named it *Zigongosaurus*, after the region in China where it had been found. Its name means "Zigong lizard."

It had a long, slender tail.

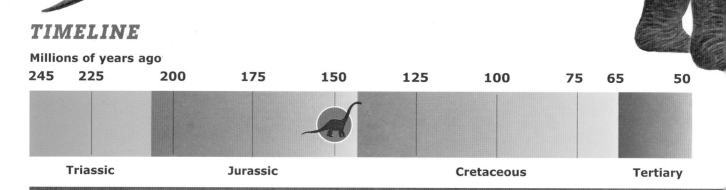

TIMELINE

Millions of years ago

245	225	200	175	150	125	100	75	65	50

Triassic   **Jurassic**   **Cretaceous**   **Tertiary**

FAST FACTS

DESCRIPTION	A quadrupedal herbivore
ORDER	Saurischia ("lizard-hipped")
NAME MEANS	"Zigong lizard"
PERIOD	Late Jurassic, about 150 million years ago
LOCATION	Asia
LENGTH	33 feet (10 meters)
WEIGHT	20 tons (20 tonnes)

Zigongosaurus had a long neck and a small head. Inside its mouth were many spoon-shaped teeth.

Where they lived

A BIT OF A MYSTERY

Scientists are puzzled about *Zigongosaurus*. Some do not think it should be classed as a separate species of dinosaur, saying that it has been wrongly identified. They think it is really a *Mamenchisaurus*, which lived at the same time and in the same part of China. More fossils will have to be found before the puzzle is finally solved.

It had chunky, elephantlike legs. Its hind legs were longer than its front legs.

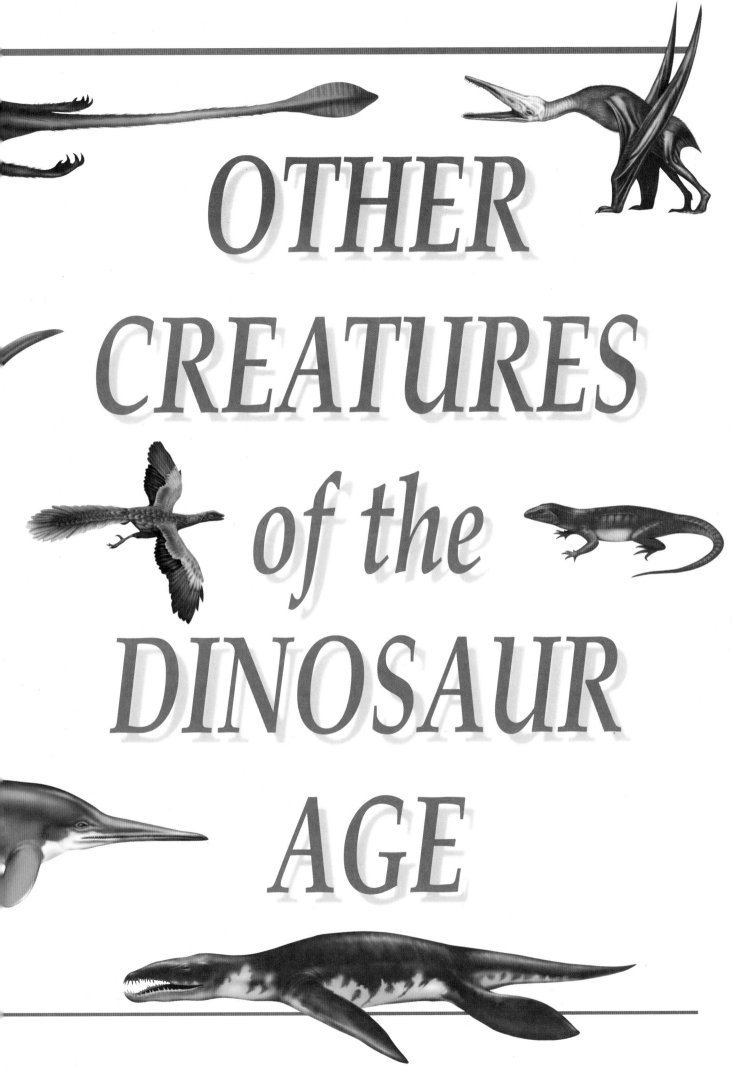

OTHER
CREATURES
of the
DINOSAUR
AGE

Eudimorphodon

Eudimorphodon was one of the first known pterosaurs. These creatures were not "flying dinosaurs." In fact, they were not dinosaurs at all. But they were reptiles, like the dinosaurs. Different kinds of pterosaurs lived at the same time as the dinosaurs, throughout the Mesozoic Era. Fossils of *Eudimorphodon* have been found in Europe, in northern Italy near Bergamo and Milan.

HOW DID PTEROSAURS FLY?

The arms of pterosaurs had evolved into wings. Pterosaurs flapped their wings up and down for flight, much like a bird does today. Some pterosaurs could only soar or glide with slow wing beats. Others were skilled fliers who could flap, swoop, turn, and dive at speed. *Eudimorphodon* was a very early kind of pterosaur. It had large wings, a lightweight body, and other typical pterosaur features.

The wings of Eudimorphodon *were probably made of thin, leathery skin supported by arm and finger bones, stiffening fibers, and muscle fibers. The skin may have been similar to the wings of today's bats.*

Eudimorphodon *was a member of the tailed pterosaur subgroup, the rhamphorhynchoids. It had a long, bony tail with a upright "paddle" at the end.*

Where they lived

TIMELINE

Millions of years ago

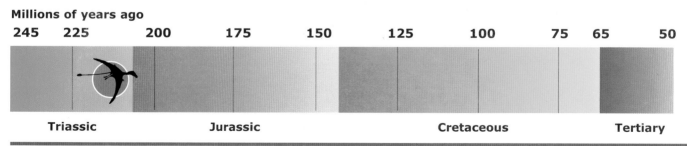

245	225	200	175	150	125	100	75	65	50

Triassic	Jurassic	Cretaceous	Tertiary

TEETH FOR FISHING

Eudimorphodon had very unusual teeth, unlike those of any other pterosaur. Their special shape was ideal for catching and eating fish. Fossilized remains of scales, bones, and other parts of fish have been found in the stomach region of this pterosaur's skeleton.

Eudimorphodon *had small, weak legs. It could probably only waddle along weakly on land, using its folded wings to support the front of the body.*

Like most pterosaurs, Eudimorphodon *had large eyes. Pterosaurs were day time animals and found their way around by sight.*

The front teeth were large, single, and fanglike. The back teeth were much smaller with three or five cusps (points) on each one.

There were over 100 teeth in jaws less than 3 inches (6 centimeters) long. The teeth were worn from biting and chewing the food before swallowing.

HOW BIG WAS EUDIMORPHODON?

Eudimorphodon was about the same size as the common duck called a mallard. Its wings measured just over 3 feet (1 meter) from tip to tip. Its length from bill tip to tail "paddle" was just over 2 feet (65 centimeters). *Eudimorphodon* probably weighed only 3.3 pounds (1.5 kilograms), little more than a bag of sugar.

Preondactylus

Preondactylus was one of the first pterosaurs, from the late Triassic Period. It was also one of the smallest, being slightly smaller than a pigeon. At a time when there were no birds in the sky, *Preondactylus* could have flapped and squawked, clambered over rocks, and landed in trees.

The teeth of Preondactylus *were small and pointy. This suggests that it fed on small creatures, such as insects and perhaps small fish.*

The extremely long bones of the fourth finger held out most of the wing and formed its front, or leading, edge. This "wing finger" formed more than three-quarters of the span of the whole wing.

The "nonflight" fingers, numbers one to three, had sharp claws. Pterosaurs probably used these to help them clamber up tree trunks or cliff faces, or to grip smooth rocks.

Where they lived

TIMELINE

Millions of years ago

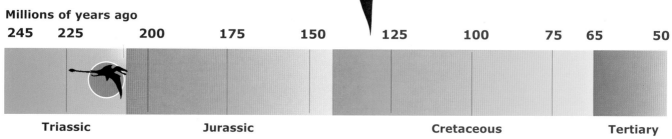

245	225	200	175	150	125	100	75	65	50

Triassic	Jurassic	Cretaceous	Tertiary

Preondactylus fossils were found in the Preone Valley and other valleys in the Alps of northern Italy. The name of this valley, and the first fossil finds which were its finger bones, gave their name to the pterosaur—"Preone finger."

The "paddle" at the end of the tail was made up of two flaps. It was not floppy, but was held up by bony rods from the tail backbones.

Like all of the early pterosaurs, Preondactylus was a member of the tailed pterosaur subgroup, the rhamphorhynchoids. It had a long, trailing tail.

Many of the bones in a pterosaur's skeleton were hollow, like tubes. They may have been filled with air spaces, making the skeleton very light.

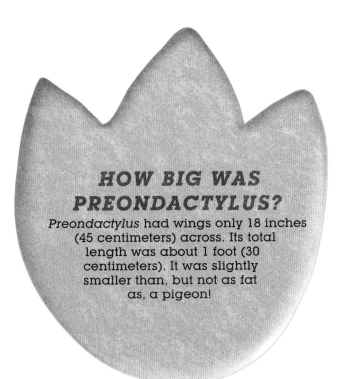

HOW BIG WAS PREONDACTYLUS?

Preondactylus had wings only 18 inches (45 centimeters) across. Its total length was about 1 foot (30 centimeters). It was slightly smaller than, but not as fat as, a pigeon!

PTEROSAUR WINGS

The wings of a pterosaur like *Preondactylus* were very different from the wings of today's birds or bats. The inner part of the wing near the body was held out by short, strong arm bones. The hand was about one-quarter or one-third of the way along the wing, at the front. It had four fingers. The first three were short with claws. The very long bones of the fourth finger held out the rest of the wing along the front, right to its tip. The fifth finger had disappeared during evolution.

ORIGINS OF PTEROSAURS

Like *Eudimorphodon*, *Preondactylus* was already fully adapted to fly and swoop. Pterosaurs may have evolved from small, active reptiles named thecodonts, which sped about on their hind legs—and which may also have given rise to the dinosaurs.

Dimorphodon

Dimorphodon was an early pterosaur with a very big head, which formed one-quarter of its total length. The head may have been big, but it was not heavy. The skull inside was very light, made of thin struts of bone rather than large slabs. Most of the head was made up of the large bill.

The remains of *Dimorphodon* were found near Lyme Regis in southern England. Its first fossils were first dug out in 1828. It was named in 1858 by the scientist who also invented the name "dinosaur," Richard Owen.

As in other tailed pterosaurs, Dimorphodon's tail was quite stiff. With its "paddle" at the end, it probably worked as an all-in-one rudder and stabilizer, for turning and moving around in the air.

The legs and feet were quite large and strong for a pterosaur. Dimorphodon could probably crawl well on all fours and maybe even stood up to run on its legs.

The fifth toe was longer and thinner than the others. Dimorphodon may have used it like a thumb to support the rear part of the wing as it crawled on the ground.

Where they lived

TIMELINE

Millions of years ago

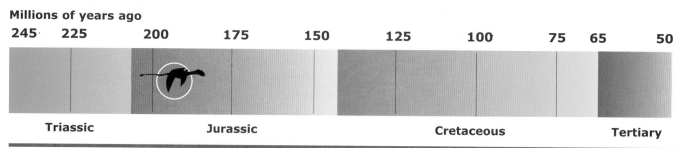

245	225	200	175	150	125	100	75	65	50

| Triassic | Jurassic | Cretaceous | Tertiary |

BIG-HEADED PTEROSAUR

Unlike a bird's bill, the bill of *Dimorphodon* had teeth. Compared to other pterosaurs the bill was tall from top to bottom but narrow from side to side. It seems much too large simply to catch food, which was probably fish, squid, and similar small sea animals. So why was the bill so big?

Such a large bill could carry a lot of food at the same time. (The puffin gathers a lot of sand eels and other small fish like this and carries them back to its nest for its chicks.)

The mouth of Dimorphodon *had four large teeth on each side at the front, in both the upper and lower jaws. The upper jaw had a row of smaller teeth behind them. In the lower jaw there were tiny, sharp teeth.*

BILL SHOW-OFF?

The bill was bigger but similar in shape to the bill of a puffin today. In the nesting season the puffin's bill becomes very brightly colored with red, yellow, and blue stripes, to attract a mate. Birds such as toucans and hornbills also have colored bills mainly for this reason. The bill of *Dimorphodon* may also have had bright colors in the breeding season. So far, we do not know for certain.

HOW BIG WAS DIMORPHODON?

Like many early pterosaurs, *Dimorphodon* had a relatively large body but short wings. Its wingspan was about 4½ feet (1.4 meters), and its total length was just over 3 feet (1 meter). It was roughly the size of a goose.

Rhamphorhynchus

Rhamphorhynchus was one of the last tailed pterosaurs, in the subgroup named after it—the rhamphorhynchoids. Its amazingly detailed fossils come from fine-grained limestone rocks in the Solnhofen region of Germany. From the same rocks come similar well-preserved fossils of the first known bird, *Archaeopteryx*. Smaller parts of fossils that may be *Rhamphorhynchus* have also been found in England, Portugal, and Tanzania in East Africa.

Rhamphorhynchus *had stick-shaped teeth pointing sideways and forward.*

Rhamphorhynchus *had big eyes at the back of its large head, small nostrils in front, and very long, slender, bill-like, point-tipped jaws.*

Rhamphorhynchus *had a short, strong neck and a large chest with a big breastbone (sternum) to anchor the powerful wing-flapping muscles. It was probably an expert flier.*

TIMELINE

Millions of years ago

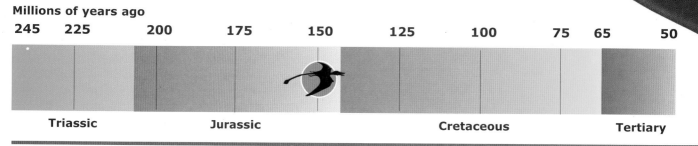

245	225	200	175	150	125	100	75	65	50

| Triassic | Jurassic | Cretaceous | Tertiary |

THE FINEST FOSSILS

The tiny grains of the Solnhofen rocks allow minute details to be seen in the fossils of *Rhamphorhynchus*. They even show elastic fibers no thicker than cotton threads in the wings. These rocks formed on the beds of shallow sea lagoons. Most pterosaur fossils are found in rocks formed on the sea bed, rather than on land. This is partly why we think pterosaurs fed on fish, swooping over the water to grab their prey in their toothed bills. Occasionally a pterosaur fell in, drowned, sank, and was preserved.

HOW BIG WAS RHAMPHORHYNCHUS?

Different kinds, or species, of *Rhamphorhynchus* were different sizes. The smallest had a wingspan of only 16 inches (40 centimeters), slightly larger than a blackbird. The biggest had wings 6 feet (1.8 meters) across, almost bigger than a swan.

A FLYING FISH-CAGE

Possibly *Rhamphorhynchus* swooped down and skimmed along the water's surface, scooping up food in its bill. The food would be trapped in the mouth, with the teeth acting like the bars of a cage. More evidence for this comes from a small fish preserved with a fossil *Rhamphorhynchus* skeleton, where the pterosaur's stomach would have been in life.

The tail of Rhamphorhynchus *had a diamond-shaped "paddle." Different kinds of pterosaurs had different shapes of tail paddles, so these help us to identify them.*

In the wing, tough fibers ran from the front to the rear. After landing, the wing could fold up like a fan as the wing bones were pulled back along the sides of the body.

Where they lived

Pterodactylus

Pterodactylus was one of the first of a new subgroup of pterosaurs. These were the short-tailed or tailless pterosaurs, known as pterodactyloids. They took over from the long-tailed pterosaurs, which died out around the end of the Jurassic Period. The tailless pterosaurs lasted right until the end of the Age of Dinosaurs.

The fossils of *Pterodactylus* have been discovered mainly in the Solnhofen area of Bavaria in Germany. Some have also been identified in southern England, France, and Tanzania, East Africa.

BIG AND SMALL

There were several different kinds of *Pterodactylus*. Some were as small as thrushes, others bigger than eagles. All were probably very good fliers, and they all had small, sharp-pointed teeth. Small *Pterodactylus* may have caught flying insects, such as dragonflies, in midair, or swooped on small creatures, such as lizards, on the ground. The bigger ones probably fed on fish.

WHAT WERE PTERODACTYLS?

The name pterodactyl means "wing finger." Pterosaurs are sometimes called pterodactyls. But the pterodactyls, such as *Pterodactylus*, were only one small subgroup. The name for the whole group is pterosaurs, which means "winged lizards."

Pterodactylus *had a very long bill compared to the smaller rear part of its skull. This was another new trend in the short-tailed pterosaurs. But like all pterosaurs, it had big eyes for good sight.*

Where they lived

TIMELINE

Millions of years ago

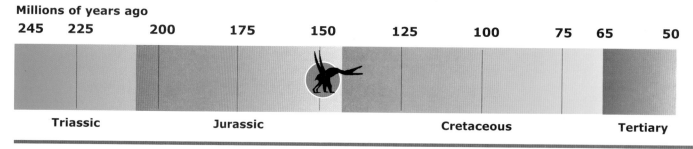

245	225	200	175	150	125	100	75	65	50

Triassic	Jurassic	Cretaceous	Tertiary

HOW BIG WAS PTERODACTYLUS?

Different kinds, or species, of *Pterodactylus* were different sizes. The smallest had a wingspan of only 14 inches (35 centimeters), about the same as a starling. The biggest had wings 8 feet (2.5 meters) across, as large as a vulture or condor.

Pterodactylus *showed exciting new trends in pterosaur evolution. It had longer wings and a shorter body compared to the earlier long-tailed pterosaurs.*

The tail of Pterodactylus *was very short, made of just a few tail bones. Also it did not have a paddlelike end as in the long-tailed pterosaurs.*

Another new trend of Pterodactylus *was a long, flexible neck that arched up from the body. The head was at an angle on the neck so it looked forward.*

As in other pterosaurs the wing was held out by the upper arm bone (humerus), then the forearm bones (radius and ulna), then the hand bones (metacarpals), and finally the extremely long fourth finger.

Pteranodon

During the Cretaceous Period, pterosaurs gradually became bigger and more specialized for soaring and gliding long distances. One of the largest was *Pteranodon*. It was almost all head and wings. It had a very small body, little weak legs, and a short stump for a tail. It could perhaps fly at about 30 mph (50 kph). Its wings were three times longer than those of the albatross, the bird with the biggest wingspan today. Its head was huge, over 7 feet (2 meters) in length. But its tail, which was so long in the early pterosaurs, had almost disappeared.

The various types of *Pteranodon* fossils come from many places, including England, several states in the United States such as Kansas, Delaware, and Texas, and possibly also Japan.

The crest of Pteranodon may have been brightly colored for display at breeding time.

Its head was almost the same length as its body. But it was very light as the skull was made of hollow, thin-walled bones.

The 3-feet-(1-meter-) long bill had no teeth at all, so it was very light. The name Pteranodon means "toothless flier." The bill may have had a flexible bag of skin on the chin for scooping up food, like the pelican today.

TIMELINE

Millions of years ago

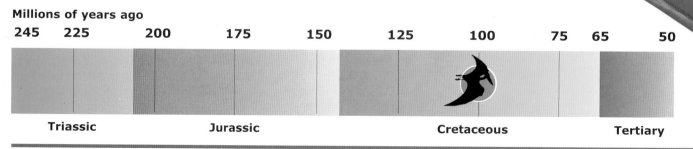

245	225	200	175	150	125	100	75	65	50

| Triassic | Jurassic | Cretaceous | Tertiary |

Where they lived

Many pterosaur fossils show signs of hair or fur on the body. Also, flying is a very active, energy-hungry process and needs a body that works fast inside. Both these features suggest that pterosaurs were warm-blooded.

The wings were so big, and the legs so small, that Pteranodon *would have had difficulty taking off by running and flapping. It probably launched itself off a crag or cliff into the wind.*

THE PTEROSAUR'S "HAT"

Pteranodon had a new pterosaur feature. This was a narrow, pointed, bony crest on the back of its head, almost like a witch's hat. It was about as long as the bill at the front. The crest balanced the head and bill over the neck— especially when the mouth was full of food! The crest probably also worked as a stabilizer and rudder for balance and steering in the air.

OUT IN THE OCEAN

Pteranodon's long, narrow wings were similar in shape to the wings of ocean-soaring birds today, such as gulls, shearwaters, and petrels. Its fossils were found in the types of rocks that formed on the ocean floor at least 100 miles (160 kilometers) from the coast. So *Pteranodon* probably made long trips over the ocean, soaring on the winds and skimming near the surface to grab fish.

HOW BIG WAS PTERANODON?

A medium-sized type of *Pteranodon* was nearly 7 feet (about 2 meters) long with wings 23 feet (7 meters) across. Yet it weighed only 35–40 pounds (16–18 kilograms). The biggest types had a wingspan of 30 feet (9 meters).

Quetzalcoatlus

Quetzalcoatlus was the largest flying creature ever, about the size of a small plane! It was also among the last of the pterosaurs, dying out with the last of the dinosaurs in the great end-of-Cretaceous mass extinction. *Quetzalcoatlus* is named after the legendary feathered serpent-god of Ancient Mexico, Quetzalcoatl.

Fossils of *Quetzalcoatlus* come from Big Bend National Park in the state of Texas. In Texas everything has a reputation for being very big! Similar fossils, perhaps from different types of *Quetzalcoatlus*, have been found in Alberta, Canada, too, and in Russia, Jordan in the Middle East, and Senegal in Africa.

LIFE OVER LAND

The fossils of *Quetzalcoatlus* were dug from rocks that formed on land, rather than beneath the ocean as with most other pterosaurs. The rocks indicate a landscape of sandy plains and winding rivers probably several hundred miles from the ocean. How did *Quetzalcoatlus* survive in such places? It may have waded and probed in the sand and mud with its long, stiff bill and neck, to find fish, crabs, worms, and similar animals.

HOW BIG WAS QUETZALCOATLUS?

Huge! Its length in flight with its trailing feet was over 26 feet (8 meters). Its wingspan was a massive 39 feet (12 meters). It probably weighed about 180–200 pounds (80–90 kilograms), as much as a large man.

The neck of Quetzalcoatlus *was very long but not very flexible. It could bend a little up and down, but hardly at all from side to side.*

The crest on the back of the skull was short, low, and thin, nowhere near as big as the crest of Pteranodon.

The jaws were long, toothless, and sharp-edged. As in other pterosaurs they were probably covered with a tough substance (like our fingernails).

TIMELINE

Millions of years ago

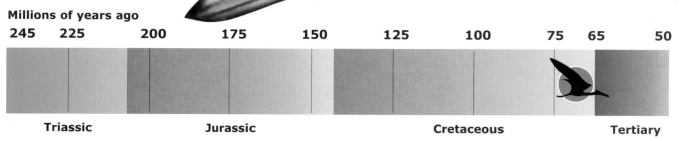

245	225	200	175	150	125	100	75	65	50

| Triassic | Jurassic | Cretaceous | Tertiary |

THE GIANT VULTURE

Another idea is that *Quetzalcoatlus* was a giant reptile version of a vulture. It soared over the land, hardly flapping its vast wings as it circled in warm air rising from the rocky plains below. When it saw a dead or dying dinosaur, it would swoop down to peck and feed on the carcass.

One of the fourth-finger bones in the wing was more than 4 feet (1.2 meters) long. Overall the four bones of the fourth finger held out nearly 10 feet (3 meters) of wing.

Where they lived

Like other tailless pterosaurs, Quetzalcoatlus had just a small stump for its tail. It must have twisted its wings and used its vast bill, head, and crest to help it turn and steer in flight.

Archaeopteryx

Birds have something no other animal has—feathers. A bird also has no teeth and no bones in its tail (the tail is made up of just feathers). During the Age of Dinosaurs a creature appeared that also had feathers. It was the first known bird, *Archaeopteryx*. But this strange bird also had teeth and a long, bony tail.

There are only seven known fossils of *Archaeopteryx,* and one of these is just a feather! They have been found mainly in the Solnhofen region of Bavaria, Germany, where many other dinosaurs, pterosaurs, and other Late Jurassic animals were preserved.

COULD ARCHAEOPTERYX FLY?
Probably, but not too well. It lacked another feature of modern birds—the large breastbone with a flat part called a "keel" where the strong flight muscles of today's birds are anchored. Perhaps *Archaeopteryx* used its clawed toes and its unbirdlike clawed fingers to clamber and haul itself up tall plants, trees, or rocks. Then it could launch into a short, flapping glide.

HOW BIG WAS ARCHAEOPTERYX?
It varied between chicken—and turkey-size, 16—24 inches (40—60 centimeters) from bill to tail-tip with a wingspan of 20–28 inches (50–70 centimeters). It weighed only 3 pounds (1.5 kilograms).

The tail had a row of bones, named caudal vertebrae, like a dinosaur or other reptile. Modern birds have tail feathers but no tail bones.

TIMELINE

Millions of years ago

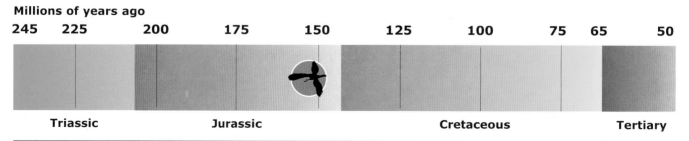

245	225	200	175	150	125	100	75	65	50

Triassic	Jurassic	Cretaceous	Tertiary

The front limbs of Archaeopteryx *were held out by long upper-arm and forearm bones. (This is quite different to pterosaurs, see page 178).*

Where they lived

The small, spiky teeth were spaced out in the long, slim, bill-like mouth. Archaeopteryx *probably ate insects, worms, lizards, mammals, and other small animals.*

Long feathers covered its wings and body. The feathers were not just for protection or to keep in body warmth. They were ideally shaped for flight, just like the feathers of modern birds.

Archaeopteryx *had three clawed fingers about halfway along each wing, near the front. No birds today have these.*

On each foot the first toe was reversed—it pointed backward so Archaeopteryx *could grasp and perch on branches.*

WHERE DID ARCHAEOPTERYX COME FROM?

For many years one *Archaeopteryx* fossil was mistaken for a small dinosaur from the same time and place, *Compsognathus* (see page 88). This shows the similarity of *Archaeopteryx* to some dinosaurs. The arm and hand bones suggest that *Archaeopteryx* evolved from a small raptor-type dinosaur in the same group as *Deinonychus* and *Velociraptor*.

Archaeopteryx was not a halfway creature, partly evolved between dinosaur and birds. Some of its body parts were fully dinosaurian, and others fully like a bird.

193

Crocodiles, placodonts and nothosaurs

Nearly all wild animals today can swim, especially to save their lives. Dinosaurs could probably swim if they had to. No dinosaurs actually lived in the water. But many of their reptile cousins did. Different groups came and went during the Age of Dinosaurs.

Protosuchus

MINI-CROCODILES

One group came and stayed—crocodiles. With birds, crocodiles are the closest living relatives of dinosaurs. They appeared about the same time, the Late Triassic Period. However the first crocodiles were not the big, heavy, armor-scaled predators that lurk in swamps today. *Gracilisuchus* and *Terrestrisuchus* were slim, light, lizardlike land animals only 1—2 feet (30—60 centimeters) long. They chased small prey, like insects, through dry Triassic scrubland.

Placodus

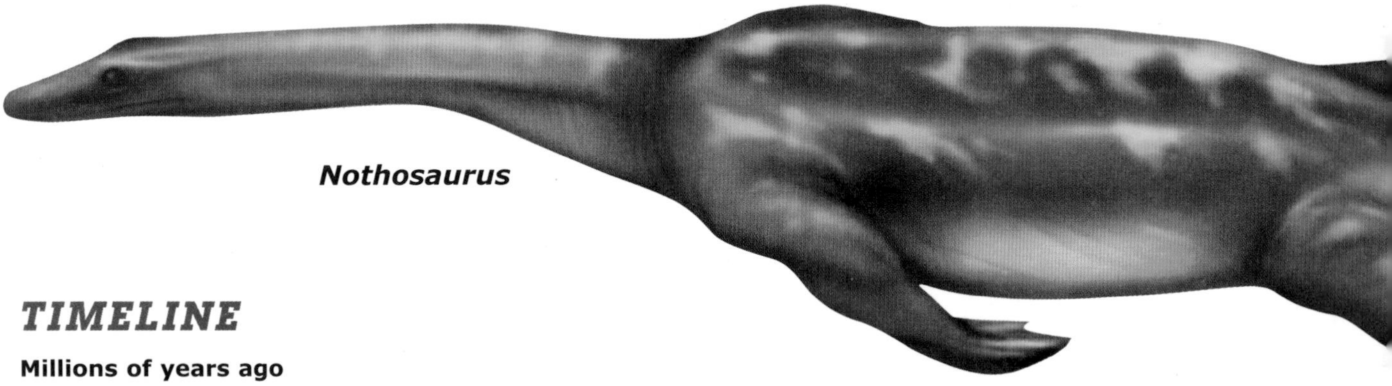

Nothosaurus

TIMELINE

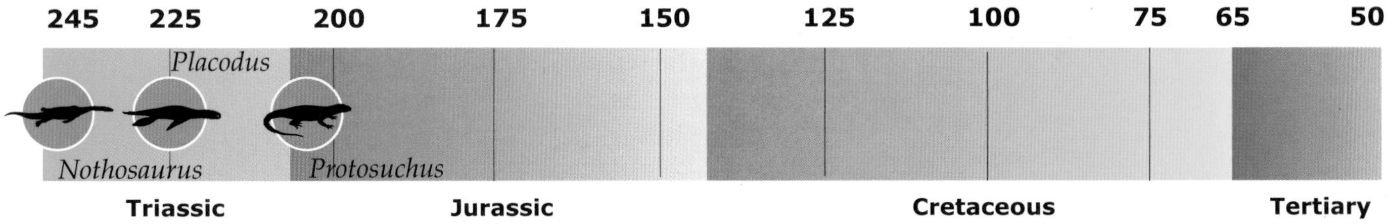

Millions of years ago

245	225	200	175	150	125	100	75	65	50

Placodus

Nothosaurus *Protosuchus*

Triassic	Jurassic	Cretaceous	Tertiary

Protosuchus looked like a big lizard, but it was an early Jurassic crocodile. About 3 feet (1 meter) long, its fossils come from Arizona, where dinosaurs, such as *Dilophosaurus*, also roamed the land. Perhaps crocodiles took to the water to avoid dinosaurs who hunted similar prey.

CROCS COME OF AGE

During the Jurassic Period crocodiles grew bigger and more powerful. By the Late Jurassic they looked more like they do today. Crocodiles thrived during the Cretaceous Period. They were widespread, successful, and enormous. *Deinosuchus* (also called *Phobosuchus*) lived in Texas. Only its fossil skull is known. But this is over 6 feet (2 meters) in length, so *Deinosuchus* could have been as much as 50 feet (15 meters) long!

PLACODONTS

Even before dinosaurs on land, placodonts swam in the water. Some looked like big, armor-plated newts—others resembled crocodiles or turtles. *Placochelys* had flipper-shaped limbs and a large body shell about 3 feet (1 meter) long. These reptiles were shellfish eaters. They scraped up mussels and clams with their long, protruding front teeth and crushed the shells with massive flat teeth on the roof and floor of the mouth.

Placodus fossils were found in southern Europe. This placodont was 6 feet (2 meters) long. It had a ridged back and a fin along its tail held up by short, bony rods.

NOTHOSAURS

Nothosaurs were streamlined, speedy swimmers similar to plesiosaurs but living before them. Some were less than 1 foot (30 centimeters) long, while others more than 13 feet (4 meters). A nothosaur flapped or rowed with its powerful front legs and used its back legs for steering. It could dart its long, flexible neck to grab slippery prey with its rows of sharp, peglike teeth.

Nothosaurus fossils are widespread in Europe, North Africa and across Asia to China. It was 10 feet (3 meters) long and hunted fish, squid, and other food, then hauled itself out on land to rest.

Plesiosaurs and pliosaurs

Liopleurodon

Plesiosaurs swam in the seas during most of the Age of Dinosaurs. They were well adapted to life in water and probably dragged themselves ashore only briefly, to lay their eggs in beach sand like sea turtles today.

LONGER NECKS

One of the first plesiosaurs was *Plesiosaurus* from the Early Jurassic Period. As time passed, the plesiosaur body changed little. But the neck became amazingly long. The Late Cretaceous *Elasmosaurus* had a neck of 26 feet (8 meters)—over half its total length! This could loop around not once but twice so that *Elasmosaurus* still looked forward!

WHY THE LONG NECK?

Perhaps a plesiosaur paddled slowly at the surface, holding its head above to look down into the water. When it saw a victim, it darted its head quickly into the water. Another idea is that the plesiosaur swam underwater, poking among rocks with its snakelike neck.

HOW BIG WAS PLESIOSAURUS?

About 8 feet (2.3 meters) long. Later longer-necked types, such as *Elasmosaurus*, reached 45 feet (14 meters).

TIMELINE

Millions of years ago

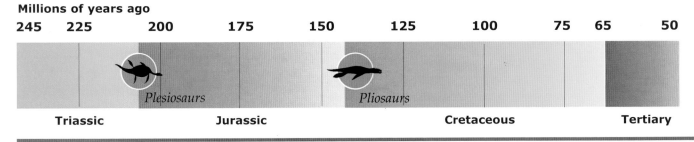

245	225	200	175	150	125	100	75	65	50

Plesiosaurs

Pliosaurs

Triassic	Jurassic	Cretaceous	Tertiary

Liopleurodon was possibly the greatest meat eater the world has ever known, even bigger than the sperm whale. This monster was 20 times heavier than *Tyrannosaurus* and its teeth were twice the size.

The short tail tapered so that water slipped off it smoothly instead of swirling around and slowing down the pliosaur.

BIGGEST OF THE BIG

Pliosaurs were a subgroup of plesiosaurs that evolved shorter necks. They kept the four flippers and the streamlined body. Some pliosaurs reached incredible sizes. *Liopleurodon* may have been over 75 feet (23 meters) long and a gigantic 100 tons (100 tonnes) in weight, rivaling the biggest dinosaurs and the great whales of today.

The neck was long and flexible, so Plesiosaurus could dart its head about. The neck had 28 bones. Some later plesiosaurs had 70 neck bones!

Plesiosaurus

Like all reptiles, Plesiosaurus had nostrils and breathed air, so it had to come to the surface regularly.

The body was long, slim, and agile. Plesiosaurus could turn on the spot by swimming forward with the flippers on one side and backward with the flippers on the other side.

Compared to other reptiles Plesiosaurus had more bones in each finger and toe, to form the long, narrow flippers.

Its small mouth and teeth could grab prey, such as fish and squid, up to about 1 foot (30 centimeters) long.

Ichthyosaurs and mosasaurs

Ichthyosaurus *had a triangular dorsal (back) fin, like a shark or dolphin.*

The rear end of the backbone kinked down into the lower tail. The tail flukes (fins) were probably made of stiff connective tissue, muscle, and perhaps cartilage (gristle), covered in skin.

The smooth, streamlined, torpedo-shaped body could slip through the ocean with ease.

Most of the ocean reptiles during the Age of Dinosaurs had paddlelike limbs and could probably waddle onto land. Ichthyosaurs could not. They were totally water-dwelling. They even bred in the oceans. And they did not lay eggs—they gave birth to live young. Amazing fossils show mother ichthyosaurs with young growing inside their bodies.

Hundreds of excellent *Ichthyosaurus* fossils were found near Holzmaden, Germany. They show the bones, teeth, and even soft parts, such as the fin and tail outlines, in great detail. Other ichthyosaur fossils come from places as far apart as Alaska, Argentina, and China.

SHAPED FOR SPEED

The shape of an ichthyosaur, or "fish-lizard," shows it was a fast swimmer. Similar-shaped animals today are marlin and tuna (fish) and dolphins (mammals). These speed through the oceans at 30 mph (50 kph) or more. An ichthyosaur swam like a fish, powerfully swishing its tail from side to side. The limb-paddles helped it to turn and slow down. The back fin stopped the ichthyosaur's body tilting or rolling from side to side.

TIMELINE

Millions of years ago

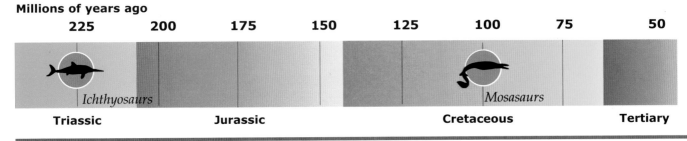

| 225 | 200 | 175 | 150 | 125 | 100 | 75 | 50 |

Ichthyosaurs

Mosasaurs

| Triassic | Jurassic | Cretaceous | Tertiary |

HOW BIG WAS ICHTHYOSAURUS?

Ichthyosaurus was up to 6 feet (2 meters) long. Some ichthyosaurs were only half this size. Others grew almost as large as today's whales. The Late Triassic *Shonisaurus* was 50 feet (15 meters) long.

The nostrils were on the upper snout, just in front of the eyes. Ichthyosaurus needed only to touch the surface with the top of its head, to take a breath and look around.

Ichthyosaurus

The four legs had become two sets of flippers, the front pair usually longer than the hind pair.

Rows of small but sharp teeth in the long, pointed jaws show that Ichthyosaurus ate marine animals, such as squid and fish.

Plotosaurus

About 70 million years ago *Plotosaurus* terrorized the sea that covered what is now Kansas. It hunted all kinds of smaller marine animals, including the last of the coil-shelled ammonites.

MOSASAURS

These fierce ocean hunters were distant relatives of today's monitor lizards. Most had four flipperlike limbs, a strong tail with long fins above and below, a huge head, large jaws, and rows of fanglike teeth. Some mosasaurs were enormous, such as *Plotosaurus*, which was 33 feet (10 meters) long.

DEATH
of the
DINOSAURS

When Did the Dinosaurs Die?

Dinosaurs were among the most numerous, long-lived, and successful animals the world has ever seen. But about 65 million years ago, something big happened on Earth. It affected global climate, oceans, landscape, plants, and animals. It was the end of an era—the Mesozoic Era—and the end of the Age of Dinosaurs.

DATING THE CHANGE

Exactly what happened is not clear, although some ideas are shown in this section. But it was enough to mark a clear, rapid, worldwide change or transition in rocks and fossils, between the Cretaceous Period and the Tertiary Period. The transition is called the K-T boundary. K is for kreta meaning chalk, the main rock formed in the Cretaceous Period. T is for the Tertiary Period. Radio-dating measures the amounts of natural radioactivity in ancient rocks, which change very slowly with time. It puts the K-T boundary at about 65–64.5 million years ago.

MASS EXTINCTION

After the Cretaceous Period there were no more dinosaur fossils. Dinosaurs were not the only creatures to die out during this period. Many other kinds of animals and plants also disappeared from the fossil record. This disappearance of many kinds of living things at about the same time has happened several times during the Earth's history and is known as a mass extinction.

OTHER MASS EXTINCTIONS

The fossil record shows many periods of mass extinctions, especially:

• End of the Cambrian, 505 million years ago.

• End of the Devonian, 360 million years ago.

• Middle and end of the Permian, about 250 million years ago. This was the greatest of all. Many larger animals disappeared, including the sail-backed, predinosaur reptile *Dimetrodon*, as well as lots of land plants. Nine-tenths of ocean life was wiped out, including the last trilobites.

• End of the Cretaceous, as shown here.

The world as it may have looked at the end of the Cretaceous Period.

Dimetrodon was one of many creatures that became extinct about 250 million years ago.

Were dinosaurs already dying out? Possibly, depending on where you look. Fossil surveys in different regions give different results. One world survey showed that at any one time during the Age of Dinosaurs, there were at least 50–100 species in 20–30 groups or families, and this dinosaur range continued right to the end of the Cretaceous Period. However, a study of North American fossils suggests that dinosaurs decreased and mammals increased over the last 10 million years of the Cretaceous Period.

Did the Dinosaurs Freeze or Fry?

Every few years a big volcano erupts somewhere on Earth. Vast clouds of smoke and ash blast into the air. They drift around the world, screen out the Sun, and affect weather for weeks or months. In June 1991 the eruption of Mount Pinatubo in the Philippines affected the world's climate for about two years.

DID THE DINOSAURS SUFFOCATE?

If many volcanoes erupted at the end of the Cretaceous Period, they could have used up the oxygen in the air. All living animals must breathe oxygen to survive. Presumably the dinosaurs did, too. Chemical tests have been done on tiny prehistoric air bubbles in lumps of fossil plant resin, amber. Results show how the oxygen in the air fell from 35 percent about 67 million years ago to 28 percent 2 million years later. Perhaps the dinosaurs could not get enough air through their small nostrils into their huge bodies to survive and suffocated to death!

COLD AND COUGHING

While some scientists believe that a giant meteorite wiped out the dinosaurs, another theory suggests that a series of volcanic eruptions was responsible. But not just from one volcano—from dozens, even hundreds of them. The mass eruptions filled the air with smoke and ash. Dust settled and cloaked plants. Poisonous sulfur fumes choked animals. Vast clouds made noon cool and gloomy. Without light and warmth, plants began to die. Dinosaurs and other animals that depended on plants began to die, too, coughing and shivering and starving.

This is how some parts of the earth may have looked at the end of the Cretaceous Period.

WHERE WERE THE VOLCANOES?

At the end of the Cretaceous Period there were probably ranges of volcanoes around the West Pacific Ocean and across North America, Greenland, and western Europe. But the main region was the vast volcanic region called the Deccan Traps, in what is now India. The Deccan eruptions may have lasted years, even centuries.

GLOBAL WARMING

Another idea is that the volcanoes released the "greenhouse gas" carbon dioxide. This made the atmosphere warmer (as is happening today because of our polluting gases). As the climate heated up, large land animals, such as dinosaurs suffered in the sweltering temperatures. They slowly fried away.

CONTINENTAL DRIFT

The massive volcanic eruptions may have been due to the great earth movements of continental drift. As landmasses moved around the globe and oceans changed shape, the world's winds and ocean currents took up new patterns.

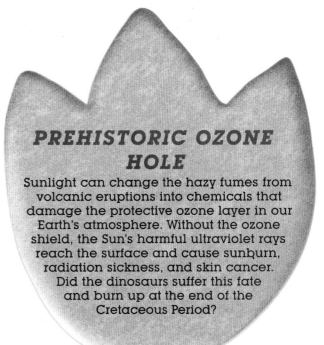

PREHISTORIC OZONE HOLE

Sunlight can change the hazy fumes from volcanic eruptions into chemicals that damage the protective ozone layer in our Earth's atmosphere. Without the ozone shield, the Sun's harmful ultraviolet rays reach the surface and cause sunburn, radiation sickness, and skin cancer. Did the dinosaurs suffer this fate and burn up at the end of the Cretaceous Period?

This brought rapid climate change. Temperatures at the equator could have fallen by 9°F (5°C), and in the midlatitudes by 36°F (20 °C). Did cold winters finish off the dinosaurs?

Death from Outer Space

Some experts say that the death of the dinosaurs happened gradually, taking a million years. Others suggest that it was fast, only a few years—maybe triggered by an event that took just a few seconds. The event was a massive lump of rock from outer space, a meteorite or asteroid, that crashed into the Earth. There is some evidence for this idea.

MYSTERIOUS METAL

In some parts of the world, Late Cretaceous rocks are separated from early Tertiary rocks by a layer of red-grey clay just under 1 inch (about 2 cm) thick. Chemical tests show that this clay has up to 30 times the normal amount of iridium, a type of metal. Iridium is rare in most rocks. But it is found in larger amounts at the center of the Earth—and in meteorites from outer space.

MASSIVE METEORITE!

From the amounts of iridium in the clay, it is calculated the meteorite was about 6 miles (10 kilometers) across—the size of a big town! It was traveling about 12 miles (20 kilometers) every second (70 times faster than a jet plane). It smashed into Earth with the same force as 100 million atomic bombs.

INCREDIBLE IMPACT

The incredible blast from such a meteorite would send sound and shock waves around the world. The impact would instantly heat and vaporize much of the rock from the meteorite and the ground it hit. The impact would also throw up gigantic clouds of spray and dust high into the atmosphere.

WORLDWIDE WINTER

Imagine how the dust cloud spread around the world, blotting out the Sun. It became night for weeks, maybe years. It was dark and cold in the gloom, just like winter. Deprived of light and warmth, plants withered and died.

OTHER RESULTS OF THE IMPACT

- The shock waves from the impact could have triggered fires, volcanic eruptions, earthquakes and tsunamis (tidal waves) around the planet.
- The dust cloud would have disturbed global winds and ocean currents.
- Extra gases in the air would have formed strong acid rain, which would acid-burn plants and animals both on land and at the surface of the sea.

Animals that ate the plants starved. Animals that ate these animals starved, too. In any case cold-blooded animals would be too cool to move. Was this how the dinosaurs met their end?

Other Extinction Theories

Can you think of a weird and wonderful reason why the dinosaurs may have died out? Each time a new discovery is made in science, someone suggests that it killed off the dinosaurs. Sadly most of these theories do not explain why many other animals and plants died with the dinosaurs. Nor do they show why other animals and plants survived.

DANGERS FROM DEEP SPACE?

There are many ideas about how events in space made the dinosaurs extinct:

• Extra-big solar flares. These vast tongues of flaming gas leap from the Sun's surface and give out extra heat and harmful rays.

• A supernova, when a giant star blows itself to bits in a gigantic final explosion. A supernova near Earth could send out deadly rays and magnetic waves to harm life here.

• A smaller star might die by collapsing into a black hole. This would release enormous bursts of atomic particles called neutrinos. They would shower Earth like invisible rain, causing cancers and other diseases.

• What about the two-sun idea? Our Sun orbits with a twin which we have not yet discovered. It is named Nemesis. Many stars have twins like this and are named binary stars. When Nemesis comes near us, about every 26 million years, its enormous gravity pulls the asteroids orbiting between Mars and Jupiter. They scatter across the solar system, hitting planets as giant meteorites.

EPIDEMICS OF DISEASE?

Maybe the dinosaurs suffered from new diseases, pests, or parasites. But it is difficult to imagine one type of germ or pest affecting all the many different kinds of dinosaurs. Also germs or parasites rarely kill off all of their animal victims. Usually some victims become resistant and slowly recover.

Dravidosaurus

RUNNING OUT OF EVOLUTION?

A more biological idea is "evolutionary old age." Just as an individual animal becomes old and weak and finally dies, so does an animal group. The group can no longer evolve to cope with a changing world. It has used up all its genes and is "worn out." The dinosaurs ruled the Earth for about 185 million years. Had they finally become too specialized to adapt? This idea is unlikely, since dinosaurs were still evolving into new types until the very end.

CHANGING PLANTS?

About halfway through the Cretaceous Period, the first flowers appeared on Earth. Perhaps dinosaurs could not digest these new and fast-evolving plants as they quickly took over the landscape. Or maybe the flowering plants made new types of chemicals to defend themselves and the dinosaurs could not survive these poisons.

Did early mammals bring about the end of the dinosaurs by eating all their eggs ...

... or were the plant eaters all poisoned as a result of eating the flowering plants that were spreading across the Earth?

THE MASS EGG-STINCTION?

Several mass extinction ideas involve dinosaur eggs. Perhaps new types of small mammals consumed more and more dinosaur eggs. Or dinosaur mothers, weakened by climate change and illness, laid eggs with shells that were too thin. These broke before the babies were ready to hatch and survive.

Did Any Living Things Survive?

Ichthyosaurs: died out

Birds and mammals, crocodiles, which are close reptile cousins of the dinosaurs, and other types of reptiles, such as turtles, lizards, and snakes, all survived the great extinction on land. In lakes and oceans, many kinds of fish and shellfish also survived and made it into the Tertiary Period.

WHO DIED?

The mass extinction is often called the "Death of the Dinosaurs." It is true that every kind of dinosaur was wiped out. But many other animals disappeared, too:

• The flapping, soaring pterosaurs all perished.
• Large marine reptiles, such as ichthyosaurs, plesiosaurs, and mosasaurs were all gone by the end of the Cretaceous Period. For some the end was sudden. Others had faded millions of years earlier.

Dinosaurs: died out

• Many kinds of fish died out, especially various sharks.
• The shelled marine animals called ammonites and belemnites did not survive. These large animals were mollusks, relatives of today's squid and octopus.
• Not just animals but many kinds of plants died out too.
Overall, some two-thirds to three-quarters of all living things perished, at or near the end of the Cretaceous Period.

WHO SURVIVED?

• Mammals—otherwise, we, as humans, might not be here! The first mammals appeared on Earth at about the same time as the first dinosaurs. They were about the size of mice or rats. As far as we know from fossils, during the entire Age of Dinosaurs no mammal was bigger than a pet cat.

• Some birds. But others which had been around for millions of years suddenly disappeared.

• Crocodiles, turtles, sharks and bony fish.

• Amphibians, such as frogs and newts.

• Insects, spiders, snails, and similar small land creatures.

• Water-dwelling creatures, such as whelks and other marine snails, crabs, shrimps, and other crustaceans, and starfish and other echinoderms.

Birds: some survived

PROBLEMS WITH THEORIES

A reason for the end-of-Cretaceous extinction must explain which life-forms died and which survived. This is a major problem. In particular, why did dinosaurs become extinct while their close cousins the crocodiles did not? The meteorite theory is the most popular, but it still leaves many questions unanswered.

Pterosaurs: died out

COULD DINOSAURS STILL SURVIVE?

There are many legends about great beasts and monsters in remote places, which might be dinosaurs that survived the great extinction:

• Loch Ness, a deep lake in Scotland, could be home to the "Loch Ness monster." Monster hunters describe a creature similar to the plesiosaurs, which lived during the Age of Dinosaurs (see page 196).

• The dense rainforests of the Congo region in Africa may hide beasts that look like sauropod dinosaurs, such as *Diplodocus*.

• The vast Amazon swamps may be home to a fierce *Tyrannosaurus*-like monster that ambushes unwary travelers.

Crocodiles: survived

HUNTING
for
DINOSAURS

How Fossils are Formed

1. When a dinosaur died, its remains could become fossilized if they weren't eaten or disturbed.

We know about dinosaurs mainly from their fossils. Most fossils are of hard and tough body parts, such as teeth, bones, claws, and horns.

FROM DINOSAUR TO FOSSIL
• A dinosaur died. Its body was washed by a flood on to a river bank. Its flesh, guts, and other soft parts were soon eaten by scavengers or rotted away, leaving the bones.
• The river flooded again and covered the bones in mud, sand, silt, and other sediments.
• This happened many times as more sediments buried the bones deeper.
• Minerals from the sediments in the water seeped into the bones. Little by little they replaced the bone, turning it to solid stone. This took thousands or millions of years.
• The sediments were also squashed by the weight above. The minerals among the sediment particles cemented them into solid rock.

• Over millions of years great earth movements tilted and twisted the layers of sedimentary rocks. Also hot sun, wind, rain, frost, ice, snow, and other forces of nature gradually wore away or eroded the upper layers.
• The fossils were uncovered at the surface. One day a fossil expert walks by, looks down, and makes another great discovery!

2. As the creature is buried under sediments, the skin and flesh rot away, leaving only the bones.

MOLDS, CASTS, AND MUMMIES
Sometimes rock formed around a body part, but the part itself was dissolved away to leave an empty place with the same shape. This is a mold fossil.

In other cases, water full of dissolved minerals seeped into the space of a mold fossil. The minerals solidified and gradually filled the gap, forming a cast fossil.

Rarely, a dinosaur perished in a very dry place, such as a desert cave. Its body dried out rapidly without having time to rot. This fast-drying process, mummification, can preserve softer body parts, such as skin. The famous *Tyrannosaurus* fossil "Sue" (see pages 162—3) was preserved like this.

OTHER FOSSILS

Not only dinosaurs left fossils. Other animals did, too, especially those with very hard body parts, such as shells. And especially those which lived in places such as the sea where sediments were plentiful and fossilization was more likely. Plants left fossils, too, especially of their hard bark, cones and seeds. These other fossils show us the animals and plants that lived alongside the dinosaurs.

THE FOSSIL RECORD

Fossils trace the evolution of dinosaurs and other life on Earth. But the fossils we have discovered are only a tiny fraction of the fossils that must exist in rocks all over the world. And

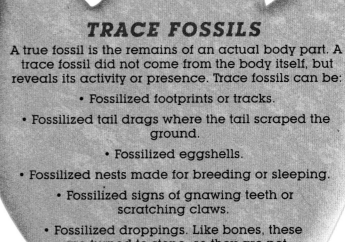

TRACE FOSSILS

A true fossil is the remains of an actual body part. A trace fossil did not come from the body itself, but reveals its activity or presence. Trace fossils can be:

- Fossilized footprints or tracks.
- Fossilized tail drags where the tail scraped the ground.
- Fossilized eggshells.
- Fossilized nests made for breeding or sleeping.
- Fossilized signs of gnawing teeth or scratching claws.
- Fossilized droppings. Like bones, these are turned to stone, so they are not soft and smelly! They are known as coprolites and often contain pieces of the last meal.

these fossils are from only a tiny fraction of all the animals and plants that ever lived. So the fossil record is very selective and patchy—a game of chance.

3. As the bones are buried deeper and deeper, they are changed into rock. They become locked into position by the force of the rocks and sediments above.

4. If the rocks above become worn away by erosion, the fossilized dinosaur bones may become exposed at the surface.

Dinosaur Fossil Hunters

Fossils of dinosaurs can tell us nothing if they are buried in the ground. Fossil hunters spend years searching remote, dangerous places for fragments of bones and teeth. Their finds have given us our knowledge of dinosaurs and prehistoric life.

Barnum Brown outside his tent during one of the digs he led in Alberta, Canada.

MANTELL AND BUCKLAND

In about 1822 English physician Gideon Mantell's wife discovered some large fossil teeth at a gravel roadworks site in Sussex, England. Mantell was a keen amateur geologist and identified them as reptilian. He showed them to important scientists, including William Buckland, Reader of Geology at Oxford University, England. In 1824 Buckland described a fossil jawbone with long teeth as that of a large, meat-eating reptile that he called *Megalosaurus*. Meanwhile Mantell had discovered the fossil teeth found by his wife were similar to, but bigger than, the teeth of the living iguana lizard. So he named their owner *Iguanodon*, "iguana-tooth."

DINOSAURS COME ALIVE

Another scientist, Richard Owen, examined these various fossils and saw that they were reptiles, but not like any living reptiles, such as lizards or crocodiles. In 1841 he described his findings to a British Association for the Advancement of Science meeting in Plymouth, England. He proposed a new name for this group of huge reptiles—Dinosauria. This is when the term "dinosaur" was invented.

THE FIGHT IS ON

Dinosaurs soon gripped people's imaginations.

The hunt was on for the biggest and best fossils. During the late 1800s in North America, two teams led by Edward Drinker Cope and Othniel Charles Marsh raced to find the most dinosaurs. They were bitter rivals, but their finds include some of the best known of all dinosaurs, such as *Diplodocus* and *Stegosaurus*.

FROM ALBERTA TO THE GOBI DESERT

Barnum Brown of the American Museum of Natural History explored the Red Deer River of Alberta, Canada, from about 1910—1917. He and his team uncovered fossils of many duck-billed dinosaurs, or hadrosaurs, from the Late Cretaceous Period. Henry Fairfield Osborn, director of the American Museum of Natural History, described and named *Ornitholestes* in 1903 and *Tyrannosaurus* in 1905. In the 1920s he helped to lead the famous fossil expedition to Mongolia's Gobi Desert when the first fossil dinosaur eggs were found, of *Protoceratops*.

NEW IDEAS

In 1964 American fossil expert John Ostrom found the remains of *Deinonychus*. In his report of 1969 he broke with tradition by suggesting it was an active, agile predator with a large brain and complicated behavior. It was possibly even warm-blooded. Ostrom also suggested that birds evolved from small theropods. From the 1970s Robert Bakker continued to champion the idea that many dinosaurs were warm-blooded. He showed the idea of enormous sauropods, such as *Brachiosaurus*, living in water was wrong. Also in the 1970s James Jensen dug up possibly the biggest of all dinosaurs, *Supersaurus* and *Ultrasaurus*. These brachiosaur types were possibly over 98 feet (30 meters) long and weighed over 100 tons (100 tonnes).

DOWN TO SOUTH AMERICA

In 1988 Dr Paul Sereno visited Argentina and found fossils of the very early dinosaur *Herrerasaurus*, a 10-foot- (3-meter-) long theropod. In 1993 he described the smaller but also very early dinosaur *Eoraptor*. In the late 1990s he explored North Africa and discovered fossils of the 26-foot- (8-meter-) long meat eater *Afrovenator* and the over 66-foot- (20-meter-) sauropod *Jobaria*.

James Jensen poses next to the shoulder blade of *Supersaurus*, one of the huge dinosaurs he uncovered.

Dinosaurs in North America

The first dinosaur fossils discovered in North America were in Connecticut, from the prosauropod *Anchisaurus*. However, this was in 1818, well before dinosaurs were recognized or even named as a group. In fact the *Anchisaurus* fossils were first thought to be human remains. In 1855 they were recognized as a reptile, in 1885 as a dinosaur, and in 1912 finally named by fossil expert, Richard Swan Lull.

Massospondylus

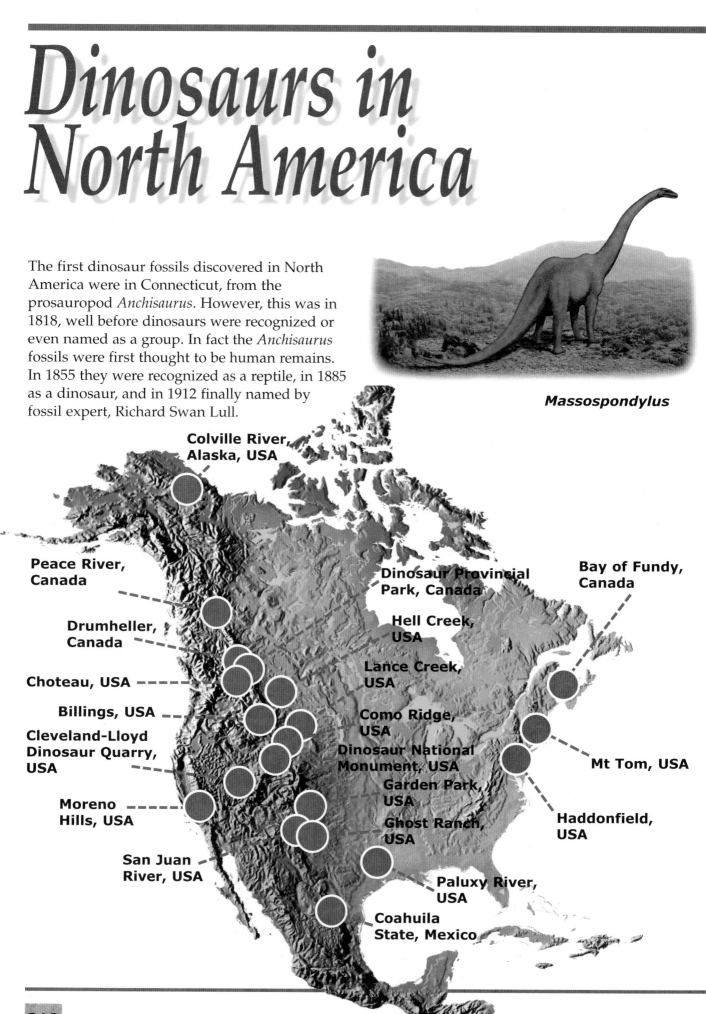

Colville River, Alaska, USA

Peace River, Canada

Drumheller, Canada

Choteau, USA

Billings, USA

Cleveland-Lloyd Dinosaur Quarry, USA

Moreno Hills, USA

San Juan River, USA

Dinosaur Provincial Park, Canada

Hell Creek, USA

Lance Creek, USA

Como Ridge, USA

Dinosaur National Monument, USA

Garden Park, USA

Ghost Ranch, USA

Paluxy River, USA

Coahuila State, Mexico

Bay of Fundy, Canada

Mt Tom, USA

Haddonfield, USA

SPECIAL SITE

The Red Deer River Dinosaur Provincial Park in Alberta, Canada, is a World Heritage Site. Since the 1880s people have explored this remote "Badlands" area where the Red Deer River cuts through 75-million-year-old rocks. Fossils include those of *Albertosaurus*, entire herds of *Centrosaurus*, many specimens of *Euoplocephalus* and *Lambeosaurus*.

THE BADLANDS COME GOOD

Dinosaurs were first studied and named in Europe during the 1840s—50s. But North America grabbed the headlines for the next 60 years. From the 1860s in the "Badlands" of the Midwest across Montana, Wyoming, Utah, and Colorado, many new dinosaurs were discovered from fossils exposed by the dry, harsh climate. The fierce rivalry between Othniel Charles Marsh and Edward Drinker Cope helped to hurry along the work.

A NEW ERA

Fossil hunting in North America received a boost during the 1960s with the remains of *Deinonychus* from near Billings, Montana. This made many experts believe that not all dinosaurs were slow and stupid beasts—some were pack hunters and "intelligent." Marvelous new specimens of old favorites, such as *Tyrannosaurus*, were discovered into the 1990s. Many fossil-rich sites have been made into parks and protected areas, especially the Dinosaur National Monument in Colorado-Utah.

LAMBEOSAURUS

One of the largest hollow-crested duck-bills, or hadrosaurs, it measured up to 49 feet (15 meters) long and 8 tons (8 tonnes) in weight. Its head crest had a front part shaped like an axehead, or hatchet, between the eyes and pointing upward, and a rear part like a back-pointing spike or spur.

MASSOSPONDYLUS

Fossils of the early prosauropod *Massospondylus* have been found in Arizona and in the Bay of Fundy region of eastern North America, and also at several African sites. It was about 16 feet (5 meters) long and lived during the Early Jurassic Period, 200—195 million years ago. *Massospondylus* walked on all fours but could probably rear up on to its back legs, perhaps using its tail as a support, to reach leaves high in trees.

MORE NORTH AMERICAN DINOSAURS

• *Orodromeus* A smallish, plant-eating cousin of *Hypsilophodon*. Its fossils were found at the mass breeding site with those of *Maiasaura* and *Tröodon*.
• *Kritosaurus* A hadrosaur 30 feet (9 meters) long with a low lump on its nose.
• *Saurolophus* Another hadrosaur with a bony ridge on its snout and a small spike on top of the head.
• *Pentaceratops* A ceratopsian like *Triceratops* but with five face horns.
• *Centrosaurus* Another ceratopsian with a single nose horn and two "tongue horns" on the top of its neck frill.

Lambeosaurus

Dinosaurs in South America

Herrerasaurus

Dinosaur fossils have been dug up in South America for more than a century. But this continent began to hit the headlines from the 1980s with exciting new discoveries. Most of these have been in the dry scrub and semidesert in Argentina and southern Brazil, and especially in the foothills of the Andes Mountains.

NEW RECORD-HOLDERS

Fossils of *Saltasaurus* were found in 1980s. This was the first sauropod known to have bony plates, like armor, over its body. *Giganotosaurus* was a meat eater similar to *Tyrannosaurus* but even bigger—up to 46 feet (14 meters) long and 8 tons (8 tonnes) in weight.

VERY EARLY DINOSAURS

Some of the most amazing recent discoveries in South America are among the first of all dinosaurs. They are from early in the Late Triassic Period, about 230—220 million years ago. They include the meat eaters *Herrerasaurus* and *Eoraptor* in Argentina, and the similar *Staurikosaurus* in Brazil. These creatures have shown us that dinosaurs were around as early as the Middle Triassic.

HERRERASAURUS

Named after the Andean farmer Victorina Herrera who found its fossils, the predator *Herrerasaurus* was about 10 feet long (3 meters). It ran fast on its large, strong hind legs. Its big feet and small hands had sharp claws. Its long, curved, pointed teeth were those of a killer.

SALTASAURUS

Found in Argentina's Salta Province, and also in Uruguay, these fossils show a 39-feet- (12-meter-) long sauropod called *Saltasaurus*, from the Late Cretaceous Period, 75—72 million years ago. It had thousands of pea-sized bony lumps in the skin of its back, like chain mail armor. Larger plates and lumps of bone were also scattered over its back.

MUSSAURUS

This prosauropod was named "mouse reptile" because its fossils are the smallest of any dinosaur, showing individuals just 8 inches (20 centimeters) long. These are babies just hatched from their eggs. The adults were similar to *Plateosaurus* but smaller, about 10 feet (3 meters) long. They lived in the Late Triassic Period.

Mussaurus

MORE SOUTH AMERICAN DINOSAURS

• *Staurikosaurus* At about 7 feet (2 meters) long, this slim, light, speedy theropod could run fast on its long back legs.

• *Eoraptor* The "dawn thief" is one of the earliest dinosaurs and shares many body features of its nondinosaur ancestors.

• *Carnotaurus* A Cretaceous meat eater over 23 feet (7 meters) long and weighing 1 ton (about 1 tonne), it had strange, cowlike horns over its eyebrows and a short-snouted, deep face, almost like a bulldog.

• *Titanosaurus* The large sauropods called titanosaurs were identified in Argentina in the 1890s.

El Breté, Argentina

Cerro Rajado, Argentina

Santa Maria, Brazil

Ischigualasto, Argentina

Neuquén, Argentina

Cerro Condor, Argentina

Santa Cruz, Argentina

SPECIAL SITE

In southern Argentina, many dinosaur fossils have been found in Chubut Province and along the Chubut River. Argentinian fossil expert José Bonaparte has discovered and named several, including *Carnotaurus* from Chubut. It probably preyed on the brachiosaurlike *Chubutisaurus*, which was more than 72 feet (22 meters) long. *Patagosaurus* was another sauropod, this time from the Late Jurassic.

Dinosaurs in Europe

The first dinosaur ever described and named in a proper scientific report was *Megalosaurus* (see pages 122—3), a large meat eater similar to *Allosaurus*. This was in 1824 even before the term "dinosaur" had been invented. In fact, the first dinosaur fossil to be written about as far back as the 1670s may have been from *Megalosaurus*, also the bones were believed to have come from a giant man!

SAFETY IN NUMBERS

Europe has since yielded many dinosaur fossils. Especially numerous are the 23-foot- (7-meter-) long prosauropod *Plateosaurus* from the Late Triassic Period and the 5-ton- (5-tonne-) ornithopod *Iguanodon*. The remains of about 40 *Iguanodon* were dug up in the 1870s from 1,000–1,150 feet (320–350 meters) deep in an old coal mine at Bernissart, Belgium.

A LONER

Other European dinosaurs have just one or two individuals. The armored dinosaur *Hyaelosaurus* is known from only one specimen found in 1833 in Tilgate Forest, Sussex, southern England. Along with *Megalosaurus* and *Iguanodon*, it was one of the three founder members of the Dinosauria when Richard Owen invented this name in 1841. An exciting recent find in Europe is *Baryonyx*, "heavy claw" (see page 78).

PROCOMPSOGNATHUS

Fossils of *Procompsognathus* come from Germany, like those of the similarly-named *Compsognathus*.
Procompsognathus was a two-legged meat eater, similar in size and shape to *Compsognathus*, but it lived earlier, during the Late Triassic. In body features it resembled the North American *Coelophysis*.

SPECIAL SITE

"Lithographic limestone" is rock with grains so small and fine that it was once quarried and used for printing (lithography). This rock is common in the Solnhofen region of Bavaria, Germany. The fine grains preserved Late Jurassic fossils in incredible detail, including the fragile bones and delicate feathers of the earliest known bird, *Archaeopteryx*, several pterosaurs (flying reptiles), and the small dinosaur, *Compsognathus*.

SCELIDOSAURUS

About the size of a pony but with a long, thick tail, *Scelidosaurus* was an early cousin of the plated and armored dinosaurs, such as *Stegosaurus* and *Ankylosaurus*. Its fossils come from southern England, and possibly also East Asia and North America.

Procompsognathus

MORE EUROPEAN DINOSAURS

• *Halticosaurus* One of the earliest large meat eaters, about 16 feet (5 meters) long, from the Late Triassic Period. It probably resembled *Ceratosaurus* and *Allosaurus*.

• *Saltopus* A very small, two-legged meat eater from the Late Triassic. It was probably slim and lightweight, like the later *Compsognathus*, yet even smaller. Its fossils come from Scotland.

• *Camptosaurus* An *Iguanodon*-type ornithopod around 23 feet (7 meters) long. Its remains were found in Portugal, England, and also North America, showing that these continents were joined 140–130 million years ago.

BIG EGGS

Some of the biggest dinosaur eggs ever found were probably laid by the Late Cretaceous sauropod *Hypselosaurus*. The fossil eggs were discovered at Aix-en-Provence, southern France. Each is about 12 inches (30 centimeters) long and the same volume as 60 ordinary hen's eggs.

Scelidosaurus

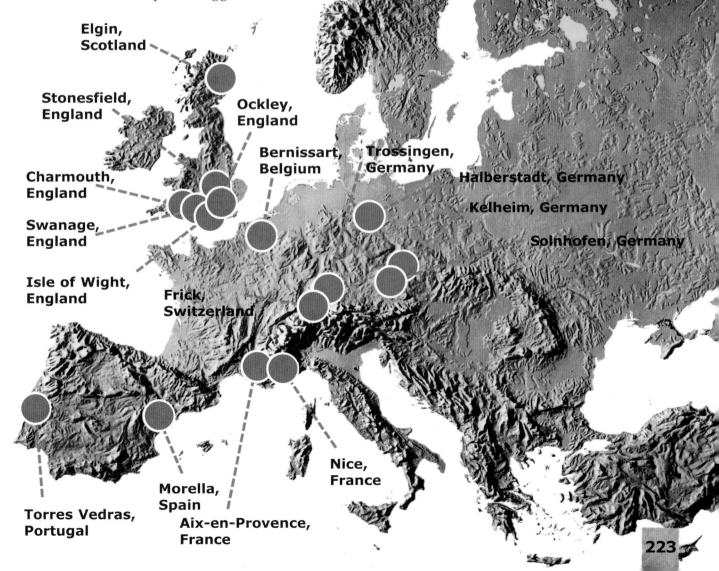

Elgin, Scotland

Stonesfield, England

Ockley, England

Charmouth, England

Bernissart, Belgium

Trossingen, Germany

Halberstadt, Germany

Kelheim, Germany

Solnhofen, Germany

Swanage, England

Isle of Wight, England

Frick, Switzerland

Nice, France

Torres Vedras, Portugal

Morella, Spain

Aix-en-Provence, France

Dinosaurs in Asia

Asia, the world's biggest continent, has provided fossils of more dinosaurs than any other continent. For thousands of years, dinosaur teeth, claws, and horns dug up in China were believed to have come from dragons and other mythical beasts. In the 1920s, expeditions to Mongolia made fantastic discoveries of great tyrannosaurs, ostrich dinosaurs, horned and plated dinosaurs, and dinosaur eggs and nests.

AMAZING FINDS
For many years few fossil finds in China were available for study. As China has increased its links with other countries in recent years, the most astonishing fossil finds are now becoming widely known. In particular there are incredible remains of various ancient birdlike dinosaurs— or were they dinosaurlike birds?

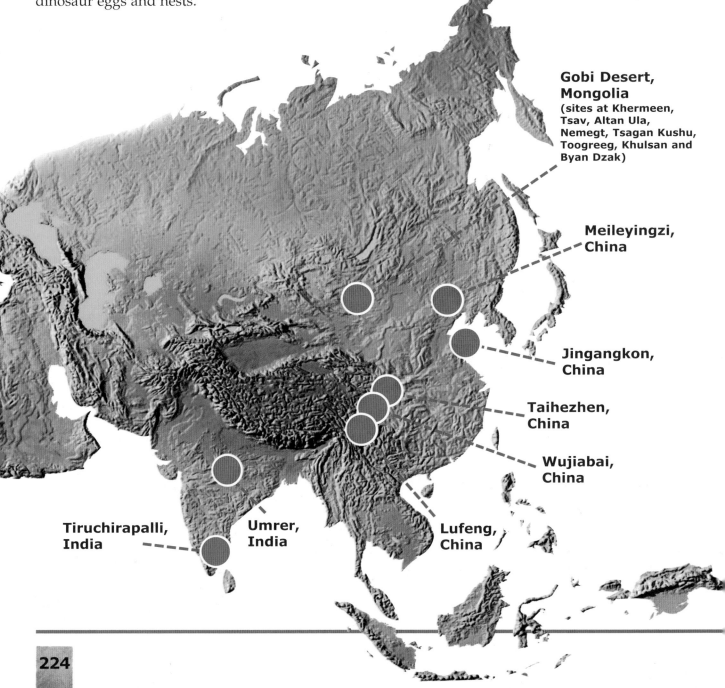

Gobi Desert, Mongolia
(sites at Khermeen, Tsav, Altan Ula, Nemegt, Tsagan Kushu, Toogreeg, Khulsan and Byan Dzak)

Meileyingzi, China

Jingangkon, China

Taihezhen, China

Wujiabai, China

Lufeng, China

Tiruchirapalli, India

Umrer, India

Tsintaosaurus

Tsintaosaurus

This 23-foot- (7-meter-) long Late Cretaceous hadrosaur from China had a very odd tube-shaped head-crest. It was thin-walled and therefore not much use as a weapon. It was not linked to the breathing passages and so could not be used as a snorkel or to blow as a "trumpet." In fact, it was probably a fossil from another animal, mistakenly put on the hadrosaur (now called *Tanius*). Like the unicorn, *Tsintaosaurus* was a myth!

The "bird mimic"

Avimimus is one of many mysteries posed by Asian dinosaurs. Its fossils were dug up from 1981 in Mongolia and China. They show a slim, light theropod, 5 feet (1.5 meters) long, from the Late Cretaceous Period. It ran swiftly on its two powerful hind legs, peered with its large eyes, and pecked with its birdlike, toothless bill. One puzzling feature is a ridge along its forearm bone. A bird's wing bone has small knobs in a similar position, where the feather shafts attach. Did *Avimimus* have feathers on winglike arms? Birds were already well established by its time. So was *Avimimus* a bird that evolved back into a dinosaur? Or did it evolve feathers separately from birds?

Pinacosaurus

A cousin of *Euoplocephalus*, but slightly smaller at 16 feet (5 meters), this ankylosaur lived in Mongolia during the Late Cretaceous Period. It had spiky, cone-shaped armor over its back and a heavy bone tail club to smash the legs of tall enemies.

SPECIAL SITE
The valley of the Nemegt Basin lies in the vast, harsh Gobi Desert in Mongolia. Blazing daytime temperatures of 104°F (40 °C) plunge to bone-chilling minus 40 °F (-40 °C), at night, windblown sand gets into everything, and the nearest town is hours away. Yet hardy fossil hunters have found fascinating dinosaur fossils here, including ostrich dinosaurs, raptors (dromaeosaurs), *Tarbosaurus*, the Late Cretaceous sauropod *Opisthocoelicaudia*, and helmet-headed pachycephalosaur *Prenocephale*.

More Asian dinosaurs

• *Tarbosaurus* This huge meat eater from China and Mongolia was so similar to *Tyrannosaurus* that some experts suggest they were North American and Asian versions of the same creature.

• *Lufengosaurus* A prosauropod very similar to *Plateosaurus* in Europe. Its fossils come from Yunnan Province in China, an area that has produced many prehistoric remains.

• *Dravidosaurus* One of the few dinosaurs from India, this stegosaur was 10 feet (3 meters) long and lived during the Late Cretaceous Period.

Pinacosaurus

Dinosaurs in Australia and Antarctica

Much of Australia is parched desert with rocks of the wrong age or wrong type for dinosaur fossils. Until the 1970s only a few kinds were known from this huge continent. They included an early sauropod *Rhoetosaurus* dug up in 1924 in Queensland, and in 1964 the discovery of a smallish armored dinosaur, *Minmi* (see pages 124—5).

DINOSAURS BY THE SEASIDE
But all this changed by the 1980s. Another Queensland find in 1981 was *Muttaburrasaurus*. It was a relative of *Iguanodon* and very similar in shape, but smaller at 23–26 feet (7–8 meters) long. It had a curious bony lump on the snout just in front of the eyes. In recent years an avalanche of discoveries has come from "Dinosaur Cove," an area on Australia's southeastern coast near Melbourne.

NEW ZEALAND AND ANTARCTICA
A fossil vertebra (backbone) from Mangahouanga on New Zealand's North Island is probably the tail bone from a theropod dinosaur. In 1986 the great frozen land of Antarctica became the last continent to reveal dinosaur fossils—although this is probably due to problems in finding fossils under ice and snow rather than lack of them. The remains of a *Euoplocephalus*-like ankylosaur were unearthed near James Ross Island in 1988, followed by fossils of a horned theropod and a sauropod.

LEAELLYNASAURA
One of the newest dinosaur stars, *Leaellynasaura* was a slim, light, fast-moving, parrot-billed plant eater. It was named "Leaellyn's lizard" (Lea-Ellyn) in 1989 after the daughter of its discoverers, Patricia Vickers-Rich and Thomas Rich. Its huge eyes could see in the wintry gloom of dense forests.

MIGRATE OR HIBERNATE?
Leaellynasaura was about 7 feet (2 meters) long and chest-high to a human. It was perhaps too small to make a long journey and migrate away from the long, dark, cold winter. It could stay in the region, protected in the undergrowth from the worst frost and ice, but would have been too cold to move. This type of hibernation in reptiles is called torpor.

Dryosaurus

James Ross Island, Antarctica

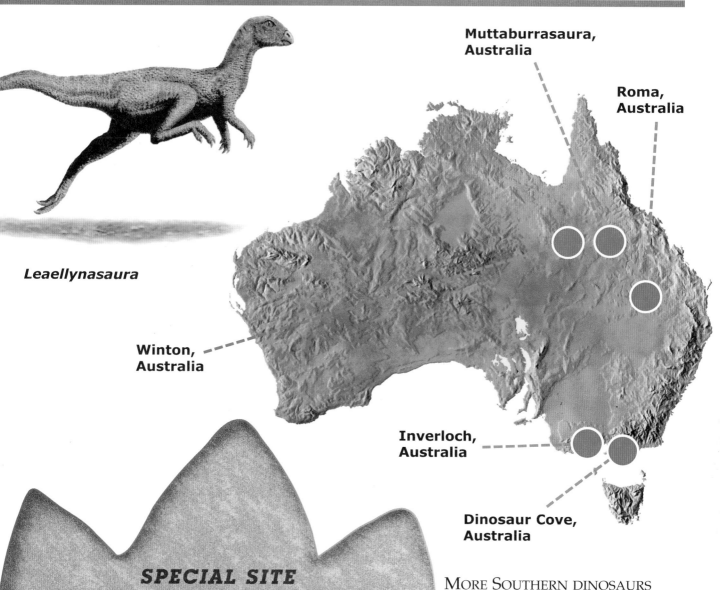

Leaellynasaura

Muttaburrasaura, Australia

Roma, Australia

Winton, Australia

Inverloch, Australia

Dinosaur Cove, Australia

SPECIAL SITE

Dinosaur Cove is a rich coastal area of Cretaceous fossils near Melbourne. At that time, around 110 million years ago, Australia was linked to Antarctica and both were near the South Pole. Dinosaurs here would survive a long, dark winter with no sun for several weeks, although not as cold as today's Antarctic! Dinosaur Cove finds include:

• Ostrich-dinosaurs or ornithomimosaurs, much earlier than North American types such as *Struthiomimus*.

• A miniversion of the great and fearsome theropod *Allosaurus*, at only 7 feet (2.2 meters) tall.

• Armored dinosaurs or ankylosaurs no bigger than sheep.

• Horned dinosaurs or ceratopsians like *Triceratops* but again only sheep-sized.

• Many hypsilophodonts—small and light two-legged runners which ate plants—including *Leaellynasaura*.

MORE SOUTHERN DINOSAURS

• *Rhoetosaurus* An early sauropod about 56 feet (17 meters) long from the Middle Jurassic. It was related to the cetiosaur or brachiosaur types.

• *Austrosaurus* Another large sauropod, about 49 feet (15 meters) long, but from the Late Cretaceous Period when most other sauropods had died out.

• A 10-foot-(3-meter-) long plant eater similar to a combined version of small *Hypsilophodon* and big *Iguanodon*. Its fossils also come from North America and Africa.

227

Dinosaurs in Africa

Wawmda, Morocco

Bahariya, Egypt

Taouz, Morocco

In Gall, Niger

Gadoufaoua, Niger

A "Dinosaur Rush" to Africa began in about 1907, with news of massive fossil bones in what was then German East Africa, now Tanzania. There have been many important finds since, mainly across North Africa and in East and southern Africa. In the Cretaceous Period some 110—100 million years ago, in what is now the Sahara Desert, the great sail-backed meat eater *Spinosaurus* (see page 146–7) stalked its possible prey, *Ouranosaurus*.

ROCKS OF ALL AGES

Africa has rocks from the other two periods when dinosaurs ruled. More than 200 million years ago in the Triassic Period lived the prosauropods *Anchisaurus* and the 13-foot- (4-meter-) long *Massospondylus*, both also known from North America. During the early Jurassic, tiny plant eaters, such as *Lesothosaurus* and *Heterodontosaurus* from the ornithopod group darted through the scrub. Later, massive sauropods, such as *Cetiosaurus*, *Barosaurus*, and *Brachiosaurus* pounded the land.

Tendaguru, Tanzania

Lake Kariba, Zimbabwe

Harrismith, South Africa

Ladybrand, South Africa

Mafetang, Lesotho

Kadzi, Zimbabwe

Herschel, South Africa

Anchisaurus

A NEW ERA

The 1900s ended with a flurry of amazing new dinosaur discoveries in and around Africa. A very early but large sauropod, *Jobaria*, was identified from fossils in Morocco. It lived 165 million years ago and was about 66 feet (20 meters) long and 22 tons (21.6 tonnes) in weight. Most stunning are the remains of prosauropod-type dinosaurs from 230—225 million years ago on the large island of Madagascar. They promise to rewrite the early history of dinosaurs, back into the Middle Triassic Period.

Barosaurus

ANCHISAURUS

This smallish, early Jurassic prosauropod was about 8 feet (2.5 meters) in length, with a body as big as a large dog but with a longer, more flexible neck. It could probably trot on all fours and also rear up to run on its two hind legs.

BAROSAURUS

At 85 feet (26 meters), this vast sauropod from the Late Jurassic Period was almost as long as its cousin, *Diplodocus*. However, its skull has never been found, so scientists have had to guess what the head looked like.

HETERODONTOSAURUS

This ornithopod had very unusual teeth. They were small and sharp like chisels at the upper front of the mouth. Behind were four long, fanglike teeth, almost like a wild boar's tusks. At the back of the mouth were flatter, crushing cheek teeth. *Heterodontosaurus* was only 5 feet (1.5 meters) long and lived 205–200 million years ago in what is now southern Africa.

MORE AFRICAN DINOSAURS

• *Cetiosaurus* The 59-foot- (18-meter-) long "whale lizard" was the first sauropod to be named by Richard Owen when he invented the word "dinosaur" in 1841. Its fossils come from Morocco and also England.
• *Massospondylus* A prosauropod 16 feet (5 meters) long from 200 million years ago, similar to *Plateosaurus*. Its fossils also occur in Arizona.
• *Ouranosaurus* A sail-backed cousin of *Iguanodon* some 23 feet (7 meters) long, from the Middle Cretaceous Period about 115 million years ago in Niger, Africa.

SPECIAL SITE

One of the biggest-ever fossil-hunting expeditions was to the Tendaguru Hills near Mtwara in Tanzania, between 1908—1912. It excavated the tallest complete skeleton of any animal ever found, a *Brachiosaurus*. Other sauropods from the site were *Barosaurus* and *Dicraeosaurus*, as well as the stegosaur *Kentrosaurus* at 16 feet (5 meters) long, and the 10-foot- (3-meter-) long ostrich dinosaur *Elaphrosaurus*.

Digging up Dinosaurs

Fossil hunters have a lot to do before their very own fossil dinosaur, named after them, can be proudly displayed for the world's news media.

THE RIGHT ROCKS

The first thing that fossil hunters look for is the correct age and type of rock. Dinosaurs lived during the Mesozoic Era, about 250–65 million years ago. Their fossils are found in sedimentary rocks, such as limestones and sandstones. Large-scale geological maps show where Mesozoic sedimentary rocks are found at the Earth's surface rather than buried far below.

FINDING A SITE

Most fossil-bearing rock is part of the top rock layer but this is often hidden under lakes, oceans, forests, grassland, and also roads, houses, and buildings. Expert fossil hunters frequently need to let nature do the work—they search places where bare surface rocks are continually cracked and worn away by hot sun, strong winds, rain, frost, and ice. With luck, the fossils will just be lying there waiting to be picked up! Unfortunately these harsh, rocky places are remote "badlands," deserts, cliffs, ravines, and coasts. There are few roads or towns, so transportation is usually a big problem. They are dangerous, too.

A team of paleontologists carefully uncover the fossilized remains of a dinosaur.

MAN-MADE SITES

Fossil hunters also search in places where the actions of people have exposed suitable rocks, such as mines, quarries, rail and road cuttings, and deep-foundation building sites. You can do this, too, but you should always get permission and always put safety first.

THE SURVEY

Next, the site must be surveyed. This involves describing the main features, making maps, taking photographs, and drawing sketches. A photograph can show a lifelike bird's-eye view. But an illustration can highlight details that may not be obvious in the photograph. The site is usually marked out with pegs and string, like graph paper, so finds can be located on a grid. These tasks are repeated at intervals as the dig continues.

Dig, dig, dig!

At last, the digging can start in earnest. Depending on the size of the specimens, the rock's hardness, and other features, fossil hunters use a variety of tools for this:

• Dynamite! Some sites are blown up to expose new rock, and the remains carted away by bulldozers and road diggers.

• Road-drills and jackhammers remove bulk material.

• Picks and shovels clear the area with greater control.

• Small power drills, grinders, and sanders move material more carefully.

• Hand-held geological picks, hammers, and chisels are used to deal with the more detailed stages.

• Fine needle-probes and even wooden or plastic toothpicks are used for delicate items.

• Brushes are used to clear away very light, crumbly rock.

• Sieves and shakers sift general debris for small bone fragments or tiny teeth.

All wrapped up

Often a fossil is left in its surrounding rock, the matrix. The whole chunk is cut out and taken back to the laboratory, where there is more time and equipment. A delicate fossil can be protected and strengthened by painting it with a resin that soon hardens, or covering it with resin-soaked layers of glass-fibre, or sacking and plaster of Paris, or by using spray-on foam that quickly dries and hardens. A wooden or metal cradle built around the entire block allows it to be lifted from a wheelbarrow to a heavy-lift cargo helicopter.

Dinosaurs in Museums

A jumbled pile of fossil bones fresh from the dig site is only the start of putting a dinosaur together. There may be years of careful cleaning, measuring, comparing, copying, and rebuilding, before the skeleton or a lifelike model is put on display in a major museum.

A GOOD CLEAN UP

First the fossils must be cleaned of their surrounding rock. This is very time-consuming. Often it is done under the microscope with small sanders, vibrating needles, and high-speed dental drills. Shot-blasting fires a powerful stream of sand or plastic grains at the area. If the surrounding rock is different from the fossil rock, acids and other chemicals can be used to dissolve it away in stages, leaving the fossil unharmed. This can take months in acid baths.

FILLING IN THE GAPS

A complete fossil skeleton of a dinosaur is a rare find. Usually the remains are bent and broken, jumbled and mixed up, with various parts missing. The gaps are "filled in" using parts from another, similar dinosaur, or from similar animals that we know from today, such as crocodiles, lizards and birds. This is the science of comparative anatomy. (Anatomy studies the structures and parts of living things.)

MAKING COPIES

A complete fossil skeleton is very heavy and awkward to handle, since it is made of solid rock. One brachiosaur toe bone is far too heavy to lift! Also a very rare specimen may be worth more than its weight in gold! So copies of the fossils are made in glass-fiber or similar material, and painted to look like the originals. Then the originals can be stored safely.

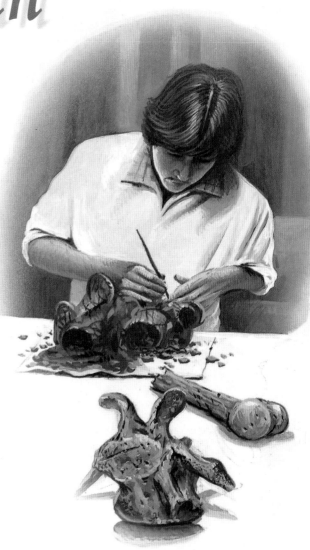

A museum worker cleans up pieces of a dinosaur fossil discovered during a dig.

MOUNTING THE SKELETON

Finally the skeleton is mounted—put together with bones linked as they would have been in life. Older mounted skeletons had thick metal bars or wires to hold them up. Today a lightweight metal or plastic frame is used. This is almost invisible since it follows the curves of the body and the insides of the glass-fibre "bones." Modern museum displays also put dinosaurs in exciting positions and surroundings that tell us more about their life. They may be fighting off a predator, looking after their babies, or roaring at the visitors.

MAKING A LIFELIKE MODEL

Comparative anatomy is also used to add muscles, guts, and other soft parts of a dinosaur to its skeleton. Living bones have roughened areas where muscles are anchored. These rough patches or scars may show on fossils, revealing the sizes and positions of a dinosaur's muscles. The position and size of the lungs and heart can be guessed at from the structure of the rib cage. The stomach and intestines are added in, again using modern reptiles and other animals as guides.

CLOTHED IN SKIN

Gradually the dinosaur is rebuilt from its skeleton outwards, layer by layer. On the outside is skin. Rare fossils of dinosaur skin show that they had scales like modern reptiles. Some had bony plates and spines too, although the positioning of these is often the result of clever guesswork.

WHAT COLOR?

The final touch is color. But this, we do not know. Fossil skin is made of stone and is the color of stone. So you can color a dinosaur any way you wish, even pink with yellow spots, and no one could say it was wrong! However, most dinosaur models have colors and patterns based on similar animals today, such as crocodiles and lizards.

Using lifting platforms, specialist dinosaur builders assemble the pieces of a model *Barosaurus* skeleton.

DINOSAUR

DATA

Frequently Asked Questions

Brachiosaurus

1 HOW LONG DID A DINOSAUR LIVE FOR?
We can only guess what the natural life
expectancy was for a dinosaur, by studying
animals that are around today. Ideas range
from a few years for small dinosaurs,
such as *Compsognathus*, to a century
or more for the giant sauropods,
such as *Brachiosaurus*, which
would have needed 20–30
years to grow to
full size.

Stegosaurus

Edmontosaurus

Gigantosaurus

Baryonyx

2 HOW MANY DIFFERENT DINOSAURS WERE THERE?
To date, almost 900 different dinosaurs have been identified and given
scientific names. But this must represent only a tiny number of all the
dinosaur species that lived during the 185 million years of the Age of
Dinosaurs. No one will ever know the true number of dinosaurs that
lived on Earth—some will have disappeared without leaving any tell-
tale fossils behind so nothing will ever be known about them.
We only have to look at the amazing variety of animals on Earth
today (there are between 10–15 million different species) to guess
that there may well have been thousands of different types of
dinosaur. As more fossils are found, many more new species of
dinosaur will eventually be discovered.

Ankylosaurus

3 WERE DINOSAURS REALLY THE ANCESTORS OF BIRDS?

Not long ago the idea that dinosaurs were related to birds would have seemed ridiculous. But not today. New discoveries, such as those made in China in the late 1990s, have shown clear evidence that some dinosaurs evolved feathers. Other similarities include these facts:

• some dinosaur bones are similar to those of birds (they are hollow and have the same shape);
• dinosaurs laid eggs in nests;
• some dinosaurs, such as *Oviraptor*, seem to have brooded their eggs in the nest.

All this evidence seems to suggest that today's birds may be the descendants of the dinosaurs. It is quite a thought.

Orodromeus egg

Archaeopteryx

Mother *Maiasaura* and hatchlings

Corythosaurus

4 WHAT COLOR WERE DINOSAURS?

Like so many questions about dinosaurs, this is almost impossible to answer. Very little dinosaur skin has ever been found, and what remains has lost all of its original color. While we know that dinosaurs were reptiles, there is still no evidence to suggest that dinosaurs were the same colors as present-day reptiles. Some scientists go as far as saying they were brightly colored, in shades of green, black, and yellow. When artists paint pictures of dinosaurs, some give them the dull colors of modern reptiles, but others brighten them up with patches of color.

5 DID ANY DINOSAURS LIVE IN THE SEA, OR FLY IN THE SKY?

No! Not all animals that lived during the Age of Dinosaurs were dinosaurs. A dinosaur was a land-living reptile that had an upright posture. Creatures that flew in the sky or swam in the sea shared the world with the dinosaurs, but they belonged to other groups of prehistoric animals.

Dimorphodon

Liopleurodon

237

6 WERE DINOSAURS WARM-BLOODED?
For a long time scientists have thought that, like present-day reptiles, dinosaurs were cold-blooded animals. But this idea is changing, and many people now think that they were warm-blooded. If they were, they would have needed to eat plenty of food to make enough energy to keep their bodies warm.

Tröodon

Meteorite

7 HOW DID THE DINOSAURS DIE OUT?
Whole books have been written trying to answer this tricky question! More than 100 ideas have been put forward to explain what happened to the dinosaurs—from the crazy (aliens took them for food), to the silly (they got bored). More serious ideas have suggested that mammals stole their eggs, and with no young being born they just died out, to some kind of epidemic or mass-poisoning. The most likely idea does have a connection with space—that a huge meteorite crashed into the Earth, sending up a cloud of dust which covered the sun from view and caused the temperature to fall. Earth descended into a long, cold winter in which the dinosaurs could not survive.

Yangchuanosaurus wounded in battle with Tuojiangosaurus

9 COULD DINOSAURS MAKE NOISES?
Almost certainly. Just like today's animals, dinosaurs had voice boxes. We cannot be certain what noises they made, but it's probably reasonable to say they could make a range of sounds from shrill squeaks and squeals to deep bellowing grunts and groans.

Inside the skull of Parasaurolophus

Gastroliths, or stomach stones

Leg and foot bones of a theropod

8 DID DINOSAURS EVER GET SICK?
Just like today's animals, dinosaurs faced problems with their health, and evidence has been found for the injuries and diseases they suffered from. They fell and broke their bones, and diseases such as arthritis attacked the bone joints, making them stiff and painful.

Parasaurolophus

Jawbone of a plant-eating dinosaur

10 WHAT SHOULD YOU DO IF YOU FIND A DINOSAUR BONE?
It could happen! Many dinosaur discoveries have been made by chance, by amateur fossil hunters all over the world. If you think you've found a dinosaur bone, the most important thing to do is report it to your local museum or college. Someone there will be able to call in the experts to take a closer look at your find. Who knows, maybe it will be a new dinosaur—and if that is so, then it may well be named after you!

Pronunciation Guide

The names of some of the creatures from the Age of Dinosaurs are quite difficult to pronounce. You will find many of these names listed here, together with a guide to their pronunciation.

A

Abelisaurus ah-bell-i-sore-us
Acanthopholis a-can-tho-fole-is
Alamosaurus al-am-oh-sore-us
Albertosaurus al-bur-toh-sore-us
Allosaurus al-oh-sore-us
Ammosaurus am-oh-sore-us
Anchiceratops an-key-ser-a-tops
Anchisaurus an-kee-sore-us
Ankylosaurus an-kee-loh-sore-us
Antarctosaurus ant-arc-toe-sore-us
Apatosaurus ah-pat-oh-sore-us
Archaeopteryx ah-key-op-trix
Avimimus av-i-mime-us

B

Bagaceratops bag-a-ser-a-tops
Baryonyx bar-ee-on-iks
Brachiosaurus brak-ee-oh-sore-us
Brachyceratops brak-ee-ser-a-tops
Brachylophosaurus brak-ee-loaf-oh-sore-us

C

Camarasaurus kam-are-ah-sore-us
Camptosaurus kam-toe-sore-us
Carcharodontosaurus car-car-oh-dont-oh-sore-us
Ceratosaurus ser-a-toe-sore-us
Cetiosaurus see-tee-oh-sore-us
Chasmosaurus kaz-mo-sore-us
Claosaurus clay-oh-sore-us
Coelophysis see-loh-fie-sis
Coelurus see-loo-rus
Compsognathus komp-so-nay-thus
Corythosaurus coh-rith-oh-sore-us

D

Dacentrurus da-sen-troo-rus
Daspletosaurus da-spleet-oh-sore-us
Datousaurus dat-oo-sore-us
Deinocheirus die-no-kie-rus
Deinonychus die-non-ick-us

D (continued)

Dicraeosaurus die-kray-oh-sore-us
Dilophosaurus die-loaf-oh-sore-us
Dimorphodon die-more-pho-don
Diplodocus die-ploh-de-kus
Dromaeosaurus drome-ee-oh-sore-us
Dryosaurus dry-oh-sore-us
Dryptosaurus drip-toe-sore-us

E

Edmontosaurus ed-mon-toh-sore-us
Elaphrosaurus ee-laf-roe-sore-us
Elasmosaurus ee-las-mo-sore-us
Eoraptor ee-oh-rap-tor
Erlikosaurus er-lik-oh-sore-us
Euhelopus yoo-hel-oh-pus
Euoplocephalus yoo-op-loh-sef-ah-lus
Euskelosaurus yoo-skel-oh-sore-us

F

Fabrosaurus fab-roe-sore-us

G

Gallimimus gal-lee-meem-us
Geranosaurus jer-an-oh-sore-us
Giganotosaurus jy-ga-no-toe-sore-rus
Goyocephale goy-oh-kef-a-lee
Gracilisuchus gra-sil-i-soo-kus

H

Hadrosaurus had-roe-sore-us
Halticosaurus hal-tik-oh-sore-us
Heterodontosaurus het-er-oh-dont-oh-sore-us
Homalocephale hom-al-oh-kef-a-lee
Hylaeosaurus hy-lee-oh-sore-us
Hypacrosaurus hy-pack-roe-sore-us
Hypsilophodon hip-sih-loh-foh-don

I

Iguanodon ig-wha-no-don
Indosuchus in-doh-soo-kus
Itemirus eat-em-ear-us

J

Janenschia yah-nen-shee-a

K

Kentrosaurus ken-troh-sore-us

L

Lambeosaurus lam-bee-oh-sore-us
Leptoceratops lep-toh-ser-a-tops
Lesothosaurus le-soo-too-sore-us
Liopleurodon lee-oh-ploo-ro-don
Lufengosaurus loo-feng-oh-sore-us
Lycorhinus lie-koe-rime-us

M

Maiasaura may-ah-sore-ah
Mamenchisaurus mah-men-chee-sore-us
Massospondylus mass-oh-spon-die-lus
Megalosaurus meg-ah-loh-sore-us
Melanorosaurus mel-an-oh-roe-sore-us
Minmi min-my
Monoclonius mon-oh-clone-i-us
Mussaurus mus-sore-us
Muttaburrasaurus mut-a-bur-a-sore-us

N

Nemegtosaurus nem-egg-toe-sore-us
Noasaurus no-ah-sore-us
Nodosaurus no-doh-sore-us
Notoceratops no-toh-serra-tops

O

Omeisaurus oh-may-sore-us
Ornitholestes or-ni-thoe-les-teez
Ornithomimus or-ni-tho-mee-mus
Ouranosaurus oo-ran-oh-sore-us
Oviraptor oh-vee-rap-tor

P

Pachycephalosaurus pack-ee-sef-a-lo-sore-us
Pachyrhinosaurus pack-ee-rine-oh-sore-us
Parasaurolophus pah-rah-sore-oh-loaf-us
Parksosaurus parks-oh-sore-us
Patagosaurus pat-a-goh-sore-us
Pelorosaurus pel-oh-roe-sore-us
Pentaceratops pent-ah-ser-a-tops
Pinacosaurus pin-ak-oh-sore-us
Placodus plac-oh-dus
Plateosaurus plat-ee-oh-sore-us
Plesiosaurus plee-see-oh-sore-us
Plotosaurus plo-toe-sore-us
Preondactylus pree-on-dak-ti-lus
Procompsognathus pro-komp-so-nay-thus
Protoceratops pro-toe-ser-a-tops
Psittacosaurus sit-ak-oh-sore-us
Pteranodon ter-an-oh-don
Pterodactylus ter-oh-dack-tee-lus

Q

Quetzalcoatlus kwet-zal-co-at-lus

R

Rhamphorhynchus ram-for-inch-us
Riojasaurus ree-o-ha-sore-us

S

Saltasaurus salt-a-sore-us
Saltopus salt-oh-pus
Saurolophus sore-oh-loaf-us
Scelidosaurus skel-ide-oh-sore-us
Secernosaurus see-ser-no-sore-us
Segnosaurus seg-no-sore-us
Seismosaurus size-moh-sore-us
Shantungosaurus shan-tung-oh-sore-us
Shunosaurus shun-oh-sore-us
Spinosaurus spy-no-sore-us
Staurikosaurus store-ik-oh-sore-us
Stegoceras ste-goss-er-as
Stegosaurus ste-go-sore-us
Struthiomimus strooth-ee-oh-mime-us
Struthiosaurus strooth-ee-oh-sore-us
Styracosaurus sty-rack-oh-sore-us
Supersaurus soo-per-sore-us
Syntarsus sin-tar-sus

T

Tarbosaurus tar-bo-sore-us
Thecodontosaurus thec-oh-dont-oh-sore-us
Therizinosaurus ther-ih-zin-oh-sore-us
Titanosaurus tie-tan-oh-sore-us
Triceratops try-ser-a-tops
Tröodon troo-oh-don
Tsintaosaurus sin-toe-sore-us
Tyrannosaurus tie-ran-oh-sore-us

U

Ultrasaurus ul-tra-sore-us

V

Velociraptor vel-oh-see-rap-tor
Vulcanodon vul-can-oh-don

W

Wannanosaurus wan-an-oh-sore-us

X

Xiaosaurus shee-ah-oh-sore-us
Xuanhanosaurus zoo-ahn-han-oh-sore-us

Y

Yangchuanosaurus yang-choo-ahn-oh-sore-us

Z

Zephyrosaurus zef-roe-sore-us
Zigongosaurus zee-gung-oh-sore-us

Timeline

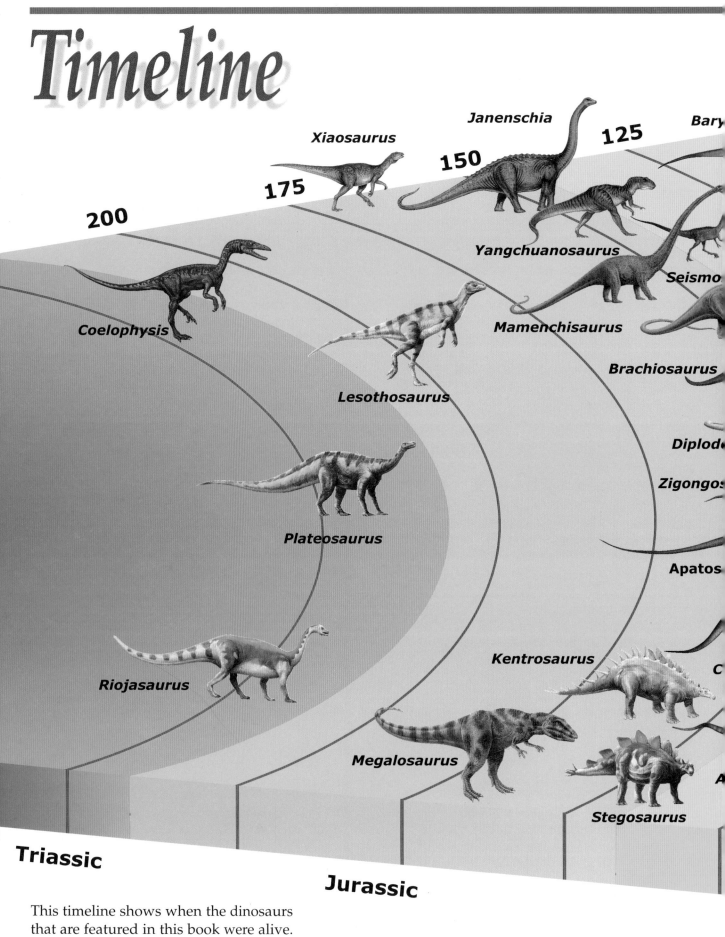

200

175

Xiaosaurus

Janenschia

150

125

Bary

Coelophysis

Yangchuanosaurus

Seismo

Lesothosaurus

Mamenchisaurus

Brachiosaurus

Plateosaurus

Diplod

Zigongos

Apatos

Riojasaurus

Kentrosaurus

C

Megalosaurus

A

Stegosaurus

Triassic

Jurassic

This timeline shows when the dinosaurs
that are featured in this book were alive.
They are not shown to scale.

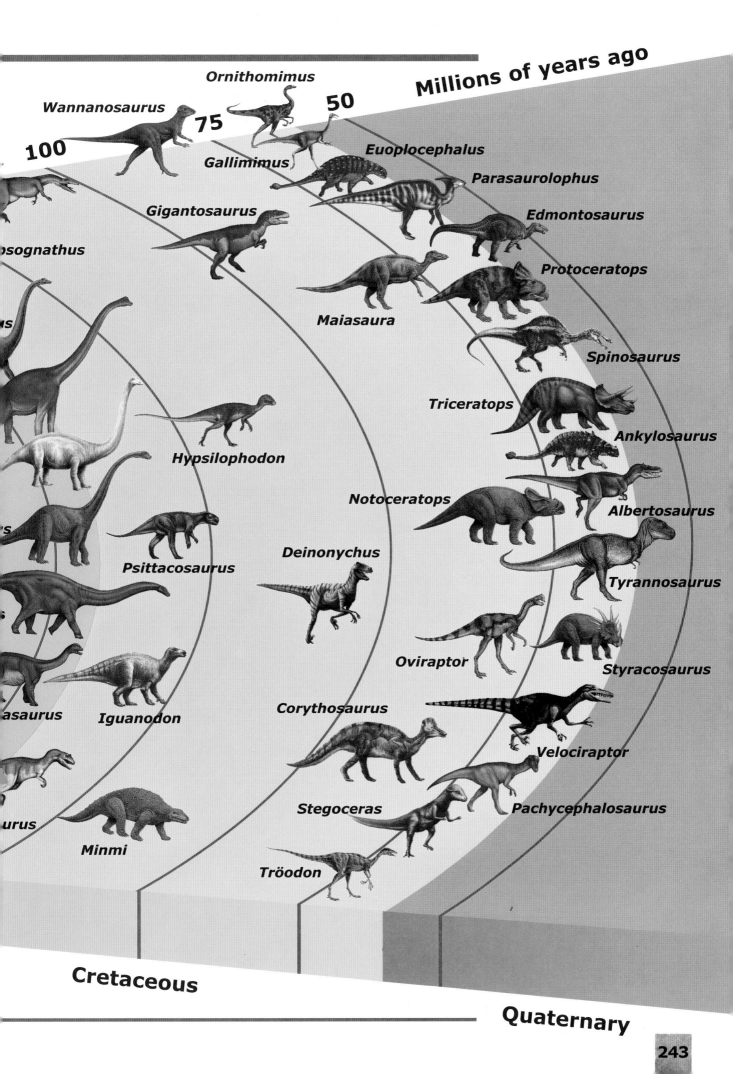

Wannanosaurus

Ornithomimus

Gallimimus

100

75

50

Millions of years ago

Euoplocephalus

Parasaurolophus

Edmontosaurus

Gigantosaurus

Protoceratops

Maiasaura

Spinosaurus

osognathus

Triceratops

Ankylosaurus

Hypsilophodon

Notoceratops

Albertosaurus

Psittacosaurus

Deinonychus

Tyrannosaurus

Oviraptor

Styracosaurus

Iguanodon

Corythosaurus

Velociraptor

asaurus

Stegoceras

Pachycephalosaurus

urus

Minmi

Tröodon

Cretaceous

Quaternary

Glossary

Amphibian An animal, such as a frog, with a backbone and four legs that lays its eggs in water. In the larval (young) stage it lives in water. In the adult stage it lives on land.

Anapsid A reptile whose skull does not have an opening behind the eye, such as a turtle.

Ankylosaur An armored dinosaur covered with bony plates, knobs, and spikes.

Biped An animal that stands, walks, or runs on its two hind legs.

Cambrian Period About 570–510 million years ago.

Carboniferous Period About 360–290 million years ago.

Carnivore An animal that eats only meat.

Cast fossil The shape of a buried animal preserved in the form of hardened minerals.

Cenozoic Era The last 65 million years, from the end of the Mesozoic Era to the present day. Also called the "Age of Mammals."

Ceratopsian A large plant-eating dinosaur with pointed horns and a bony frill growing from the back of its skull.

Cheek teeth Teeth used for chewing behind the front teeth or bill, especially found in plant eaters.

Cold-blooded A popular term to refer to an animal that receives most, or all, of its body heat from sources outside its body, usually the sun.

Conifer A tree or shrub that produces seed cones, such as fir and pine.

Continental drift The process by which the continents slowly drift around the globe.

Coprolites Fossilized animal droppings.

Cretaceous Period About 144–65 million years ago. Dinosaurs died out at the end of this period.

Crust The rocky outer layer that forms a thin "skin" over the surface of the Earth.

Cycad A nonflowering plant with a thick trunk, no branches, and palmlike leaves. Related to today's conifers.

Dental battery A large number of interlocking teeth that form a shearing and grinding surface.

Devonian Period About 410–60 million years ago. Also called the "Age of Fish."

Diapsid A reptile whose skull has two openings on either side, such as a lizard.

Dinosaur An extinct reptile with an upright posture.

MEANINGS OF THE PARTS OF NAMES

acro – top
allo – strange
alti – high
brachio – arm
brachy – short
bronto – thunder
cera – horned
cheirus – hand
coelo – hollow
compso – pretty
corytho – helmet
derm – skin
di – two
diplo – double
docus – beam
echino – spiny
elaphro – light
hetero – different
hypsi – high
lepto – slender
lopho – ridge, crest
mega – huge
micro – small
odon(t) – tooth
ophthalmo – eye
pachy – thick
physis – body
plateo – flat
pod, pus, pes – foot
poly – many
ptero – winged
quadri – four
raptor – thief
rhino – nose
salto – jumping
saurus – lizard, reptile
stego – roofed
thero – beast
tops – head, face
tri – three
tyranno – tyrant
veloci – fast

Ecosystem A community of living things and their environment.

Embryo The early stages in the development of a plant or an animal.

Evolution The process by which a plant or animal changes through time.

Extinction The disappearance of a species of animals or plants.

Family A group of animals or plants that are related to each other.

Fern A nonflowering plant with finely divided leaves named fronds.

Fossil Any evidence of past life. Dinosaur fossils are bones and teeth, footprints, coprolites, gastroliths, eggs, and skin impressions.

Gastroliths Stones found in the stomachs of some plant-eating dinosaurs to help them break down and digest vegetation.

Geologist A scientist who studies rocks.

Gingko A tree that looks like a conifer but which sheds its leaves in fall. The only living species of gingko is the maidenhair tree.

Gondwanaland The southern supercontinent made up of Africa, Australia, Antarctica, South America, and India.

Hadrosaur A large plant-eating dinosaur with a long, flat bill, also called a duck-billed dinosaur.

Herbivore An animal that eats only plants.

Horse-tail A plant with an upright stem and tiny leaves. Horse-tails are related to ferns.

Ichthyosaur A dolphinlike reptile that lived in the ocean.

Iguanodont A plant-eating dinosaur with hooflike nails on its hind feet and spikes on its hands in place of thumbs.

Invertebrate An animal without a backbone.

Jurassic Period About 206–144 million years ago. Dinosaurs became common throughout the world during this time.

Laurasia The northern supercontinent made up of North America, Europe, and Asia.

Mammal A warm-blooded animal covered with hair and which feeds its young with milk.

Mesozoic Era The time from about 250–65 million years ago. Also called the "Age of Dinosaurs."

Mold fossil Where the remains of a buried animal have been dissolved, and all that is left is a hole in the shape of the creature.

Omnivore An animal that eats both meat and plants.

Order A group of animals or plants that belong to related families. There are two orders of dinosaurs—*Ornithischia* and *Saurischia*.

Ordovician Period About 510–440 million years ago.

Ornithischia One of the two orders of dinosaurs. This order includes bird-hipped plant-eating dinosaurs, such as the ankylosaurs, ceratopsians, and stegosaurs.

Ornithomimid A fast-running, meat-eating dinosaur with a long neck and slender legs. Similar in appearance to a present-day ostrich.

Ornithopod A two-footed plant eater, some of which had crests on their heads.

Pachycephalosaur A two-footed plant eater with a thick skull.

Paleontologist A scientist who studies fossils and the history of life.

Paleozoic Era The time from about 600–250 million years ago.

Pangaea The single land mass or supercontinent of the Permian Period. It broke up during the Triassic Period.

Permian Period About 290–250 million years ago.

Plesiosaur A long-necked reptile that lived in the ocean.

Precambrian Period
About 3,500–570 million
years ago.

Predator An animal that
kills other animals (prey)
for food.

Prey The animal that is
killed by a predator.

Quadruped An animal that stands, walks, or
runs on all four limbs.

Reptile A cold-blood animal with scales and a
backbone that lays its eggs on land.

Saurischia One of the two orders of dinosaurs.
Saurischians were lizard-hipped dinosaurs that
included all theropods and sauropods.

Sauropod Bulky, long-necked, long-tailed plant
eaters that walked on all four feet.

Scute A bony plate set in to the skin of a dinosaur.

Serrated Sharply notched along an edge, such
as the teeth of theropods.

Silurian Period About 440–410 million
years ago.

Stegosaur A large plant-eating dinosaur with
rows of triangular, bony plates on its back and
spikes on its tail.

Synapsid A mammallike
reptile whose skull has
one opening on
either side.

Tertiary Period The
period after the Mesozoic
Era, from about 65–2
million years ago.

Thecodont A big, heavy reptile that crawled on
all four legs. Thecodonts were probably the
ancestors of dinosaurs.

Theropod A two-legged meat-eating dinosaur,
such as *Allosaurus* and *Tyrannosaurus*.

Trace fossil A fossil that is not part of the
actual body of an animal. Dinosaur trace
fossils are footprints, eggs, gastroliths, and
coprolites.

Triassic Period About 250–206 million
years ago.

Vertebra A bone of the spine. Vertebrae is
the plural.

Vertebrate An animal with a backbone.

Warm-blooded A popular term for an animal
that can control its own body
temperature, such as a mammal
or a bird.

Index